DURATION

ST. ANSELM AND HIS CRITICS

ST. ANSELM
AND HIS CRITICS

A RE-INTERPRETATION OF THE
CUR DEUS HOMO

BY

JOHN McINTYRE, M.A., B.D., D.Litt.
Principal of St. Andrew's College
within the University of Sydney

OLIVER AND BOYD
EDINBURGH: TWEEDDALE COURT
LONDON: 39A WELBECK STREET, W.I.

FIRST PUBLISHED .   .   . 1954

PRINTED IN GREAT BRITAIN BY
T. AND A. CONSTABLE LTD., EDINBURGH
FOR OLIVER AND BOYD LTD., EDINBURGH

ACKNOWLEDGMENT

I WISH to make grateful acknowledgment of the assistance given towards the publication of this book by The Mrs. Frances Mary Gillespie Memorial Fund, which is administered jointly by the Faculty of Theology of the Presbyterian Church of Australia in New South Wales and the Council of St. Andrew's College.

CONTENTS

CHAPTER ONE

REMOTO CHRISTO : METHODOLOGY

CHAPTER TWO

AUT POENA AUT SATISFACTIO : HAMARTIOLOGY

PART A

PART B

CHAPTER THREE

DEUS-HOMO : CHRISTOLOGY

CHAPTER FOUR

ILLA REDEMPTIO : SOTERIOLOGY

REMOTO CHRISTO : METHODOLOGY

THE problems which have exercised most, if not all, of the historians of soteriology in regard to the *Cur Deus Homo* of St. Anselm might, with certain justification, be described as secondary. These problems have ranged from the alleged Tritheism and Monothelitism of St. Anselm, through such questions as his dependence upon Teutonic legal concepts and the early medieval penance system, to the issue of whether St. Anselm ultimately reconciles the justice and the love of God. An undue concern with such problems has, in the history of Anselmic study, obscured the primary problem presented to us by the *Cur Deus Homo*, namely, what is the relation of this work, and the method which St. Anselm employs in it, to his famous principle of *credo ut intelligam*? [1]

Nowhere that the matter is mentioned is it taken to be a problem at all, the assumption being that the *Cur Deus Homo* is just another example, similar to the *Monologion*, of the principle in operation. Now, while this view may be the only one which is in the end permissible, it would be a grave mistake to treat it as an unexplored assumption, or yet as immediately self-evident in the *Cur Deus Homo* itself. More often, however, the matter is not raised, largely because those writers who have discussed the *credo ut intelligam* principle (such as C. C. J. Webb, E. Gilson and E. L. Mascall, to name but a few) have been more interested in St. Anselm's theistic philosophy than in his soteriology; whereas those who have been writing about the latter (such as J. K. Mozley, James Denney, T. H. Hughes, A. Ritschl, A. Harnack and many others) have not had the more strictly theistic theme before them. St. Anselm, therefore, is presented in two different, and at the same time unrelated, rôles: on the one hand, as the first Christian formulator of the Ontological Argument, an argument which was to have a famous, if not notorious, history at the hands of St. Thomas, Descartes, Kant and Hegel, and as the first theist really to put the *credo ut intelligam* principle explicitly and continuously

1

into action; and, on the other hand, he is presented as the theologian who gave us the first systematic account of the Atonement. It is rather surprising that his commentators—no matter how divergent their own theological or philosophical positions may be —are almost unanimous in their praise of his performance in the first rôle, and equally categorical in their condemnation of him in the second. This outrageously disproportionate assessment of St. Anselm's abilities in the two, not unrelated, spheres of theological enquiry has arisen because of a failure to realise that it is one person who is playing the two rôles, that his thought is not twofold but single, and that consequently any assessment of his abilities in the one sphere intimately affects that of his accomplishments in the other. The outright condemnation of St. Anselm's soteriological work has had this other deplorable result, that it has led to the neglect by dogmatic theologians in general—Karl Barth is a conspicuous exception—of St. Anselm's views on the other great themes of dogmatics, such as the Doctrine of the Trinity, the attributes of God, the procession of the Holy Spirit, the freedom of the will, and so on. It is, therefore, only when we seek to understand St. Anselm's thought in its integrity, and cease to regard him merely as a stage, either on the way that led from St. Augustine to St. Thomas, or on that which led from Athanasius to Abelard, that this problem, which has been called the primary problem in interpreting the *Cur Deus Homo*, emerges. No major Christian thinker has suffered quite so much as St. Anselm from the hit-and-run tactics of historians of theism and soteriology.

This problem of the relation of the *Cur Deus Homo* to the *credo ut intelligam* principle is not raised at this stage of our discussion simply for polemical reasons, or because there is any intrinsic value in adding to the many problems to be found in the writings of St. Anselm. Occam's razor would deter us on the second score, and the vastness and grandeur of St. Anselm's thought make polemics at any time a course not lightly to be embarked upon. We dare not, except at grave peril of missing much that is good for us, dismiss unthinkingly anyone who prays as St. Anselm prays, and who at times makes his theology a prayer, a height to which few theologians have risen. On the contrary, this problem is raised for two reasons. On the one hand, by examining it we shall be the better qualified to understand what St. Anselm is endeavouring to do in the *Cur Deus Homo* and to appreciate the method by which he is doing it. The importance of theological procedure or methodology was for St. Anselm paramount, and it is therefore worthy of consideration in relation to all his works, and not solely to the *Monologion* or the *Proslogion*, with which it has been most closely associated in the past. On the other hand, this problem is held to be primary because it provides a setting in which to place the others. If we are first clear about what St. Anselm thinks of himself as seeking to achieve in the *Cur Deus Homo*, then we shall be the better able to decide whether he has fallen short of his self-imposed standards. Too many criticisms of St. Anselm's soteriology have sprung from his failure to comply with the soteriological theories of his critics, and too few of his critics have been sympathetic enough to realise that any great thinker must first be interpreted in terms of his own premises before extraneous criticisms are undertaken. A study, therefore, of this primary problem will take us directly, it is hoped, to the central meaning and purpose of the *Cur Deus Homo*.

Interestingly enough, F. S. Schmitt, by placing the *Commendatio Operis ad Urbanum Papam II* and the *Praefatio* in sequence before the actual text of the work, in the most recent edition of the *Sancti Anselmi Omnia Opera*,[2] has enabled us to discover the problem *in parvo* within the *Cur Deus Homo* itself. The problem of the relation of the *Cur Deus Homo* to the *credo ut intelligam* principle does arise there in miniature, though it can be seen in its true perspective, and its fullest implications appreciated, only when the *Cur Deus Homo* is set in relation to the rest of St. Anselm's writings. The *Commendatio*, as we briefly call it, is, according to F. S. Schmitt, a covering letter written by St. Anselm when he sent the *Cur Deus Homo* to Pope Urban II. One of the manuscripts places it between the *Praefatio* [3] and the list of chapter headings, others between the chapter headings and the text of the work,[4] one at the end of the work.[5] Of the remaining manuscripts, some place it in the appendix to the letters of St. Anselm,[6] and others treat it as the *Prologus* to the *Epistola de Incarnatione Verbi*.[7] Thus, in view of the evidence, F. S. Schmitt takes rather a bold line in placing the *Commendatio* where he does. In the *Commendatio*, St. Anselm states what we

recognise from his other works to be the *credo ut intelligam* theme.
"I judge no one to be blameworthy," he writes,[8] "if, being
established in his faith, he should wish to employ himself in the
search for its reason." Adding that Holy Scripture invites us to
seek out the reason for our faith when it says: "You shall not
understand unless you have believed,"[9] he affirms [10] that "the
understanding which we have in this life stands midway between
faith and sight: the more one advances to that end, so much the
more, in my judgment, does he approach sight, to which we all
aspire". This theme of the *Commendatio* appears early in the
Cur Deus Homo,[11] when Boso, the interlocutor, says, "Just as
correct procedure demands that we believe the deep things of the
Christian Faith before we discuss them with our reason; so it
appears to me to be negligence on our part if, after we have been
confirmed in our faith, we do not endeavour to understand [12]
what we believe." In other words, faith is a necessary precondition of intellectual comprehension of Christian truth. So far from
being reprehensible, intellectual searching is obligatory upon
believers, and unwillingness to understand what it is they believe
and the grounds upon which they believe it is moral negligence.

In the *Praefatio*, however, we find what appears, on the surface
at least, to be a very different position, and now our problem
comes into view. After explaining that he proposes to deal with
the subject of why there should be a God-man, St. Anselm says
that he will divide his material into two books. In the first, after
disposing of certain arguments of unbelievers who try to show
that the Christian faith is contrary to reason, he promises that
"Christ being set aside (*remoto Christo*) as if He had never been,
he will prove by logically necessary steps that apart from Him
salvation of man is impossible".[13] In the second book, he continues, upon exactly the same premise—that nothing is to be
assumed as known about Christ—he will demonstrate, by logically accurate reasoning, that man was created for the purpose of
enjoying immortality; that this end could be accomplished only
through the God-man; and that all we believe concerning Christ
is necessarily so. The *remoto Christo* position is reaffirmed
throughout the book [14]; it is not a rhetorical boast or a mere slip
of the pen. Besides, the whole temper of the book leaves the
reader in no doubt that St. Anselm is seeking to advance argu-

ments that will refute the objections of unbelievers and win them over to Christianity; indeed, at I.25,[15] he invites unbelievers to recognise the cogency of his reasoning, to desist from ridicule and to embrace the faith and be saved. At times the book seems to be quite openly apologetic rather than strictly dogmatic. St. Anselm is, therefore, not simply attempting to build up the faith of believers by suggesting reasons for the faith that they hold. He offers arguments which, in his opinion, will convince unbelievers; for even if "Christ is set apart", St. Anselm claims to lead them by steps which they must admit to be logically necessary to conclusions which they will hold only on grounds of reason and which will be identical with statements accepted by Christians on faith.

Here, then, is the difficulty which the comparison of the *Commendatio* with the *Praefatio* raises. In the *Commendatio* understanding proceeds upon faith; without the latter, the former is impossible. Understanding moves within the boundaries of faith, and while it may map out the territory with a thoroughness and an accuracy which faith cannot possibly achieve, it never abandons faith or goes beyond it. "I believe in order that I may understand." But in the *Praefatio* faith and the subject of faith, Jesus Christ, are set aside so that no presuppositions concerning the Person or the Work of Our Lord are permitted to enter into the premises from which the argument begins or to affect the argument as it develops. The claim is made that unbelievers can be led to the doctrines of faith, in this case to the Incarnation and the Atonement, by way of reasoning which is as convincing for them as it is for Christians. The aim outlined in the *Praefatio* is borne out by the method of argumentation used throughout the book. Unbelievers are shown how they can come to understand even though they do not believe. The implication is that the logic by which they thought to substantiate unbelief in fact carries them to understanding of the faith, if not also to belief in Christ Himself as their only Saviour. The principle involved almost becomes: *intelligo ut credam.*

Two "short-cut" solutions of the problem thus presented and a third, much longer, suggest themselves. First, it could be argued that the *Cur Deus Homo* is, in view of the phrase *remoto Christo*, definitely not an example of the *credo ut intelligam* principle operating in regard to the doctrines of the Incarnation and the Atonement, and that this work constitutes a departure on St. Anselm's part from his customary theological methodology. On this solution the *Cur Deus Homo* is not written in faith, by faith and for faith; it is not faith's attempt to understand its own inner intellectual structure. It is, rather, faith's logical refutation of the objections of unbelievers, who maintain its irrationality. To resolve the difficulty created by the explicit statement of the *credo ut intelligam* theme in the *Commendatio*, we might resort to textual criticism and say that there is good documentary evidence for removing it from the place allocated to it by F. S. Schmitt, before the *Praefatio*, and for setting it with the *Epistola de Incarnatione Verbi*, and some internal theological evidence, too, for such removal, in that the theme of the *Commendatio* is more completely in line with the first chapter of the *Epistola* than it is with the *Cur Deus Homo*. In this fashion the immediate problem would be solved, but we should still have to answer the question of why St. Anselm makes such a departure, and whether there are any other examples in the rest of his writings. Besides, this procedure only perpetuates what may be regarded as a quite false isolation of the *Cur Deus Homo* from these other writings.

Secondly, it could be maintained that the *Cur Deus Homo* is an instance of the *credo ut intelligam* principle in action but that St. Anselm has not carried out his task thoroughly, or that he has introduced a conception—that of *remoto Christo*—which, though he does not realise it, conflicts with the main aim of his work. To support such a solution relevant evidence could again be adduced. For example, the entire work stands within what we might call a framework of faith. In I.3 we are reminded that it is by God's love and compassion that Atonement occurs at all, and in II.20 God's mercy, which might seem to have been obscured by so lengthy a discussion of His justice, is reaffirmed. All St. Anselm's logical deductions and inferences could then be said to take place within that framework. What would result from this solution would be an unresolved contradiction both in the letter and in the spirit of the work, a conflict between, on the one hand, the devotional quality of St. Anselm's mind and the personal character of his own faith, seen so clearly in the opening chapter of the *Proslogion* and in so many of his letters, and, on the other hand, the rationalism of his age, which he felt obliged to accept. This solution, however, rests upon such a low estimate of St. Anselm's intelligence that it is suspect from the start.

Since it has already become obvious that there is no easy short-cut to the solution of the problem posed by the comparison of the *Commendatio* with the *Praefatio*, a problem which, we have begun to see, is not confined to these two short statements but extends to the interpretation of the entire *Cur Deus Homo* and of what St. Anselm is trying to accomplish in this work, it remains for us to state and discuss the third and longer way already mentioned of solving the problem. Apart from the individual difficulties raised against the two "short-cut" solutions, two other major criticisms of them may be made. On the one hand, they fail to realise the importance of treating St. Anselm's works as a whole and of approaching the *Cur Deus Homo* with a general understanding of his main themes and special theological techniques. Conversely, they have not been able to appreciate the extent to which the *Cur Deus Homo* may, in its turn, assist in the comprehension of St. Anselm's other works. On the other hand, they both rest upon an unexamined and supposedly self-evident interpretation of the saying *credo ut intelligam*, an assumption totally unwarranted by the history of the interpretation of the phrase. The method which it is here proposed we follow for the solution of this primary problem of the *Cur Deus Homo* is: (1) to bring together the evidence of St. Anselm's own statements about, and of his actual employment of, the principle *credo ut intelligam*, and to state, with the minimum of elaboration, the main features of that evidence; (2) to examine interpretations of the principle which have appeared in the history of theology; (3) to indicate the conclusions yielded by that examination; and (4) finally, to relate the phrase *remoto Christo* to these conclusions.

1

Apart from the brief reference in the *Cur Deus Homo*, I.1, the most important accounts of the principle *credo ut intelligam* occur in the *Proslogion*, 1; the *Epistola de Incarnatione Verbi*, 1; and the *Commendatio* of the *Cur Deus Homo*, which we have already discussed.[16] The accepted examples of the principle in action are the *Mono-*

logion and the *Proslogion*; the *Cur Deus Homo* is here omitted because it is *sub iudice*. It is significant that the other more strictly dogmatic works of St. Anselm, such as the *De Processione Spiritus Sancti* or the *De Concordia,* have never been considered in discussions of the principle in action.

(1.1) *Proslogion*

The first explicit statement of the principle is given to us in the *Proslogion* at the end of c. 1, and its occurrence there deserves careful attention. The whole of the chapter is a prayer to God, of great devotional intensity; in it St. Anselm, aware of the inaccessibility of God and of his own inability to accomplish that for which he was made—knowledge and vision of God—beseeches God to teach him how to seek, and to show Himself to him when he does seek. In sentence after sentence St. Anselm traces the emptiness of the life that has not found God and entreats God to give him his heart's desire. Then he says: "I do not attempt, oh Lord, to soar to Thy height because I do not in any way compare my understanding with Thine; but I do desire to understand Thy truth as far as my heart believes and loves it. For I do not seek to understand in order that I may believe, but *I believe in order that I may understand.* For this also do I believe: that 'I shall not understand unless I believe'." [17] Throughout the rest of the book this method of personal address to God, even in the course of argument, is sustained to a degree which makes the whole work a perfect example of Martin Buber's saying: "God is not to be expressed but addressed."

St. Anselm begins c. 2 of the *Proslogion* ("That God truly exists") with the words: "Therefore do Thou, oh Lord, Who givest understanding of faith, grant to me that . . . I may understand that Thou art as we believe (Thee to be), and that Thou art that which we believe. And certainly we believe that Thou art that than which no greater can be thought." [18] Even the fool who says in his heart, "There is no God," understands what he hears when this definition of God is spoken. From that point the logic of the entire work stands revealed; it is designed to demonstrate that the fool of whom the Psalmist spoke in Psalm 14 is committed by his thinking of this notion—"having it in the understanding" is St. Anselm's phrase—to affirming not only the existence of God but also the several attributes of God: His goodness, self-existence, omnipotence, impassibility and so on.

It does not further our immediate purpose to examine the much discussed question of whether St. Anselm's argument is valid, or whether he has dealt satisfactorily with Gaunilo's *Pro Insipiente*, the defence of "the fool", for we are more concerned with St. Anselm's methodology than with his logic. The evidence yielded by the *Proslogion*, which is likely to prove valuable in our determination of what the *credo ut intelligam* dictum truly means, must therefore be indicated. It is with such evidence, too, that any interpretation of the dictum must ultimately come to terms.

(1.1.1) While it is true to say that in c. 1 of the *Proslogion* St. Anselm is aware of God's existence—in fact, it would not be untrue to say that when God withdraws Himself from him he is more sure of God's existence than he is of his own—nevertheless, his faith is uncertain of itself. "O Lord, Thou art my Lord, and never have I seen Thee. Thou hast made me and re-created me, and hast bestowed all good things upon me, and yet I do not know Thee. Above all, I was made so that I might behold Thee, and I have not yet done that for which I was made." [19] The will to believe is there, but the reality seems to be lacking. If the phrase *Deo remoto* were too extreme as a description of c. 1, then certainly *Deo longinquo* would be quite appropriate. That mood, that attitude, of St. Anselm's is not a pious outburst which is out of relation to the rest of the work; on the contrary, it is an essential part of the dramatic unity of the book, and it sets the problem in the light of which the remainder of the book is to be understood.

(1.1.2) When we reach c. 26 of the *Proslogion* we discover that St. Anselm's mood has changed. Now he speaks of the joy which he has found—"an abundance, yes! and a superabundance" [20]— and he wonders (for he has not yet found his completest certainty) whether this is the joy which "eye hath not seen nor ear heard". This change of mood from c. 1 to c. 26 is so marked that it appears permissible to conclude that the address to God which occupies cc. 2-25 is the process in and through which St. Anselm has been taken from uncertainty concerning God to joy in His presence.

B

Yet it is in these chapters that he has been discussing the implications of the definition of God as "that than which no greater can be thought". He has been seeking to understand (*intelligere*) what is involved in believing (*credere*) that God is such,[21] and this understanding has led to fuller faith.

At the same time, however, this understanding of the implications of the definition is calculated to convince "the fool" of the falsity of his thoughts concerning God. This issue is left in no doubt when the details of the correspondence between St. Anselm and Gaunilo are carefully examined. Therein lies what might be called the dual character of the process of *intellectus*: on the one hand it leads St. Anselm to fuller faith, and on the other hand it is intended by St. Anselm as the means by which the unbelief of "the fool" will be dissolved.

(1.2) *Epistola de Incarnatione Verbi*, 1[22]

In the *Epistola de Incarnatione Verbi* Roscelin (who is not mentioned by name but can be easily identified from the *Epistola Iohannis ad Anselmum* [23] and the *Epistola Anselmi ad Fulconem*,[24] where his views are expressly stated) provides the subject of attack, but before proceeding to show how Roscelin is himself a Tritheist and has confused orthodox Trinitarianism with Sabellianism, Anselm gives a lengthy account of the *credo ut intelligam* position. Condemning the "unspeakable boldness" of some who reject articles of the Christian faith on the ground that what they cannot understand cannot therefore exist, he affirms that no Christian ought to dispute about the Catholic faith until he has loved and lived according to it. It is preposterous to try to ascend by understanding and without faith to the positions which faith holds. The faith which must precede understanding, therefore, is not simply intellectual assent; the heart must be established by faith and the eyes illumined by keeping the Lord's commandments. The necessity for a good will, as well as true faith and a correct understanding, is similarly emphasised by St. Anselm in the *De Concordia*, I, q.2: "He is not said to have correct understanding who does not regulate his will according to understanding; nor is he said to have anything but a dead faith who does not rightly will to act according to faith, for to that end is faith given." Only then, with will morally upright, are we qualified to embark upon the intellectual understanding of our faith. In c. 1 of the *Epistola de Incarnatione Verbi* the whole situation is tersely summarised: "He who has not believed shall not understand. For he, who has not believed, has not experienced; and he, who has not experienced, shall not know." [25] First-hand experience surpasses second-hand hearsay. As the work develops a certain apologetic interest shows itself. Catholic Trinitarianism is being defended against Tritheistic and Sabellian interpretations and the necessity for the Incarnation of the Word rather than of either of the other two Persons of the Trinity is demonstrated.

The *Epistola* yields valuable additions to the evidence of the *Proslogion*:

(1.2.1) On the one hand, it is more definite in its account of the nature of the *credo* which is the precondition of the *intelligo*, or of the *fides* which is necessary for the proper *intellectus*. Faith involves the entire personality of the believer—conation, affection and cognition. He must live according to the commands of God; his heart must be strengthened by God, and his attitude to God be worshipful and humble; and his eyes must be illumined so that he may see the things of faith. It is in the latter mode of the believer's consciousness that the beginnings of *intellectus*, of understanding, are to be found. It is because of the presence of this cognitive element even in *fides* that the latter should not be antithesised to *intellectus*, as if it were irrational, or prerational. Of course, this comprehensive character of *fides* is noticeable in the *Proslogion*, c. 1, in St. Anselm's statements about his spiritual longing for God and his desire to know God, but the *Epistola*, which is less devotional and more theological in its quality, brings out that character very emphatically. There is no doubt in St. Anselm's mind that it is only the committed believer who can possibly understand the content of the faith, as may readily be seen in his negative propositions: "He who has not believed has not experienced, and he who has not experienced shall not know." [26]

(1.2.2) On the other hand, if we relate cc. 2 ff. of the *Epistola* to c. 1 and regard the whole work as a theological and dramatic unity, then we are led to the same interesting conclusion as was reached with regard to the *Proslogion*: that the process of refuting the unbeliever is at the same time a process in which faith seeks to understand the content of the faith. Now admittedly the unbeliever, Roscelin, is not in this instance an atheist, a "fool who saith in his heart, There is no God". He is, however, an unbeliever to the extent that he denies the true nature of the Holy Trinity. St. Anselm's refutation of the Tritheism of Roscelin, and of the Sabellianism with which the latter identified orthodox faith, forms a single texture of argument with the exposition of the orthodox position. The heretical views are presented not simply for the purpose of their being refuted, but serve also to elicit the orthodox doctrines. Faith comes to fullest *intellectus* through a conversation, a dialectic, with unfaith. The double purpose is achieved of indicating the fallacies involved in unfaith and of building up a true understanding of his faith within the believer.

(1.3) *Monologion*

The *Monologion* is, together with the *Proslogion*, regarded as the *locus classicus* of the *credo ut intelligam* principle in action. Nowhere in the work, or in the covering *Epistola ad Lanfrancum Archiepiscopum*, or in the *Prologus*, is any mention made of the principle. In fact, in the *Prologus* St. Anselm tells us that those who constrained him to write this work laid upon him the condition that he should not appeal to the authority of Scripture but conduct his enquiry in a simple style, using commonplace arguments and enforcing his case solely by the necessity of reason. The *Monologion* fulfils the prescription to the letter.

In the *Prologus* St. Anselm tells us that there is nothing in the work which is in conflict with what St. Augustine says in the *De Trinitate*. Starting from the empirical generalisation that "all men seek to enjoy those things which they think to be good", he affirms that by reason alone anyone can be persuaded as to the existence of "one nature, the highest of all things that exist, self-sufficient in his eternal happiness . . . and as to the many other things that we necessarily believe concerning God and His creatures". [27] He so maintains his argument that in the end he has proved, by a liberal use of the Platonic Doctrine of the Forms, not only the existence and attributes of this *summum bonum* and *summe magnum* but also his three-in-oneness. It is only in the last chapter [28] that he says: "Therefore it appears, indeed it is generally asserted, that this is nothing but what is called God, and to this highest essence alone is the name of God assigned." At no point in the previous seventy-nine chapters has St. Anselm, in his own opinion, drawn on the Catholic faith of the Church; at no point has he even gone so far as to mention God. He has taken the unbeliever from a premise that he would admit to the fullest Christian conclusions.

(1.3.1) In the *Monologion*, therefore, St. Anselm does not explicitly quote his well-known principle, yet the method which he follows here is so completely identical with that of the *Proslogion*, cc. 2 ff., that it must be regarded also as a genuine instance of the *credo ut intelligam* in operation. His use of two phrases draws attention to two important features of his methodology. The first is "*auctoritate scripturae . . . nihil*".[29] The example of St. Augustine's *De Trinitate* is obviously in front of him, with its repeated appeal to, and exegesis of, Holy Scripture, but St. Anselm chooses to avoid such an appeal, no doubt thinking of those who would not accept Scripture as authoritative for them. Once again he puts himself alongside the unbeliever, making no assumptions which the unbeliever would not grant, and endeavouring to be as honest as he possibly can be in doing so. The second important phrase, which occurs later in his works, is the *sola ratione* of c. 1.[30] It is the positive complement to the "*auctoritate scripturae . . . nihil*", and is an indication of the common ground which he and the unbeliever will both recognise in the discussion which is to follow.

(1.3.2) If the *Monologion* is properly interpreted as *fides quaerens intellectum*, then the previously mentioned dual character of St. Anselm's method reappears. For the discussion takes as its starting-point a proposition which is not an ingredient of the faith situation and proceeds nevertheless to the completest of faith's conclusions. Faith wins through to *intellectus fidei* by means of an argument which is designed to convince someone who does not know "the one nature . . . which is alone self-sufficient in its eternal happiness ".[31] In the process of the argument one can see how the dual purpose of the discussion is fulfilled: the transition from the empirical generalisation to the complete statement of the Doctrine of the Trinity is made by way of one simple form of the Platonic Doctrine of the Forms, and the *sola ratione* condition is thereby observed. At the same time, every opportunity is taken to draw out the fullest implications of the Doctrine of the Trinity and of the Attributes of God, and the *intellectus* has left far behind the empirical observation from which it started. It is this willingness of St. Anselm to make explicit the inner logic of the Doctrine of the Trinity and of the Attributes of God which is thought to constitute the claim of the *Monologion* to be regarded as an example of the *fides quaerens intellectum*.

(1.3.3) As has been observed, it is not until c. 80 of the *Monologion* that St. Anselm mentions the name of God. He has led the unbeliever by a rationally developed argument to the point at which he must affirm the existence of a *summum bonum*, who is also a *summe magnum*, one Essence existing in three persons, eternal, omnipresent, and so on. That "highest Essence", St. Anselm affirms, is what the Christian means by God. The very manner in which St. Anselm makes this affirmation shows that the rational argument by which he has reached it is not the ground upon which he himself believes in God. Obviously he would require evidence independent of that supplied by the argument to enable him to make this concluding identification. Clearly, of course, St. Anselm means that the rational argument has helped him to understand more adequately the nature of the belief which he had held previously on other grounds.

(1.3.4) When we compare St. Anselm's starting-point in the *Monologion* with that of the *Proslogion* and the *Epistola de Incarnatione Verbi*, we readily discover that no general principle can be established about the point of departure which the *intellectus fidei* will assume. Sometimes it may be a general statement, sometimes a definition, or perhaps some misrepresentation of the Catholic faith. The qualified conclusion may, however, be taken as established: that *intellectus fidei* does not always commence with the propositions of the faith,[32] nor yet always with statements to which both believer and unbeliever would readily subscribe. Any account of the meaning of *credo ut intelligam* which endeavours to be fair to St. Anselm's methodology must therefore take full account of this qualified conclusion.

2

The variety of the Anselmic evidence on the maxim *credo ut intelligam* leads us to expect a certain variety in the interpretation of that principle, but it does not quite prepare us for the immense variety, nor yet for the actual contradictoriness, of the interpretations which have been offered in the history of the study of St. Anselm. A consideration of these interpretations is a necessary next step towards the definition of St. Anselm's method and purpose.

(2.1) C. C. J. Webb

In his *Studies in the History of Natural Theology* Webb has many kind things to say of St. Anselm. In his judgment St. Anselm has laid the proper foundation for philosophy of religion, by maintaining that this philosophy cannot begin *in vacuo* but requires material which can be assimilated only in faith, from the corporate religious experience of the community into which the philosopher is born. Refusing to be trapped by any false distinctions between Natural and Revealed Theology, St. Anselm sought "to discover in the content which faith gave him the rational connection with principles which were, or seemed to be, on grounds of reason, indisputable".[33] In both the *Monologion* and the *Proslogion* the methodology is the same: "the starting-point of faith, the free employment of rational methods, the absence of any dogmatic authority to divert or interrupt the course of speculation".[34] Accordingly, Webb translates *fides quaerens intellectum* as "belief in search of rational self-justification".[35] Writing particularly with reference to the *Proslogion*, he adds that, while the treatise is "able to serve as a 'short way with unbelievers'", the purpose of St. Anselm's method is to offer justification for faith in two ways: on the one hand, by demonstrating that it is logically inferrible from general principles of reason, and, on the other, by exhibiting the logical self-contradiction involved in the denial of the faith.

A close examination of Webb's account of St. Anselm's views yields the following criticisms:

(2.1.1) Webb does not do sufficient justice to what might be called the "apologetic interest" of St. Anselm's writings. It would be wrong to say that this interest is predominant in St. Anselm, but "the fool who saith in his heart, There is no God" is never far from his mind all through the *Proslogion*, and Gaunilo does not allow him to forget him in the later exchanges. The subtlety of St. Anselm's thought consists in the manner in which he weaves the apologetic interest into his dogmatic pattern. It is not simply that St. Anselm in establishing his own position happens to refute "the fool"; rather does faith use the views of "the fool" to understand itself the better. Whatever else we shall have to say concerning St. Anselm's method, we cannot deny that, for example in the *Monologion*, he considers himself as using premises accepted by unbelievers to form part at least of the basis for Christian conclusions, and therefore as endeavouring to carry conviction to these unbelievers.

(2.1.2) On the other hand, by translating *fides quaerens intellectum* as a type of self-justification, Webb places *fides* too much on the defensive and understates the nature of *intellectus*. The former criticism is made because in fact St. Anselm nowhere conceives of himself as obliged to apologise abjectly for his faith, or to justify it at the bar of contemporary reason as if that were the final criterion of the truth of his *fides*. Defensiveness of that kind belongs more properly to the nineteenth than to the twelfth century. Professor John Baillie puts the matter thus: "St. Anselm never regards it as the function of reason to *justify* . . . saving faith in God; but only to understand it—a very different and far more modest office." [36] The latter criticism follows from what has been said already about the dual character of St. Anselm's method. He establishes the nexus between the content of faith and the rational principles of the day because these principles are accepted not only by those against whom he is arguing but also by himself. If he is going to understand his faith, if he is going to appropriate it and not simply accept it on the authority of Scripture or the recommendation of the Fathers, then it is in terms of the common intellectual categories of his day that he will do so. There are no others in terms of which he could possibly appropriate the faith. In this respect St. Anselm proves himself both wiser and more honest than thinkers of other generations, who thought to dissociate themselves from the metaphysics of their time and to construct a non-metaphysical theology, but all too plainly demonstrated their acceptance of the majority of the categories held by their contemporaries.

(2.1.3) Further, Webb's account of St. Anselm's procedure— "the starting-point of faith, the free employment of rational methods, the absence of any dogmatic authority"—is consistently obscure. In what sense, for example, is faith St. Anselm's starting-point? Clearly, Webb cannot mean that St. Anselm begins his arguments from propositions assented to by faith, for faith's propositions come as the conclusions of each work. Webb may mean that it is his faith which has started St. Anselm off on this kind of argument against the unbeliever, but then some less ambiguous phrase than "the starting-point of faith" should have been used to make this intention clear. Somehow it would appear that Webb wants us to link the phrase with his statement that St. Anselm provides the proper basis for philosophy of religion by seeking to construct it within the living experience of a worshipping community. Faith, that is, religious experience, provides the data upon which the rational methods may freely work. Webb is also somewhat idealistic in his imputation to St. Anselm of "the free employment of rational methods", for this "free employment" invariably yields Christian conclusions. A brief reminder of the very different ends to which utilitarian ethical systems have employed the original presupposition of the *Monologion*, namely, that "all men seek to enjoy those things which they think to be good", should be sufficient to cause us to doubt such "freedom". St. Anselm may forswear the authority of Scripture, but nevertheless it is clear that he moves within the limits which Scripture defines. To allow to St. Anselm freedom beyond these limits is to assign to him a freedom which he would himself be most unlikely to accept.

(2.2) E. Gilson

Webb [37] differentiates his interpretation of St. Anselm from what he regards as two false accounts of his theology. The first account is given by "the adherents of the later scholastic systems", who charge St. Anselm with attempting to deduce the Doctrine of the Trinity from general principles of reason. The second comes from those who find in his *credo ut intelligam* the classic instance of a "tied philosophy", a philosophy bound to a dogmatic authority. In contemporary literature are to be found examples of each type of interpretation; here E. Gilson is selected as the representative of the former and A. E. Taylor of the latter.

Etienne Gilson treats of St. Anselm's methodology in a manner which implies the inferiority of St. Anselm to St. Thomas Aquinas. The order to follow in the search for truth, according to St. Anselm, is as follows: to believe first the mysteries of faith before discussing them with reason; to compel oneself, next, to understand what one believes.[38] Even if it is necessary to believe in order to understand, Gilson asks, is it possible that everything we believe can be made intelligible? For St. Anselm such a problem never arose, because he did not hesitate to prove the necessity even of the Trinity and the Incarnation. St. Anselm's position is therefore one of Christian rationalism. He will have nothing to do with anything but reason alone. He begins from rational principles and proceeds to rational conclusions, and establishes by the evidence of reason and natural knowledge the truth of all that an independent study of revelation could show to be true.[39] However, either because he has become a little conscience-stricken over his extremely rationalistic interpretation of St. Anselm, or because he now realises that there is more to St. Anselm than simple rationalism, Gilson adds that, in St. Anselm's view, if reason wishes to be completely reasonable, if it hopes to satisfy itself as reason, it can best achieve these ends by exercising itself on the rationality of the faith. Faith, Gilson would finally say, is for St. Anselm continually endeavouring to transform itself into understanding, though faith does not rest upon the logical arguments which reason provides for faith's positions.

Gilson's treatment of St. Anselm I find both confusing and enlightening. It is confusing to this extent that he does not attempt to reconcile what are either incongruities in his own analysis of St. Anselm or obscurities in St. Anselm himself. Thus he sets side by side the two views, first that we must believe before we understand, and secondly that we come to an understanding of the propositions of faith without reference to Scripture and solely by means of rational principles. Moreover, in his affirmation of the rationalism of St. Anselm, he ignores the place which faith as devoted trust and consecration of will occupies in St. Anselm's religion, for example, in the *Proslogion*, c. 1. Gilson's account, however, also proves enlightening, in that it points, albeit inconsistently, to two possible solutions of the *credo ut intelligam* principle. First, it could be taken to mean that faith prescribes the conclusions towards which the understanding may move by means of logical argumentation. If we had not faith we should be unaware of what the conclusions were which reason ought to establish by its own principles. Faith, that is, indicates *a priori* the direction in which reason should move. Secondly— and this point follows from the first—it is only in proceeding in such a direction that reason fulfils its true nature. It is in seeking to establish as logical conclusions the propositions which faith holds on trust that reason is really rational. In other words, it is only as I believe that my understanding functions properly.

(2.3) A. E. Taylor

A. E. Taylor [40] outspokenly attributes to St. Anselm that view which we have seen to be present, somewhat contradictorily, in Gilson's account, namely, that for St. Anselm faith provides the goal towards which the understanding is constrained to move. St. Anselm is understood as saying that when you think things out you are inevitably led to the positions which faith holds. Taylor goes so far as to suggest, parodying Bradley, that theology is, like metaphysics, "the finding of good reasons for what we believe on instinct". Finally, we are told that *fides quaerens intellectum* will be led to western Christianity in the atmosphere of eleventh-century Paris or Canterbury, to Islam at the Court of Baghdad or Cordova. Taylor, who shared with a small number of great thinkers an outstanding ability to state sympathetically even views with which he radically disagreed, shows himself at this point curiously unsympathetic towards St. Anselm, a fact no doubt due to his well-known predisposition towards St. Thomas Aquinas. His lack of sympathy, in fact, leads to actual misunderstanding of St. Anselm in the following ways:

(2.3.1) If we were to take Taylor's view of the relation of *fides* to *intellectus* seriously, we should be obliged to regard the *intellectus* either as a piece of sheer self-deception or as a bit of nonsense, and to dismiss St. Anselm as a somewhat unworthy representative of Christian theology, a pygmy beside the giant that was St. Thomas Aquinas. Now what I may call "the feel" of St. Anselm's argumentation is not that of a man who is engaged in either of the pursuits just mentioned. The impression one gains—and the impression increases the more one reads of St. Anselm—is that he is genuinely working out a case. There is an earnest dialectic of belief and unbelief, and the issue of that dialectic is, one is convinced, important; nor is it foreclosed. In the *Proslogion* there is genuine reality in the struggle which St. Anselm carried out to secure his own faith, through the complexity of the dialectic of the *intellectus*. His soul is in his writing, and to deny this fact is to miss the sincerity which is one of the supreme qualities of St. Anselm's writing.

(2.3.2) It is a mistake, too, to reduce St. Anselm's method to an attempt to discover "good reasons" for dogmas accepted on authority. St. Anselm categorically rejects the double standard of theological truth which Taylor attributes to him—that of authoritative tradition, and that of rational, or pseudo-rational, justification. He may have come to know his theological conclusions through his acquaintance with the Church's traditional doctrine, but in his writings he nowhere allows that such a standard is authoritative for him. His chief purpose throughout is to understand his faith, and naturally he does so in the categories of Canterbury rather than in those accepted in Cordova. This criticism of Taylor's is only another form of the "rational self-justification" interpretation given by C. C. J. Webb and it need not further detain us.

(2.3.3) It is no criticism of St. Anselm to suggest that arguments which would convince the native of Canterbury would be rejected by the member of the court at Cordova. St. Anselm never thought otherwise. In each of his writings those with whom he is arguing must be willing to accept certain premises from which to begin. If they rejected these premises the discussion could not continue. In most of St. Anselm's writings these premises include propositions which no Mohammedan would ever accept; no Mohammedan therefore would be expected by St. Anselm to accept the arguments which in his opinion lead to certain propositions of the

Christian faith. In other words, Taylor pictures St. Anselm as failing to be a pure rationalist, which in fact St. Anselm never attempted to be.

(2.4) John Baillie[41]

We have from the pen of Professor John Baillie a much more appreciative and penetrating analysis of St. Anselm's maxim *credo ut intelligam* and of his concept *fides quaerens intellectum*. Translating the latter phrase as "belief in search of understanding", Professor Baillie maintains that for St. Anselm the *intellectum* is preconditioned by *fides*, which is not simply blind acceptance of an established theological tradition but a total response of the human personality to the prevenient grace of God. The *intellectus*, therefore, does not induce *fides*, nor does it rationally justify *fides*, but it does provide the believer with a deeper comprehension of what it is that he believes. *Fides*, in other words, formulates the conclusions towards which the *intellectus* must work, and here, in direct opposition to A. E. Taylor, Professor Baillie has a high word of commendation for St. Anselm, who in his opinion has brought to light one of the essential characteristics of the methodology of the so-called *Geisteswissenschaften*, namely, what R. G. Collingwood termed "the reversible character" of their argumentation. In the philosophical and theological sciences we not infrequently know our conclusions to be true independently of the truths we may adduce to prove their truth. In such cases the proofs do not therefore constitute the grounds of our conclusions (or beliefs) but they do assist us in understanding the nature and content of the conclusions. St. Anselm, therefore, would fall completely within this tradition, and his proofs concerning God's existence, nature and attributes would be taken to further the believer's appreciation of what he in fact believed on other grounds.

While Professor Baillie's treatment of St. Anselm is illuminating, and while it does justice to aspects of his theological procedure which are obscured by others, nevertheless there are in regard to certain details difficulties worthy of comment:

(2.4.1) Professor Baillie's analysis of the relation of *fides* to *intellectus* rests on the assumption that throughout the process of *intellectus* the *fides* as *fides* remains unchanged. He refers on page 137 [42] to the proofs supplied by St. Anselm as "a better understanding of a belief *already firmly held*".[43] One interpretation of St. Anselm's writings would cast doubt on the truth of these last three words. They would not correctly apply, for example, to the *Proslogion*. Chapter I of that work could not be said to imply in St. Anselm, at that point, the existence of a "belief firmly held". The firmness of the belief is reached only through the lengthy process of the *intellectus*. Accordingly, it must be maintained that the proof (Professor Baillie's word) does enter in, for St. Anselm, as a factor which affects the acceptability of the conclusion; and, *per contra*, failure to complete the proof would have led to a debilitation of the conclusion. In fact, it would be difficult to see how Professor Baillie could in the end escape that stultification of St. Anselm's method which A. E. Taylor enunciated so forcefully.

(2.4.2) While it is true to say that St. Anselm's proof is not intended to lead us to full belief in God, nevertheless we ought not to underestimate the weight which St. Anselm thought his arguments would carry with unbelievers. He may not have expected to argue "the fool who saith in his heart, There is no God" into living faith in God, but he did estimate that his closely knit argument would remove not a few of the difficulties which were keeping "the fool" from faith. By a process of inference it may not be possible to reach faith, yet assuredly, as long as faith is not "blind" faith, the process of inference must assist faith. So, if it cannot be denied that "it is not as a result of an inference of any kind . . . that the knowledge of God's reality comes to us", this latter proposition must not be taken as a denial of the possibility that faith may follow upon an inferential process. In fact, that possibility must always be left open so long as men are rational and, one might add, rationalising beings.

(2.4.3) Professor Baillie,[44] following along the same line which we have just discussed, further maintains that it is St. Anselm's intention "not to show us *why* we already believe in (God), but only to convince us *that* we already believe". This estimation of St. Anselm's intention is scarcely in agreement either with Professor Baillie's description of St. Anselm's method or with St.

Anselm's actual writing. Professor Baillie's interpretation had been that St. Anselm, in the *fides quaerens intellectum*, is endeavouring to understand the faith and not to convince himself or the unbeliever *that* he believes; and, further, that St. Anselm's conviction ("belief already firmly held") rests on grounds other than the arguments he advances. If St. Anselm does not seek to show us why we already believe, still less does he seek to show us that we already believe. If, on the other hand, we do allow that St. Anselm aims at convincing, the questions at once arise: whom? and of what? St. Anselm's writings offer answers to these questions. Several answers would have to be given according to which of his works we were considering. Thus, he aims at convincing his intellectual opponent (who may variously be "the fool" of the *Proslogion*, or the person in the *Monologion* who agrees that "all men seek to enjoy those things which they think to be good") that certain beliefs which he accepts logically imply certain other beliefs which he does not accept, but which are affirmations of faith. In both the *Monologion* and the *Proslogion* St. Anselm does appear to be attempting to convince his opponent, who does not believe in God, that his unbelief commits him to logical self-contradiction; in short, he is attempting to show him *why* he should believe that God exists.

(2.4.4) To the question of how, if faith in God does not rest upon an argument, the construction of an argument can be expected to lead to correct understanding of faith, Professor Baillie gives an answer as follows: the argument is "the clear explication of a logical structure which had been already 'implicitly' contained in the mental process by which the faith was originally acquired".[45] Professor Baillie, advancing this account as a suggested defence of St. Anselm's method of theological procedure, goes on to reject it. The reason he gives [46] is that since knowledge of the reality of God comes through "our personal encounter with Him in the Person of Jesus Christ", it cannot be derived from any series of inferences. Even if we agree with Professor Baillie and allow that the principle *credo ut intelligam* does imply faith of some kind or to some degree as a precondition of the *quaerens intellectum*—and such agreement is possible even though we would disagree as to whether this faith were firmly held at the beginning of the search or were deepened as a result of the search—nevertheless we may join issue with the attempt to find a logical structure "implicit" in the initial act or attitude of faith. For this suggestion, to my mind, carries with it the implications that it is this "implicit" logical structure which constitutes the ground of that initial act or attitude of faith, and that the *intellectus fidei* is the bringing into the conscious field of something which, unknown to the believer, was already present and operative in his mind. It is highly improbable that either of these implications would be acceptable to St. Anselm. He would, perhaps, rather say that the ground for the *credo* which "seeks understanding" is the authority of Scripture, the testimony of the Fathers, but supremely —to use Professor Baillie's own phrase—the God Who has mediated Himself to him through both. With reference to the *Proslogion*, it is impossible to see how a logical structure is implicit in the "unbelieving belief" of c. 1; if it were, St. Anselm would be a much happier man at that point. The following chapters of the book supply something which is neither implicit nor explicit in c. 1 but which satisfies the need so skilfully there stated. Quite apart from any appeal to St. Anselm's works, we could simply say, in criticism of Professor Baillie's suggested defence of St. Anselm, that it is not ultimately possible to understand what it means. If the logical structure is properly "implicit" in the *credo* which goes on to seek understanding, the believer is not *ex hypothesi* aware of it at that moment. When at a later time he is presented with an explicit piece of reasoning, he will be unable to say whether it is or is not an explication of the conditioning structure of his belief, for he has no awareness of any such structure with which to compare the so-called explication. Finally, in most of St. Anselm's arguments, as we have already observed, his purpose is to convince certain intellectual opponents, who, so far from having "implicit" grounds for the article of faith which he establishes, are on the contrary quite convinced of the untruth of that article. In such cases it would be playing with words to say that they implicitly believe what they explicitly disbelieve.

(2.5) Karl Barth[47]

Having listened to Gilson's structures upon the rationalism of St. Anselm, and having observed the delight with which Webb

hails the fact that St. Anselm has laid the proper foundations of
a philosophy of religion, we come, not without some surprise,
upon Karl Barth's most commendatory treatment of St. Anselm's
methodology.   His *Fides Quaerens Intellectum*, which is an
analysis of and a commentary upon St. Anselm's proof of God's
existence as given in the *Proslogion*, is a work of paramount
importance for any examination of Karl Barth's own works and of
his own methodology.   In this essay Barth virtually declares,
through his praise of St. Anselm, that his own writing will follow
a pattern somewhat similar to that of St. Anselm—a fact which
can easily be illustrated from the frequent, and still commendatory,
references to St. Anselm which recur throughout the later and
much longer *Kirchliche Dogmatik*.   In fact, it could with some
fairness be maintained that St. Anselm exerts a greater determining influence upon the methodology of Karl Barth, if not also
upon the content of his writing, than any of the other thinkers,
such as Kierkegaard, Dostoievsky, Luther and Calvin, with whom
his "source critics" so often associate him.   He is appreciative of
St. Anselm almost to the degree of being uncritical.   While, therefore, Barth's treatment of St. Anselm is invaluable as a clue to the
understanding of Barth's own method in theology, his very en-
thusiasm makes it difficult for the reader to discriminate between
Barth's exposition of St. Anselm and his elaboration of the latter's
statements along lines which represent his own thoughts more
than they do St. Anselm's.   Nevertheless, Barth's account of St.
Anselm's theology is the most comprehensive of all the writings
on the subject and deserves the most careful treatment.

(2.5.1) What Barth has to say concerning the *credo ut intelligam*
maxim or the phrase *fides quaerens intellectum* may be grouped
around his characterisation of *fides* and *intellectus*:

(2.5.1.1) Drawing on the *De Incarnatione Verbi*, c. 1, Barth
makes it plain that for St. Anselm the *fides* is obedience-belief.
It involves the right act of will in relation to God,[48] and until the
enquirer has placed himself at the point of that obedience he is
not qualified to embark upon the intellectual enquiries that follow.
Belief and obedience are to be comprehended within the single
experience which St. Anselm calls *fides*, for only as faith takes
place within an act of living obedience to God is it truly faith.

C

Barth sees St. Anselm here as standing within what J. V. Langmead Casserley [49] calls the "Existentialist tradition".

(2.5.1.2) *Fides* or *credere* is under no circumstances, however, to be regarded as irrational, or illogical, or distinct in kind from *intellectus*. *Intellectus* is necessary in order that faith may understand what is said in the Sermon, that it may hear the Word of Christ which is identical, by God's grace, with the Word of those who preach Christ. (Here Barth is elaborating St. Anselm's position by means of what he later developed into a Doctrine of Proclamation.) Faith involves the intellectual apprehension of a certain set of words occurring in a logical and grammatical context, or, as Barth says,[50] the knowing of a *vox significans rem*. This knowing, this hearing, faith shares with unfaith; in unfaith, the hearer has the matter only *in intellectu*, whereas faith is consciously aware of the reality (*res*) of what it hears. In *fides*, then, there is present an *intellectus*, with which *fides* is one in kind though it differs in degree.[51]

(2.5.1.3) Further, faith seeks for a fuller understanding of itself. Barth refers to St. Anselm's use of such words as the "longing", the "hungering", the "thirsting" of faith after understanding, this desire of faith being proper or essential to its very nature. The fact that I believe in itself constitutes a challenge to me to understand the faith that I believe.[52] Faith does not pass out of itself—there is no μετάβασις εἰς ἄλλο γένος—to understand itself. It so proceeds by means of its own inner logic and by the sheer compulsion of that logic.

(2.5.1.4) At the end of the process of *intellectus* a further affirmation of faith takes place. Then faith declares that the truth at which *intellectus* has arrived by proof is the Truth, which is Christ, in Whom faith believes. The beginning and the end of *intelligere* lie in faith. According to Barth's account of the situation, the procession in St. Anselm is as follows: understanding (of the *vox significans rem*); faith; the understanding by faith of itself; faith.

(2.5.1.5) The success or non-success of the *intellectus* in arriving at its conclusions, Barth most emphatically points out,[53] does not affect the reality of *fides*. It is not the function of theology to lead believers to deeper faith, or unbelievers from unfaith to faith, nor yet does it remove any doubts from faith. The believer is too sure of his faith to be shaken in any way if in the process of *quaerens intellectus* he can discover no *ratio* for his belief.

(2.5.2) *Intellectus*, as we have already seen, is the continuation of a process already present in *fides*. As such, it is described by Barth as a meditation upon what is put before it by faith. *Nachdenken* (literally, thinking afterwards or reflection) is the word by which Barth translates the *intelligere*. This reflection is circumscribed in its limits, beyond which it cannot at any time pass, by the *fides*. This general description of the relation of the *credere* to the *intelligere* Barth makes specific in several directions:

(2.5.2.1) There is a description,[54] to begin with, which, as has been indicated above, Professor Baillie was to state in kindred terms some years later. It is that the *intellectus* is a continuation and explication of a body of affirmations already contained implicitly in the *fides*. The act of faith, while apparently simple and unreasoned, carries within it a full logical structure which the understanding by reflection is able to draw forth. The relation of the *fides* to the *intellectus*, on this account, would be not dissimilar to that of the ordinary person who knows that $2+2=4$ to the mathematical logician who understands the vast conceptual system upon which this simple arithmetical equation rests and which it involves for its truth.

(2.5.2.2) Next, it is maintained [55] that the believer in saying "*credo*" affirms that such-and-such is the case. When he goes on and is *quaerens intellectum*, he is endeavouring to discover *how* or *how far* it is the case, *quomodo sit*. The *intellectus* can never come within reach of doubting the *that*: immediately it does, it ceases to be *intellectus*. In other words, the *intellectus* has to recognise that there are certain limits set to enquiries about the *how* and *how far*; beyond these limits the questions are directed at the *that*, and must forthwith be restrained. Barth adds, by implication, that the *intellectus* does not endeavour to discover *why* it is so,[56] for the foundation of the *credo* is to be found in the fact of the Divine Revelation. Faith does not at any point of its progression in *intellectus* rest upon the arguments which *intellectus* explicates.

(2.5.2.3) At a later stage of the *Fides Quaerens Intellectum* Barth employs an argument from derivation at some considerable length. *Intelligere*, he points out, is derived from *intus* and *legere*; the faith, in understanding itself, *reads* what is within the *credo*, but this *intelligere* is a deepened *legere*.[57] At this point, in order to bring out more clearly the distinction between the *intelligere* and the *legere* of the believing person, Barth introduces a distinction, not to be found in St. Anselm, between an "exterior text" and an "interior text". The "exterior text" (of Holy Scripture or Creed) is that which the believer and the unbeliever alike may read; the "interior text" is the full "sense, reason and context" contained in that text, which the believer has to understand and therefore knows as the truth of the text. For us, as "sons of Adam", the "exterior" and "interior texts" are not one. We cannot read off the latter from the former. The "exterior text" poses the problem which the understanding must solve, namely, the problem of what it "means". The "exterior text veils in darkness" the truth of its meaning, which is the "interior text"; nevertheless, it is within the "exterior text" and not elsewhere that that truth is to be discovered, or, more accurately, is to be revealed by God. It is in the *intelligere—intus legere—*that this event takes place. Barth's use of the distinction creates its own problems, for the "exterior text" seems sometimes to mean, as above suggested, the words which infidels in their scorn, and believing Christians in their honest doubts, as well as the educated and the uneducated,[58] can all understand, and also the inner significance which the faithful who have not embarked upon the search for understanding have grasped. Alternatively, *legere* seems sometimes to be applied to the activity in which believers and unbelievers alike read off the words written in Scripture or Creed, and to that activity which the believer as a believer performs in affirming his *credo*, before proceeding to *intellectus fidei*; thus Barth speaks of "faithful *legere*".[59] This apparent ambiguity in Barth can be dissolved—and this may be his intention—if we see that the *legere* of the faithful who reads his Scripture or his

Creed is already an *intus legere*; or, altering the significance of a
sentence previously attributed to Barth, that *fides* is an elementary
form of *intellectus*.

(2.5.2.4) Barth has now laid down the foundation for his
analysis of the relation of the *intellectus fidei* to Holy Scriptures
with their authoritative claim.   Scriptures rest upon the solid
foundation of their authoritative given-ness by God, a fact which
is revealed to faith.   But understanding which seeks after a
deepened *legere* of the "interior text" cannot be content with any
appeal to authority.   In the *probare*, which is an alternative description of the *intelligere*, St. Anselm, so Barth argues, refuses to
"lead into the field"[60] quotations from Scriptures as proof of the
credo or as the means for understanding the faith; such a method
would amount to a mere repetition of the *legere*.   The *probare* or
the *intelligere* emerges only when we think through to the truth
of what is affirmed in the *credo* or the Holy Scriptures.   Putting
the same point in a slightly different way, Barth says elsewhere [61]
that the Truth of Revelation is God's giving of Himself, but in
Dogmatics this revealing action does not take place in a flash, but
through a laborious advance from one partial human insight to
another.   In this laborious advance the dogmatic enquirer must
not rely simply upon the authoritative given-ness of Scriptural
statements; rather will he assume the responsibility of discovering the thought and language in which the Church can say to the
contemporary generation what the Apostles and Prophets said
to theirs.   It was, therefore, this refusal to rely simply on the
authority of Scripture which St. Anselm intended by "his well-
known but not quite unobjectionable formula" of *remoto Christo*.
On this reading of the situation, the *intellectus* has in advance the
solution of its problems, the solution being given in the "exterior
text" of the Scriptures or the *credo*.   The goal of the *probare* is
known *a priori*.   For this reason, Barth can maintain that the
intellectus fidei does not reject Holy Scriptures as the source and
norm of its thinking, and that the Scriptures and *credo* never
cease to be the precondition and the object of the understanding.
St. Anselm argues not from an arbitrarily constructed possibility
to its reality, but from the reality to its possibility.[62]

(2.5.2.5) In the light of what has been expounded of Barth's analysis of St. Anselm's methodology, the reasons for Barth's denial of the alleged rationalism in St. Anselm are plain. For St. Anselm, as for Barth, *intellectus fidei* is "open only at one end". The believer who seeks to understand his faith is not reconstructing his *credo* out of elements of knowledge derived from elsewhere. St. Anselm is under no circumstances to be regarded as "a patron saint of natural theology".[63] Barth, however, is not unaware of the possibility of a rationalistic interpretation of some of St. Anselm's own accounts of his methodology, and so he prefers to refute the charge of rationalism by demonstrating what St. Anselm has actually *done* in his *intellectus fidei*. This demonstration is much more convincing than Barth's general explanation of his concern to deny the rationalism of St. Anselm, and it is as follows:

Some article of faith is taken as the fact to be probed in the process of *intellectus fidei*, this fact being designated as "the unknown x". St. Anselm, then, proceeds to show how certain other articles within the *credo*, *a b c d*,[64] logically imply x. The person, therefore, who accepts *a b c d* cannot, without logical self-contradiction, at the same time deny x. St. Anselm uses what such a person believes to prove what he denies; for example, in the *De Processione Spiritus Sancti*, he claims to lead the Greeks from premises which they accept to affirmation of the *Filioque* which they would normally deny.

The other example which Barth cites at length in this respect, and which is of the utmost importance in our present examination of the *remoto Christo*, is that of the *Cur Deus Homo*. The x of the *Cur Deus Homo* is the necessity of the Incarnation and of the reconciling Death of Christ. Although he does not explicitly say so, Barth could well be taken to mean that the unknown-ness of the Christological x is intended by the phrase *remoto Christo*. The *a b c d* are: the existence of a Divine plan for humankind; the essential obligation of man to obey God, his Creator; sin as infinite guilt of man in the sight of God; God's relentlessness in His negation of sin; the incapacity of man to redeem himself; and, finally, the aseity and honour of God.[65] Commenting upon an almost identical list,[66] Barth draws attention to the fact that these, the given elements of St. Anselm's proof, are not universal truths, such as a rationalist might employ as his premises, but knowledge derived from revelation. In fact, not only is the goal of the *intellectus fidei* an affirmation of faith but its premises are also propositions which the believer accepts. Premises and conclusion are co-ordinate—all articles of faith. The reasonable and necessary in the *intellectus fidei* are so in terms not of any philosophical categories but of the Holy Scriptures and the Creed.

Barth is not slow to point out that, in the light of such an interpretation of St. Anselm's method, the *Monologion* and the *Proslogion* would appear to occupy a somewhat equivocal position, and he asks the question honestly, whether in these two works St. Anselm is writing what he calls "aprioristic theology".[67] He gives several replies. First, he feels that what might be called the Anselmic method of theological enquiry is so clearly defined and established in the later works, notably in the *Cur Deus Homo*, that St. Anselm would not have changed from some other method (for example, a completely rationalistic method) to that maturer method without exhibiting some embarrassment or giving some indication of a break in his development. This argument is really analogical, the method of the earlier works being determined from an examination of the later. Secondly, says Barth, it is precisely in the earlier works, notably the *Monologion*, that the principle is affirmed that faith is the foundation of the entire *intellectus*. Accordingly, such is the implication, we must also in the early works postulate an *a b c d* as the starting-points recognised by faith in its search for understanding of itself. Thirdly, in these works also it is possible to discern the elements of faith in the starting-points of the discussion: in the affirmation of the incomprehensibility of God, of the indirectness of all knowledge of God, of creation by God, and of His singularity and aseity. Or, as Barth puts it elsewhere, God is present to the enquirer in the earlier works "generally as the discoverable object of his search".[68] In these ways Barth endeavours to bring the earlier works into line with the methodology which he has so convincingly established for the later works. Fourthly, Barth endeavours [69] to draw a distinction between the *Monologion* and the *Proslogion* and to argue that the *Monologion* deals not with the question of whether God exists but with that of the nature of God. The *Monologion* uses the Neo-Platonic technique to ascend from the notion of the relatively good, great and being, to the highest good and the proper and only great and being, but it does not ask whether there is in reality anyone of this sort—an open question for the *Monologion* and that with which the *Proslogion* deals.

(2.5.3) The merits of Karl Barth's contribution to the study of St. Anselm are so outstanding (for example, his appreciation of the devotional quality of his writings; his emphasis on St. Anselm's account of faith as a total response to the initiative of a gracious, self-revealing God; his integration of *fides* with *intellectus*; and his forthright defence of St. Anselm against the charge of rationalism) that it is only with a certain diffidence and with an acute awareness of our debt to Barth that we can embark upon any criticism of his analysis of St. Anselm's thought. It is just because Barth has taught us so much about St. Anselm that we are able to make such criticisms as we do offer.

(2.5.3.1) There are certain matters of minor importance which need only briefly be mentioned. For example, Barth seems to mis-state even his own case (apart from St. Anselm's) when he affirms that the faith from which the *intellectus* begins is firmly held, and that no success or failure in theological enquiry affects the certainty of faith. Barth often draws attention to the prayer of c. 1 of the *Proslogion*, with its longing not merely for fuller knowledge but for deeper assurance of God's nearness. Faith at that stage is not "firmly held"; it is only after the endeavour to understand, which covers cc. 2-25, that something approaching assurance appears. But, further, allowing as he does that *fides* and *intellectus* are integral to each other, Barth could have been expected to go on to say that any advance in the *intelligere* (*intus legere*) affects the manner in which *fides* reads the sentences of Scripture and the *credo*, and therefore affects *fides* itself. Barth would not have compromised his own principles in any way by making this further assertion; as he so often says, the *intellectus* is *intellectus FIDEI*. Of course, it is most probable that Barth feels unwilling to go as far as we have suggested because he at times equates the *intellectus fidei* with theology, and, understandably, he is not prepared to say that theology, which is for him a science, can in any way affect faith, which is a total response of the human personality to God's address. He has to allow, too, for the person who may be intellectually incapable of the intricacies of theological enquiry but who yet has a very deep faith in God, for nowhere does St. Anselm suggest that *fides* can only remain *fides* by completing itself in *intellectus fidei*. Even so, St. Anselm is equally aware that for some people at least the *intellectus* may be the means by which *fides* is deepened, if it is not actually created by the *intellectus*.

Barth, as we have seen, suggests the view also put forward by Professor Baillie, that the *intellectus* is an explication of a logical structure implicit in the initial act of faith. The criticism made previously [70] is here also relevant, though the further question may be raised of whether this account of the *intellectus* agrees with that which Barth gives later in the *Fides Quaerens Intellectum*, that the *intellectus* consists in proving that an x, unknown at the beginning of the process, is established by logical inference from $a\ b\ c\ d$, certain sentences of the *credo*. Barth could, no doubt, answer this question in the positive, but then he would be virtually affirming that the *intellectus fidei* has a double nature. On the one hand, it demonstrates to the believer the logical interrelation of the several articles of the *credo*. The believer, before such a demonstration, accepts x; it is not "unknown" for him, though the relation of x to $a\ b\ c\ d$ is unknown. On the other hand, to the person who disbelieves x, the relation of logical implication between x and $a\ b\ c\ d$ is proved, and he is shown the impossibility of not accepting x. The questions of whether a single method of demonstration can really serve this double purpose, of which purpose is prior in St. Anselm's mind and of which therefore determines the form of the argument are matters with which Barth does not deal, but they are of paramount importance in the decision as to the "apologetic" character of his writings. But it can be fairly clearly seen from the writings of St. Anselm what conclusion is to be reached on these matters: it is the *probare* (to convince the person who disbelieves x) which determines the form which the *intelligere* (for the benefit of the believer) takes, and not *vice versa*. The x is determined in each case by the unbeliever (sometimes in a restricted sense) who will not accept this or that sentence of Scripture or *credo*, whether that x be the existence and nature of God, as in the *Proslogion*, or the Incarnation of the Second Person of the Trinity, as in the *De Incarnatione Verbi*, or the Incarnation as a historical fact and the reconciling and atoning Death of Our Lord, as in the *Cur Deus Homo*, or the

Filioque, as in the *De Processione Spiritus Sancti*. If, therefore, Barth is willing to agree that the *intellectus* may be described equally well as an explication of the inner logical structure implicit in simple faith and as the proving of an unknown *x* to a person who accepts articles *a b c d* of the *credo*, then he is obliged to face the consequences of that argument, and, not least of these, the fact that St. Anselm's concern with the unbeliever does determine the form which the explication takes and the line which it follows.   If the *intellectus* is defined as both explication of a structure implicit in *fides* and as demonstration of the logical necessity of *x*, then immediately Professor Baillie's objection is relevant, namely, that *fides* is an implicit inference.   The only way of avoiding the objection is to affirm that in the *intellectus* the *probare* (for the benefit of the unbeliever) is the sole motive. Another consequence of defining the *intellectus* as both logical explication and demonstrative proof is that it is doubtful if, in face of such a methodology, the claim of "no apologetics in St. Anselm" can still validly be maintained.

(2.5.3.2) Barth's most important contribution to the analysis of the Anselmic methodology is to be found in his contention that the *intellectus* consists in proving that an *x* not accepted by his theological opponents can be reached by a process of logical inference from certain premises, *a b c d*, which these opponents do accept, and that the denial by them of *x* involves them in logical self-contradiction.   Barth, it will be remembered, also holds that the *a b c d* which logically imply the *x* are all sentences of the Creed or Scripture.   The importance of this analysis obliges us to consider it carefully.

The first question that must be asked is whether Barth's formula explains all of St. Anselm's works.   Clearly he has a good case for the later works, for as he points out[71] nobody has yet claimed that the conclusions reached in them are derived from generally accepted philosophical truths.   The premises in each instance are obviously articles of faith, a point well illustrated from Boso's implication that St. Anselm has assumed a few premises "from our books" in his proof of the necessity for a God-man in the *Cur Deus Homo*.[72]   But it must be remarked that these works are of a more strictly dogmatic character than the earlier ones, which take account of the positions of unbelievers in the more extreme sense of the term and which have at least a *prima facie* apologetic purpose. Accordingly, it is inevitable that in the later works St. Anselm's starting-point should be the premises of faith, or, more precisely, propositions asserting the truth of certain articles of the faith. Further, it has to be recognised that in them St. Anselm's opponents do not deny the entirety of the Christian faith (as does "the fool" of the *Proslogion*); rather do these opponents accept many of the views to which St. Anselm subscribes. The *a b c d* of the later works, therefore, are also articles of faith, and they appear as the premises of his argument not primarily because St. Anselm wants to remain within the domain of "revealed truth" but because his opponents accept them. Again, the premises of the later works can be shown to be the conclusions of the earlier; for example, the Three-in-Oneness of God established in the *Monologion* and the *Proslogion* is the basis for a discussion of the relation of "nature to Persons" which we have in the *De Incarnatione Verbi*, and of the relation of Holy Spirit to Father and Son which appears in the *De Processione Spiritus Sancti*. St. Anselm is a most systematic theologian, and his writings form a very precise progression. Therefore it is no more true to say that the *a b c d* are articles of faith, or sentences of the Creed, though they obviously are so, than it is to say that the *a b c d* are the conclusions reached in the earlier works. If this view is correct, then Barth argues invalidly when he endeavours to find the method of the later works in the earlier ones, for the earlier works form the systematic foundation for the later. To establish his case he must demonstrate that the alleged Anselmic method of deriving an unknown *x* from Scriptural or credal sentences, *a b c d*, is to be found in the early writings of St. Anselm.

Such a demonstration, as we have seen, Barth does claim to give, but the several reasons given for the view that the argument from *a b c d* (being Scriptural or credal sentences) to an unknown *x* is present in *all* his works are not adequate. Thus, his contention that if St. Anselm had changed from one method to another in his writings we should have had some indication of a break in his development, wrongly assumes that the methodology of the later works is the norm and that consequently the earlier works are to be interpreted according to that pattern. I should

agree with Barth that had St. Anselm altered his method of
theological enquiry we should have had some indication of it.
But such agreement leaves open the question of whether the later
works are the key to the earlier or *vice versa*, a question which
must be decided on grounds other than the unargued statement
that St. Anselm's methodology is uniform throughout his writings.
Nor does Barth really solve the problem when he maintains that it
is in the earlier writing of St. Anselm that the *credo ut intelligam*
maxim is first clearly formulated. If Barth interprets the *credo
ut intelligam* to mean argumentation from *a b c d*, accepted by
both parties to the discussion, to an unknown *x*, then he cannot
invoke the *credo ut intelligam* principle in support of one interpretation of the argument from *a b c d* to *x*. Again, Barth claims to
find in the *Monologion* and the *Proslogion* the elements of faith
in the starting-point from which the discussion sets forth, namely,
the incomprehensibility of God and the indirectness of all knowledge of God, etc. But surely here Barth is misconstruing the
evidence in order to establish his thesis. For, on the one hand, it
is incorrect to maintain that either of these elements is a premise
from which the general argument proceeds to its conclusion.
Certainly they are mentioned at the beginning of these works, but
such mention does not constitute them "premises" for the sake
of argument. In fact, in the *Proslogion* the incomprehensibility
of God is something which St. Anselm feels to be an obstacle in
the way of fuller faith, and he longs to comprehend God better.
The rest of the work is devoted to that end. On the other hand,
if we look closely at the *Monologion*, we find that the whole argument hinges on the Platonic Doctrine of the Forms, and, moreover, on a fairly uncritical acceptance of that doctrine.

Nor is it accurate to say that while his technique is Neo-Platonic,
the content of his proofs is not to be so regarded, for technique
and content are interdependent and interrelated. It is difficult to
see how a Neo-Platonic technique could work other than upon a
content which was, partially at least, Neo-Platonic. In addition,
the chief premise of the work, as we have already seen, is the
empirical generalisation that all men seek after that which they
think to be good. It would be absurd to regard this proposition
as an *articulum fidei*. In the same way, too, in the *Proslogion*,
while St. Anselm says that God for him is "that than which no

greater can be conceived", nevertheless he is not saying something that belongs peculiarly to the Christian faith. In fact, it is only because St. Anselm believes many other things concerning God that he knows this account of God's Being to be true. Even "the fool" could be expected to agree to this account of God in the initial stages of the argument, because he is unaware of the implications of such an account, and because he could be understood to say that if there is a God, then He must comply with such a description of Him; anything less would not be God. Even in the *Cur Deus Homo*, from which Barth draws a lengthy list of first principles of faith, there are among the premises of the work certain concepts, notably that of *satisfactio*, upon which the entire argument depends and which are not to be found in either Creed or Scripture. Finally, it has to be said that the *Monologion* does not depend upon the *Proslogion* in the way which Barth suggests, namely, as leaving to the *Proslogion* the question of God's existence and itself dealing only with the nature of God. Obviously St. Anselm regarded the *Proslogion* as a more concise proof than that given in the *Monologion* of the same conclusion.

In fact, Barth in his efforts to show that St. Anselm is not a "natural theologian" seems almost to forget what he himself has so emphatically affirmed, namely, that St. Anselm does not argue from the authoritative given-ness of Scriptural or credal sentences to certain dogmatic conclusions. There lies the greatest weakness in Barth's analysis of St. Anselm's methodology, and it is a weakness which amounts to self-contradiction. All that Barth shows is that St. Anselm does not accept as authoritatively given, but as to be proved, the relation between the premises $a\,b\,c\,d$ and the unknown x. What he does not succeed in showing is that, on his reading of the situation, St. Anselm does not accept $a\,b\,c\,d$ as authoritatively given. In fact, Barth gives his position away quite clearly when, dealing with the $a\,b\,c\,d$ of the *Monologion*, he mentions St. Anselm's use of the well-known Augustinian *vestigia Trinitatis*, *memoria*, *intelligentia* and *amor*, and affirms that St. Anselm regards it as a "Biblical-ecclesiastical-dogmatic presupposition".[73] If St. Anselm regards it as a "presupposition", then he must also regard it as "authoritatively given". Barth enforces his own position a few lines later when he speaks of St. Anselm in his use of $a\,b\,c\,d$ reminding us of the "factuality of the

Revelation", which "cannot be dissolved into any causal or teleological construction but is reasonable and necessary in itself".[74] Coming in the context of his discussion of the nature of the *a b c d* which St. Anselm employs as premises for the proof of *x*, this statement cannot but mean that the "factuality of Revelation" is attributable to the *a b c d*, and that these premises therefore are "reasonable and necessary" in themselves. There, to my mind, we have the explicit contradiction of Barth's previous assertion that St. Anselm rejects the authoritative given-ness of Scriptures and Creeds and seeks through the *probare* and the *intelligere* to find contemporary reasons for the *fides*. While, therefore, Barth has made very clear what we might call the internal logic of St. Anselm's method, he has, by virtue of his own dogmatic views and of his desire to bring St. Anselm into line with them, failed to give us an accurate account of the premises (*a b c d*, as he calls them) which St. Anselm uses in his different works.

The conclusions to which this general criticism of Barth has brought us may now be summarily stated. The premises in St. Anselm's arguments are not always entirely Scriptural. St. Anselm's choice of premises is determined not by himself but by the views held by his opponents. In the *Monologion* and the *Proslogion*, where the *principia* of faith are the subjects of discussion, among the *a b c d*, which are the basis of arguing to the unknown *x*, there do not appear many sentences from Scriptures or Creeds. In the later works, where the opposition is prepared to allow many of the articles of the faith, it is almost inevitable that many of the elements of the faith should not be called in question. If then we follow up our previous suggestion as to the systematic construction by St. Anselm, we can see how he has used the contemporary criticism to provide him with the milieu of such a construction.

3

It would, therefore, now appear that the meaning of the sentence *credo ut intelligam*, as it is used by St. Anselm, cannot be rendered simply by the translation of it into the words, "I believe in order that I may understand". Nor can it be rendered by a neatly logical elaboration of that English text into a series of propositions which it could be said to imply, for example, that it is only the believer who can go on to apprehend the inner meaning of faith's propositions; or that the initial act of faith is irrational and that it is rationalised (in the best if also in the worst sense of the term) by pseudo-logical proof. The truth or falsity of such elaborations may be interesting, but it is irrelevant. For the meaning of the sentence can be determined only in relation to what St. Anselm in fact does, that is, in relation to his actual methodology, of which that statement is a precise recapitulation. In other words, his actual methodology must decide what the statement means, and not the reverse. In the light of this contention we may bring together the several facts which have emerged in the previous discussions of the different interpretations of the Anselmic sentence, recognising that there is no simple definition of his method but that by reason of its complexity it can only be set forth at length.

(3.1) It cannot be denied, at the start, that for St. Anselm the *credo* provides the *intelligenda*, or the *probanda*, the conclusions which he endeavours to establish by his argument. These conclusions prescribe *a priori* the line which his argument will take, and to that extent he is not free " to follow the argument whithersoever it goes ". To admit so much is not to accuse St. Anselm of insincerity, for while he knows in advance which conclusions he wishes to prove, he still honestly endeavours to give an argument which is convincing not only to the believer but also, and particularly, to the unbeliever. It is always an open possibility throughout the argument that he may not be able to prove his conclusions, or that the arguments he submits will not convince the unbeliever, but at all times he is patently sincere in his endeavours to be honest in his thinking—of which no better evidence can be offered than the manner in which in the *Cur Deus Homo* he so often returns to the objections which Boso raises. In fact, it is strange that the suggestion that St. Anselm knows his conclusions in advance should ever have been taken as ground for suspecting his sincerity. No one, be he scientist, mathematician or logician, ever embarks upon his demonstration without having in his mind in some form or other the conclusions which he wishes to establish. Yet the fact of knowledge of conclusions is never regarded as an indication of the insincerity of the thinker, or as proof that his argumentation is dishonestly accommodated to the conclusions he wishes to reach. The claim can be legitimately made on behalf of St. Anselm that he be treated with like justice. St. Anselm's conclusions, then, are the conclusions of faith. Whatever his premises are—and these we must shortly discuss— he does not reduce the dogmatic content of the Christian faith in order to make it more acceptable to the unbeliever, or to bring it into line with premises that will not support such a full content. In that sense his subject is the revelation of God in Jesus Christ, and a dogmatic which sets forth that revelation in fully theological terms. If we are compelled to say that St. Anselm is also an apologist, he is not so in the nineteenth-century sense which regards the faith as something for which apology must be made, and which introduces the unbeliever to a mere fraction of what the Church believes. His themes are the great dogmatic themes of the Incarnation and the Atonement, the nature of God, the Trinity, the Procession of the Holy Spirit, Providence and Freedom of the Will, the nature of Man, and so on. It is the facts of the *credo* and nothing less of which he seeks an understanding.

(3.2) Having said so, we are at once confronted with the task of showing how, in St. Anselm's opinion, faith proceeds upon such understanding of itself; or, how exactly *intelligo* is related to *credo* in his famous saying. The relation may be stated in several ways, no one of which is by itself exhaustive, though all together cover most of his statements about, and his applications of, his principle.

(3.2.1) The defence of the *credo* is the motive for the *intelligo*. While it would be too extreme to affirm that if the faith had had no critics it would never have been understood—a caricature as shallow as it is irrelevant, because it is based upon what might have happened in a world of infinite possibilities—it is nevertheless justifiable to go so far as to maintain that it is St. Anselm's avowed intention to defend the faith against the attacks of unbelievers which has led him to fuller understanding and exposition of his faith. It is no accident that he begins almost all his works with a reference to some theological or even atheistic theory which contradicts an article of faith—no accident, because it is in defending his own beliefs that he has been motivated to understand them the better.

St. Anselm, it would appear to me, makes an explicit methodological technique of a process which takes place continually in the history of theology. The Church's faith is most clearly expressed, and most clearly understood, at the points where she has met the severest criticism. The Christological controversies of the fourth and fifth centuries yielded conciseness of doctrine, which would have been almost impossible without the attacks of the heretics and the critical defence which such attacks evoked. It has even been suggested that the absence of such forthright attack on the doctrine of the Holy Spirit accounts for the fact, mentioned variously by Bishops Thirwall and Westcott, Berdyaev and Professor Raven, that the Church has no concise view of the nature and work of the Third Person of the Trinity. "Religion without revelation" was bound almost inevitably to produce in the course of theological development "religion only where revelation takes place", because the attack upon revelation compelled theologians to examine the rightful place of revelation within Christianity and to lay an entirely fresh emphasis upon the whole conception. There is nothing in the whole history of theology comparable to the view of revelation held by the Barthian theologians, for the reason that there was no previous phenomenon comparable to the attack which elicited just that response. St. Anselm, therefore, differs from most other theologians in that he consciously adopts a technique which remains only implicit in their writings.

(3.2.2) Not only is the defence of the *credo* the motive for the *intelligo* but, further, it is the *vehicle* of such understanding. It is in the actual process of defending his faith that the believer comes more fully to understand not simply the implications of his faith, but also what his faith means. The *id quo nihil maius cogitari potest* of the *Proslogion*, the Platonic Ideas of the *Monologion*, the notion of *satisfactio* of the *Cur Deus Homo*—to mention but a few of St. Anselm's conceptions—all accepted by the critics of the article of the faith which St. Anselm is defending, are woven by him into the texture of his understanding of the faith. In other words, the process by which St. Anselm defends the *credo* and proves its truthfulness is the same process as that by which he understands it. The process of *quaerens intellectum* is, then, a dialectic of faith with unfaith, and the unfaith is not necessarily always or only that of the unbeliever who is attacking Christian beliefs. The moment St. Anselm, or those correspondents of his who encouraged him to defend the faith, decide not to rely upon the authority of the Scripture or the Creeds or the writings of the Fathers, they find themselves open to the doubts of the various unbelievers who appear in the different works. It is this pressure of unfaith from within as well as from without which gives the tone of sincerity to St. Anselm's argumentation; the outcome of the examination is as important for himself as it is for his correspondents or for the critics.

Our assessment of the validity of this aspect of St. Anselm's method plays a major part in our final determination of St. Anselm's worth as a theologian, and so it is necessary to examine carefully the implications of what has been stated. Exception could be taken at once, and in this way. St. Anselm, it might be said, is affirming that our understanding of a proposition is dependent upon our ability to verify it or justify it. Now, in the faith-situation it is very often the case that the simple unbeliever can understand without being able to supply any defence for the articles of his belief. This criticism could easily be met in either of two ways. First, Barth's contention in interpreting St. Anselm that the initial act of faith is one in which understanding is present, and that it is not therefore irrational, obviates the difficulty in a single sentence. St. Anselm plainly does not mean that the simple believer accepts something which he does not understand. Secondly, the understanding with which St. Anselm is concerned is a self-critical theological type of understanding, and not the simple, unthought-out understanding of the believer who is not troubled by "intellectual difficulties".

When this exception is set aside, it becomes clear that St. Anselm conceives of the process of *fides quaerens intellectum* as one in which faith endeavours to see for itself why the propositions which it affirms are true. The use of the phrase "sees for itself" has to be understood in a manner which precludes the suggestion that faith does so without the assistance of Divine Grace. The prayer of *Proslogion* c. 1 indicates that what faith "sees" it sees as a result of the Divine initiative and through Divine assistance.

Understanding, no less than faith, is a gift of God. This process in which the believer sees for himself the truth of the propositions seems, on St. Anselm's view, to imply two things, both of which are definitely correct. First, in the *intellectus* the believer sees why the articles of his faith are not false; why, that is, they are not contradictory to certain propositions accepted by believers and unbelievers alike. Much of St. Anselm's argumentation is directed to this end. The achievement of such an end is not sufficient in itself for St. Anselm's purpose: it only proves that faith's propositions are not necessarily false. It is amazing how large a part this kind of argument plays in theological discussions. Those who are actively interested in the relation of science to religion employ it frequently. For example, they maintain that the Doctrine of God the Creator is not proved to be false by the theory of evolution as so many of the scientists of the nineteenth century had believed, because while science deals in its theory with the origin and development of species, with all the subtle differentiation involved, the Christian Doctrine answers the questions of why there is something at all to evolve, rather than nothing, and of how all that exists, whether in early or late development, is related to the Lord and Giver of Life. In much the same way the modern scientific rejection of mechanistic determinism is regarded by some Christian apologists as at least leaving open the possibility of the occurrence of miracles of the type recorded in Scripture, even if it does not prove their actual occurrence. Likewise, certain theistic philosophers claim that logical positivism does not negate *a priori* the possibility of veridical religious experience, even though such experience is of a kind denied to many logical positivists. This type of argument does seem to be permissible in theological enquiry, where the propositions thus defended are held on grounds other than scientific or philosophical ones, where, that is, it is not necessary to prove that the propositions of faith are logically implied by scientific or philosophical premises. Therefore, if St. Anselm had done no more than this one thing for his day and generation—and the sequel aims at showing that in fact he did accomplish much more—he did a useful service to the faith, for he at least demonstrated that contemporary general principles did not contradict the articles of belief.

Secondly, the account just given of St. Anselm's method repre-

sents a minimal interpretation: he believes at least that he has
shown why the faith is not to be negated. But clearly he intends
a good deal more. *Fides quaerens intellectum* discovers that certain
propositions, accepted at the beginning of each work by both the
believer and the unbeliever, logically imply conclusions accepted
by the believer and denied by the unbeliever. The conclusions,
the *probanda* or the *intelligenda*, provided for the *intellectus* by
the *fides* are seen by the believer to be true when he relates them
to other propositions which he holds, and observes that they are
logically coherent with them. They—shall we say?—"make
sense" when taken together with the other beliefs which the
Christian holds, not simply as a Christian but as a man who shares
with his contemporaries many beliefs which he does not share
with Christians of other periods of history. What, in fact, St.
Anselm is saying is that the truth or even the meaning of any
proposition, including propositions of faith, is not contained
within the four corners of the proposition. Its meaning and truth
emerge only when it is set within a specific context. The difference, therefore, between the simple believer and the believer who
undertakes the intellectual discipline of *fides quaerens intellectum*
lies not in the fact that the simple believer has no context into
which to fit his articles of faith while the other has a vast cultural
framework to provide for his, but rather in the kind of context
to which the two believers endeavour to relate their faith. Using
Barth's progression, understanding—faith—understanding—faith,
we can say that the first understanding involves, in fact consists
in, relating faith's propositions to a meaningful context, and is
the same in kind as the second, though there is a difference both
in the complexity and in the nature of the contexts. *Intellectus*,
then, is the sustained attempt on the part of the Christian to
relate the *credo* to the rest of his beliefs.

St. Anselm does seem here to have stated what is the perennial
task of the believer, the preacher and the theologian. The believer
who claims to understand what his faith is about—and it is doubtful if there has at any time existed in the Church anyone who had
what the critics call "blind faith"—is able to understand because
he has been able, or rather been enabled, to make the facts of
faith cohere with the rest of his opinions and ideas. Admittedly,
this coherence is never complete: even his non-religious beliefs

do not cohere with any completeness or perfection. But if there is no such coherence his religious beliefs will be not only irrelevant but indeed meaningless altogether. The preacher, commissioned to proclaim the Word of God, is continually faced with the responsibility of making that Word meaningful to his generation. The Word of God is, as Barth himself declares, "a rational event". He has to say to his contemporaries what the Apostles and Prophets said to theirs, but in the language of *his* contemporaries. He can do so only by relating the *fides* to the concepts, categories and beliefs of the contemporary *intellectus*. But the theologian is of all perhaps most in danger of sloughing the responsibility of St. Anselm, by remaining satisfied with thought-forms of another day. It is no disgrace to any theology that it should employ the categories of a contemporary metaphysic—provided that that metaphysic remains the servant and does not become the master. It is at this very point that much of the modern so-called Biblical Theology is more of an etymology than a theology, because it tends to regard its responsibility as exhausted in the definition of certain Biblical terms by means of the concepts used in Biblical times. It is better that a theologian should use modern metaphysical terms and his words be meaningful to his readers than that he should use only the strictly Biblical terms and his words remain meaningless. "Speaking with tongues" is no more commendable in our time than it was in St. Paul's. The conclusion emerges that St. Anselm has much evidence to support his position that understanding a proposition consists in seeing it to be true for ourselves, that is, in relating it to the other beliefs which we hold, so that we can see how and even why it is true.

One genuine criticism of this view of St. Anselm should, however, be considered. Is it not the case that he makes the truth of revelation dependent upon premises and principles not given in revelation? Does he seek the criterion of revelation beyond revelation? On first thoughts it would appear somewhat difficult to exculpate St. Anselm from the implied charge. Taking Barth's symbolism, which pictures St. Anselm as arguing from *a b c d* $\rightarrow$ *x*, and recognising, as we must, that some of the premises *a b c d* are not always *articula fidei*, then it appears valid to conclude that the truth of *x* is determined by the fact that it is implied by *a b c d*. In other words, the truth of revelation for St. Anselm is determined by certain principles, some of which at least do not belong to revelation itself. This conclusion may, however, be fairly avoided if we recognise that just as *x* depends upon *a b c d*, so it is no less true that *a b c d* is affected by *x*, and particularly those premises in the *a b c d* which are not articles of faith. For example, the Platonic Doctrine of the Forms appears in the *Monologion* in a very different form from that which it possesses, say, in the *Phaedo* or the *Sophist*. Even those idealistic philosophers who have interpreted Plato in such fashion as to credit him with developed theism have never gone so far as to maintain that his doctrine of ideas could by itself yield either the Trinitarian God or the Personal God of Christianity. So in the *Proslogion* "that than which no greater can be thought" is gradually filled with an entirely Christian content, which differentiates it from the interpretation which might be given it in some non-Christian setting. Likewise, in the *Cur Deus Homo*, the concept of *satisfactio* is so precisely defined by St. Anselm in a Christian sense that only wilful misunderstanding could assign to it significances which were only feudal or legal.

Virtually, what St. Anselm does is to indicate that some contemporary concept which has several possible meanings, one of which is presumably employed by his opponents, has a specifically Christian meaning which is just as valid as the others and the employment of which enables his argument to proceed with conviction. Further support for this explanation of St. Anselm's method may be found in his steadfast unwillingness, already mentioned, to reduce the full force of his Christian conclusions. The revelation of God in Jesus Christ, which is the source and ground of his dogmatics, is determinative of his entire argumentation. What, therefore, St. Anselm places before his opponents is not so much a conclusion, or set of conclusions, which are claimed to be credible because dependent upon certain premises, as a whole pattern of thought which challenges the credence of those who follow St. Anselm as he weaves his way through it. It is the whole argument, premises and conclusion, an argument through which revelation is understood, which is up for consideration, and not simply the conclusion by itself. It is in these terms, therefore, that the charge of rationalism so often brought against St. Anselm would be finally refuted: in terms, that is, of his concern about revelation—God's revelation in the Word Incarnate and in the Atonement, God's revelation of his Triune Nature and of His infinite attributes, and so on—and, in terms, too, of his deep desire, his hungering and thirsting to understand the nature of God's revelation of Himself. Revelation is his theme and all else is subordinated to that.

(3.2.3) Reference has already been made to the nature of St. Anselm's premises, both in the immediately recent indication that the Christian setting of the premises does affect the kind of interpretation which St. Anselm places upon those which he shares with unbelievers, and also in the analysis of Barth's account of them in his $a\ b\ c\ d \rightarrow x$ symbolism. It remains to make clear what considerations affect St. Anselm's selection of his premises for the different works. We have already found reason to disagree with Barth's view that his premises are all drawn from revelation, and this contention can now be enforced by stating the case positively. St. Anselm's presuppositions seem to fall into certain definite groups, and in any one work his presuppositions may easily be a mixture made up from all the groups, or from some; in other cases they may be drawn from only one group.

(3.2.3.1) Thus there are in some cases certain theological presuppositions which his opponents are prepared to grant while they deny certain other articles of faith. St. Anselm's task is to show that those which they do grant imply those which they deny. For example, in the *De Processione Spiritus Sancti* the Greeks hold belief in the Trinity and in the procession of the Holy Spirit from the Father, but they deny procession from the Son also. In the *Cur Deus Homo* the critics believe in God, in His goodness and justice, in His mercy and love; they recognise man's obligations to God and the sinfulness of man but they deny the necessity of salvation through the Death of Jesus Christ.

(3.2.3.2) Among his presuppositions, too, we have to note certain ideas commonly accepted in his time but not self-evident to any other age of human thought, particularly to our own. The simple form of the Doctrine of the Forms used in the course of the argument and his conception of the *summum bonum*, together of course with the empirical generalisation from which the *Mono-*

logion begins, the *id quo maius cogitari non potest* of the *Proslogion*, which cannot have been a definition of his own making, the ideas of *satisfactio* and of *necessitas* in the *Cur Deus Homo*, to mention but a few instances, belong to this class of presupposition. It would be idle to quarrel with St. Anselm because he admits this type of presupposition into his argument, for no age is ever completely critical of many of the presuppositions which are shared by all its members, believers and unbelievers alike. It is only the historian who, looking back, detects their wide influence, and he is able to do so only because they conflict with those of his own day. Yet these presuppositions are all-important in each age, because they constitute the fabric of civilisations, and of cultures. We are only now able, for example, to detect the immense influence which the concepts of progress and evolution exerted upon all thinkers in the second half of the nineteenth century and the early part of the twentieth, upon philosophers, historians, economists, Biblical critics and theologians, as well as upon scientists themselves. To suggest as Barth does that St. Anselm neither shares nor employs any of the general principles held by his contemporaries is both to ignore the plain facts and to fail to understand how even the greatest thinkers are the children of their times.

(3.2.3.3) A further group of St. Anselm's presuppositions appearing in certain of his works is formed of the conclusions which he has established in other works—a point already made in our discussion of the distinctly "systematic" quality of his writing. This interrelatedness of his works must be kept in mind; otherwise, we are led into saying that St. Anselm seems to accept certain authoritative statements from the Holy Scriptures or the Creeds in violation of his self-imposed limitation of not arguing "*ex auctoritate*". The case therefore seems complete for the contention that it is impossible to say that St. Anselm invariably uses the same kind of premises in his writings. These vary from work to work, and are determined on the one hand by the conclusions which he wishes to establish, and on the other by the opinions of those who are at any given time his opponents in discussion.

(3.2.4) Accordingly, the question of St. Anselm's relation to Scripture has almost answered itself—the question, that is, of why he does not base his arguments upon quotations from Scripture. That he does not do so is a matter of great interest, for on the one hand St. Augustine, some at least of whose writings St. Anselm appears to have known fairly well, was very liberal in his quotation and was always ready to substantiate a theological position by an elaborate exegesis of a text, and St. Thomas and the Reformers, on the other hand, elaborately used the proof-text method. St. Anselm strictly disciplined himself in the matter of Scriptural quotation for two reasons. First, as has already been suggested, the appeal to authority was one which did not carry weight with his opponents, who were out of sympathy either with the whole of the Christian faith or with certain parts of it. He could not, therefore, entirely choose his own premises for his arguments. Whether St. Anselm in other circumstances or in other days would have been more "Biblical" in his technique is a question which need not be asked. He had a missionary task to perform and he did it in his own way. Secondly, it would be wrong to suggest that St. Anselm's purpose was purely apologetic. His method was designed to help not only unbelievers but also believers—believers who recognised that in a great measure the difficulties raised by the unbelievers were their own difficulties, especially when they endeavoured to establish thought connections between their faith and the contemporary culture so much of which they accepted. *Credo quia absurdum* did not satisfy the intellectual believer of St. Anselm's day, if indeed it ever really has been accepted as a believer's attitude to his faith. "Seeing the faith to be true", clumsy though the phrase is, is a necessary part of the act and process of believing. It is in this respect interesting to find that the late Professor B. B. Warfield, who is in many ways the ablest modern exponent of what is known as the Old Protestant Doctrine of the authority of Scripture, should state his method, albeit inconsistently with certain of his other views, in a fashion which presents it as not entirely dissimilar to the kind of operation which St. Anselm executes in his *intellectus fidei*. Warfield writes: "We first prove Scriptures authentic, historically credible, generally trustworthy, before we prove them inspired." [75] I should even go as far as to say that Warfield has here given us an excellent statement of what St. Anselm continually attempts in his theological writings. But the doubt with which we are left is whether anyone in the history of theology has ever consistently relied solely on the appeal to Scripture.   At any rate it is clear that St. Anselm's rejection, for purposes of theological discussion, of the authority of Scripture as a premise of argument was due not simply to his apologetic motive but also to his discernment of the true nature of dogmatic exposition, which seeks to make the faith comprehensible without thereby forfeiting its essential autonomy, or forgetting its rootedness in revelation.

(3.2.5) We have now before us the evidence upon which we can rightly assess St. Anselm's greatness as a theologian.   We cannot use any simple formula or phrase to describe him.   For example, to say that he was a great philosopher of religion is to class him with a group of writers whose methods and principles were in many ways different from his.   Few, if any, philosophers of religion have ever been so exclusively concerned with the full dogmatic themes which occupied St. Anselm.   For that very reason he cannot be called a rationalist either; historically, rationalism has whittled down the Christian faith to a degree which robbed it of its unique content.   Nor can we swing to the other extreme with Barth and, seeing in him the prototype of the Barthian dogmatic theologian, deny that he had any apologetic interest.   Besides, his sparing use of Scripture would prevent us from classifying him unquestionably with dogmatic theologians. The fact that so many widely differing schools of theology can look to St. Anselm for inspiration and for actual methodological direction reveals the danger of prematurely assigning to him the title of any single school, and points to the anachronism involved in describing him in terms which became meaningful only centuries after he had lived and written.   We may put the situation thus.   St. Anselm was the first to formulate the principles of theological methodology and in doing so he included principles which could be used by one school and rejected by another, and *vice versa*.   In a comparable manner, we might say that all the twentieth-century forms of Existentialism stem ultimately from the writings of Kierkegaard; each could appeal to him as its inspiration, and yet we can see how each has developed one aspect of Kierkegaard's philosophy or theology to the neglect of some other which he regarded as equally important. In St. Anselm's case, the apologist can cite his regard for the unbeliever and his willingness to accept premises offered by the unbeliever; the dogmatic theologian can point to St. Anselm's devotion to the great themes of dogmatics and his unwillingness to yield any dogmatic position in his efforts to win the unbeliever; the rationalist even can call attention to the manner in which St. Anselm endeavours to establish rational connections between faith and contemporary culture; while the philosopher of religion can present St. Anselm as one who reflects upon the logical implications of a religious experience which he first receives within a believing and worshipping community. That each exponent can find justification for his method in St. Anselm does not validate the charge of inconsistency in the latter; it merely confirms our view that with St. Anselm theological methodology was in its formative period, and that therefore different methods are to be expected in his writings. Further, it should be maintained that in St. Anselm these different methods are held in proper equilibrium, so that none is allowed to go to excess, each being held in check by the other. Again, in regard to Kierkegaard, we could say that in many cases modern Existentialists have neglected those other aspects of his thought which Kierkegaard himself held in even balance and which would have acted as a corrective of excess in any one direction. St. Anselm's greatness as a theologian, then, lies in the facility with which he checks one method by the other, and demonstrates clearly that all are necessary to a successful prosecution of theological enquiry. Above all, it is the spirit in which St. Anselm writes—a spirit of reverent devotion towards the God Whose nature and mighty acts he seeks to describe, of profound humility which recognises that theological reflection is itself a gift of God Who is both *Deus absconditus* and *Deus revelatus*, and of sympathetic patience with those who have not been given to see what he has seen—which secures for him a place in the forefront of Christian theologians.

4

It remains now to relate the phrase *remoto Christo* of the *Praefatio* of the *Cur Deus Homo* to the conclusions reached concerning the meaning of the dictum *credo ut intelligam*, and to state what exactly St. Anselm is seeking to do in his construction of a soteriology. A clear understanding of his intentions is a necessary precondition of our judgment both of that work and of the many criticisms to which it has been submitted in the history of theology. The commentary upon the phrase *remoto Christo* will take the form of the application of the general principles established as to the interpretation of the dictum *credo ut intelligam* to the particular work with which we are concerned.

(4.1) The presence of the phrase *remoto Christo* in the *Praefatio* indicates that St. Anselm is consciously following the method which he has pursued in his other works, and that the *Cur Deus Homo* is not to be separated from them as if it introduced some entirely new principle. It is the existence of the God-man together with the atoning value of His Death which constitutes the *intelligendum* or the *probandum* of the work, the *x*, the logical necessity of which is implied by the *a b c d* accepted by the critics of the faith whose views are presented by Boso, the interlocutor. It is, therefore, wrong of Barth to describe the phrase as "not quite unobjectionable", for St. Anselm's whole method does involve setting Christ upon one side as if He had never been, and acceptance of St. Anselm's method implies acceptance of the several parts of it. If Barth genuinely chooses to take exception to "the well-known phrase", then he is obliged to be much more critical of St. Anselm's method than in fact he is. The occurrence of the phrase in the *Cur Deus Homo* is most important, for it serves to bring out the true character of the *credo ut intelligam* type of theological enquiry and to make explicit certain features of it which are only implicit in the other works, particularly his refusal to accept as a premise in his argument that which his argument is designed to prove, or which his opponents will not allow. By this phrase at the outset he declares that he will not employ the appeal to authority.

(4.2) It should next be observed that by emphasising the *Christo* in the phrase *remoto Christo* St. Anselm does not reject from his premises all the facts of the faith. Those he does employ we have already enumerated *in extenso*, and their presence in the work is evidence that it is not a rationalistic deduction of the Incarnation and the Atonement from general first principles. It is the Life and Death of Our Lord only which he does not premise. That is, the discussion does not involve the complete abandonment or cessation of faith as its starting-point. A good deal of faith is required of those who grant the *a b c d* of his argument, but for the unbeliever who denies Christ *remoto Christo* is a true description of his spiritual condition. How, then, can the believer also say *remoto Christo*? He does not surrender his faith in Christ but rather by "a willing suspense of judgment" awaits the argument's conclusion. The best comparable philosophical analogy —and it is only an analogy—is to be found in the doubt whereby Descartes suspended all belief except in clear and distinct ideas, and in those which were logically deducible from them, until he could be certain of the existence of the objects of his beliefs. It is as if St. Anselm said: "We who believe in Christ shall for the present place ourselves where the unbeliever is, denying Christ yet accepting many other facts of the Christian faith."

(4.3) While the phrase *remoto Christo* represents the "excluded premise" of the *Cur Deus Homo*, it draws attention as we have noticed to the conclusion which the work seeks to establish. As such, it is not known in the first instance by means of the argument. It is given to faith aroused in the believer through his reading primarily of the Scriptures, but also, St. Anselm would add, of the Fathers of the Church. In rejecting the given-ness of the Incarnation and the Atonement St. Anselm emphasises the necessity for the intellectual appropriation of the great facts of the faith on the part of the believer. He must see them to be true for himself. It is not satisfactory for him to reiterate Biblical or credal statements about Jesus Christ. He must assimilate them by discovering their *ratio*, and their *ratio* is not simply the humanly discoverable reason for their occurrence but, as Barth so frequently points out,[76] the reason which seemed good to God.

(4.4) In this process of intellectual appropriation the believer's attitude to the Atonement undergoes a change. This change is not merely that of moving from awareness of a belief to awareness of the reasons why we hold a belief. Rather does St. Anselm believe that if we follow the enquiry he submits we shall come to know more fully what the Atonement means, and means for us.

It is transition not from faith to reason but from a less complete to a more complete understanding *and* faith. Barth's emphasis upon the *credo ut intelligam*, as a principle of dogmatic enquiry in particular, does not allow sufficiently for the influence that *intellectus fidei* exerts upon *fides*. In so far as the believer is always *in via* to full understanding and faith, to the "sight" of which St. Anselm speaks in the *Commendatio, remoto Christo* will be from time to time not an *ad hoc* premise for a theological discussion but a spiritual fact for the soul that gropes in the darkness for the light of fuller understanding.

(4.5) For the unbeliever (as distinct from the believer) whom St. Anselm hopes to take with him on his journey to the intellectual understanding of faith the *remoto Christo* will mean exactly what it says. It is assumed that he will grant St. Anselm all his other starting-points, without committing himself to faith. But St. Anselm's intention for the unbeliever is not that he should be led to intellectual assent to the conclusions of faith which the book will yield, nor that he should simply feel embarrassed by the logical self-contradiction of not believing. On the contrary, because advance in *intellectus fidei* is so integrally linked with the development or, more exactly, with the creation and renewal, of faith, St. Anselm's hope is that the unbeliever will come to faith as well as to understanding of mind and obedience of heart. Anything which heightens one can, on St. Anselm's interpretation of faith, understanding and obedience, be expected to react upon the others.

(4.6) Considering, therefore, what St. Anselm's purpose in the *Cur Deus Homo* thus appears to be, a critic might be tempted to say that he is aiming at the impossible, namely, the establishing of historical fact by means of logical enquiry. Historical events—for these are what the Incarnation and the Atonement are—it could be said, are established by means of historical criticism; the interpretations of them, of course, are left to philosophical or theological enquirers, who may erect upon them any theory which pleases them. This criticism raises the large issues of the nature of historical interpretation and of whether there are any such entities as uninterpreted historical facts. But the answer to the criticism in St. Anselm's case is fairly clear. His purpose is to establish not the bare fact that at a certain date in a certain country a man who was called Jesus lived and died—that fact his opponents would allow—but rather the facts that it was necessary for man's salvation that there should exist on earth a God-man, that this Person should die for man's sin, and that the historical man Jesus was this God-man. These facts are entitled to the name as much as any bare events to which no meaning has been attached—indeed, are more entitled to the name. In other words, theological interpretation is an essential part of the determination of the facts which constitute the Christian faith, and so-called impartial historical criticism is by itself unqualified to achieve that end. Of course, the wider implications may be indicated, though they do not now concern us, namely, that elaboration of interpretation and erection of theory are necessary parts of the determination of all historical fact, and that there is no such process as impartial historical criticism, or, if there is, it yields but the barest of events, and these almost meaningless. Facts in order to be facts must be the bearers of meaning; they must be integrated with the rest of human thought, volition and action. It is just such meaning that St. Anselm seeks to discover in answering the question *Cur Deus Homo*? and such integrated facts that he hopes to discover.

(4.7) With regard, therefore, to the motivating problem of this chapter, we may say that the following conclusion has been reached. The *Cur Deus Homo* is of one piece with the rest of St. Anselm's writings in its determination of a dogmatic theme, in its selection of its premises and in its method of argument. It is an example of the *credo ut intelligam* principle in action, and in fact serves to illustrate several of the most important features of the Anselmic methodology. *A fortiori*, there is no inner self-contradiction in the work between the *Praefatio*, with its phrase *remoto Christo*, and the chapters of the book itself. As to method of treatment of its subject, the *Cur Deus Homo* stands or falls with the rest of St. Anselm's writings. If there are any internal difficulties within the work, these must, of course, be dealt with separately and independently. They must also be dealt with only in relation to the method which St. Anselm is seeking to follow, and which has so much to commend it.

CHAPTER TWO

AUT POENA AUT SATISFACTIO: HAMARTIOLOGY

PART A. INTRODUCTION

ST. ANSELM'S systematic account of the Atonement, along the methodological lines indicated in the previous chapter, does not really begin until towards the end of Bk. I, c. 10, of the *Cur Deus Homo*, and in the earlier section of Bk. I he clears the ground for his later work. This section is not, however, merely introductory, for not only does it embody St. Anselm's criticisms of views on his subject held by his predecessors in the field of soteriology, but it supplies us with his own motive for embarking upon yet another theory of the Atonement.

In cc. 1-10 of Bk. I he deals with the following subjects: (1) his reason for writing the book; (2) views previously held concerning the Atonement; (3) objections to these views; and (4) preliminary examination of topics integral to his own systematic account of the Atonement.

1

Many requests, St. Anselm tells us, had been made to him to set down in orderly fashion the answers which he had from time to time given to people who wished to understand "the reason of the faith that is in us"; particularly, questions had been asked for what reason, and by what necessity, God was made man, and brought life to the world by His Death. Out of the desire to meet this expressed need, but primarily because it is blameworthy indolence not to seek to understand what we believe, St. Anselm accepts the task, putting on record his reasons for his reluctance to do so. For example, any failure on his part might lead the sceptics to say that the truth on these matters did not exist; again, a discussion of the necessity of the Atonement involves the investigation of the difficult problems of power, necessity and will, among others; finally, a perfect account of the Atonement is beyond human possibility, and his religio-aesthetic taste deters St. Anselm from what might turn out to be a crude demonstration of his subject. Nevertheless, he decides to defer to the requests, recognising that his treatment may turn out to be of assistance to some of the enquirers. Here, then, at the outset of the book, St. Anselm states the *credo ut intelligam*, clearly showing that it is not simply a methodological principle but a means by which the religious life of believers may be strengthened in faith, and by which they may be enabled to deal with those who criticise their beliefs.

2

In a very brief review (I.3 and I.8) St. Anselm recapitulates the accounts which have traditionally been given of the Atonement, and uses them to illustrate a general principle which he enunciates concerning the nature of the Atonement. Thus, the extremities of misery from which God delivered us, and the wealth of unmerited blessings with which He endowed us, are evidence of the greatness of the love which He bore to us. The very appropriate or fitting manner in which God effected this restoration or reinstatement of sinners is sufficient in itself to silence the derision of those who mock the simplicity of believers, and to constrain them also to praise God's wise generosity. The appropriateness of the mode of redemption is illustrated by St. Anselm in three analogical inferences:

(2.1) It was fitting that, as death laid hold on the human race through man's disobedience, through man's obedience should life be restored. The *oportebat*[1] echoes the *convenienter*.[2]

(2.2) As sin, which was the cause of our damnation, had its origin in woman, so of woman should the author of our righteousness and salvation be born.

(2.3) In the same way as the Devil conquered man by persuading him to taste of the tree, so should man conquer him by bearing death upon the tree.[3]

(2.4) To these three accounts may be added a fourth, not cast in analogical form, given by St. Anselm in I.4, namely, that it was not proper (*non decebat*) that God's destiny for man, His precious creation, should be frustrated, and that this destiny could not be achieved except through the action of the Creator Himself. This account links up logically with the other three through St. Anselm's use of the word *decere*. The importance of this review of the theories previously held concerning the Atonement is to be noted not so much because of any intrinsic or historical value in it—for it is very sketchy and brief—as for St. Anselm's reactions to the theories mentioned, stated by Boso,[4] the interlocutor. To these we now proceed.

3

Boso's criticisms follow two lines, the one directed to the analogical inferences and the other to the general principle which they illustrate. On the one hand, Boso objects to the analogical inferences as being both *picturae*[5] and *convenientiae*.[6] They are *picturae* in the sense of fictions, or, more accurately, images, as Dr. Austin Farrer [7] has now popularised the term. They are, we should say, the vehicles of analogical description, and not of analogical inference, as they were thought to be. It is not so easy, however, to find a single word or phrase to convey St. Anselm's notion of *convenientiae*, which is variously translated as "logical harmonies" or "congruities". Both these translations miss the connection between Boso's criticism here and St. Anselm's use of the words *convenienter* and *oportebat* in the previous chapter. Boso resents the fact that these arguments are drawn from the realm of the "appropriate" and do not establish necessity. They assume that God has decided to save the human race and are concerned only with the manner in which that salvation may most *fittingly* be accomplished. Boso presses his point home and insists that St. Anselm expound his answer to the question, why it was *necessary* that God should become man, suffer and die, in order that mankind should be saved. In view of all that is involved in the term *convenientiae*, it may perhaps most adequately be translated by some such word as "proprieties" or "conventions".

On the other hand, Boso's criticism goes deeper [8] when he attacks the principle which the several accounts of the Atonement illustrate, namely, that the love of God for men is appropriately

shown forth in the manner in which He has redeemed them from
the extremities of evil and suffering. Boso maintains that if the
matter is left there God's omnipotence, wisdom and love—as
well as His goodness—are compromised: His omnipotence,
because surely God by His Word could simply have accomplished
redemption of mankind from sin, from His wrath, from hell and
the power of the Devil; His wisdom, because a wise person will
not do with great exertion that which can be accomplished with
less; His love, because it has not been demonstrated that in no
less painful way could man have been saved; and, finally, His
goodness, because God condemned the innocent Jesus Christ in
order to save the guilty.[9]

On the basis of these two sets of criticism provided by Boso
the themes of Bks. I and II of the *Cur Deus Homo* can be clearly
defined. Bk. I deals with the general topic that it is impossible
for man to achieve salvation for himself; Bk. II with the topic
that Jesus Christ, the God-man, is the necessary means of salvation, and that God's nature is in no way compromised thereby.
As has previously been said, these criticisms are of the greatest
importance, for reasons which may now be explicitly stated:

(3.1) The distinction between the *conveniens* and the *necessarium*
is one by which St. Anselm abides throughout the book. As will
later be observed, he does not reject the notion of *conveniens*, and
in fact uses it quite frequently, but he does so, as it were, with his
eyes wide open, and he does not confuse the two types of argument.
He uses the *conveniens* very often either after he has established
the *necessarium*, or to elucidate some point for the benefit of
believers, who might not quibble over the *conveniens* so much as
would unbelievers. Sometimes St. Anselm uses the full verbal
forms to make the same distinction, e.g. between "*oportet*" and
"*necesse est*", and the intention is always the same. "Necessity"
is the quality of such relations as are self-evident to, or accepted
after proof as true by, believers and unbelievers. "Fittingness",
on the contrary, can be applied only to such relations or situations
as are seen by believers to be the case. Believers may apply the
term in these instances for two reasons. On the one hand, from
the general premise which they hold, namely, that whatsoever
God does is fitting ("rational" is another term that St. Anselm

uses in precisely this connection, cf. I.8, p. 59, l. 11), they conclude that any relation set up by Him or situation created by Him is fitting on that account.   On the other hand, believers, perceiving the way in which God works, or apprehending through revelation this nature of God, may create analogies or patterns of similarity between the different elements in the subject-matter of the Christian faith.   The classical example of such a process is St. Augustine's enumeration of the *vestigia Trinitatis* in the *De Trinitate*.   These *vestigia* are wrongly regarded as the basis of natural theology in St. Augustine; rather are they analogies which he discovers in the created order to the revealed Triunity of God, as does also St. Anselm in the *Epistola de Incarnatione Verbi*, c. 13.

(3.2) These criticisms reveal St. Anselm's real motive in writing the *Cur Deus Homo*, namely, a dissatisfaction with the customarily accepted accounts of the Atonement.   He sees them as alternative descriptions of what happened when God delivered mankind from sin, none of them seriously attempting to understand why God should have willed to save men, or to save them in just the manner in which He did.   None of them is a genuine theory of the Atonement, a systematic account of the nature and necessity of Christ's Death.   St. Anselm's swift treatment of the earlier descriptions shows how differently he conceived his task from his predecessors, and constitutes his claim to be the first theologian to give a systematised treatment of the Atonement.

(3.3) In these criticisms St. Anselm virtually indicates the limiting conditions of any adequate theory of the Atonement.   It must be such as to bring out the true nature of the necessity of Christ's Death, but it should not compromise God's essential attributes of omnipotence, wisdom, love and goodness, either singly or all together.   Whatever else we may say of St. Anselm's discussion of his subject, we must admit that he keeps these limits ever in sight.

(3.4) It must be observed also that St. Anselm does not endeavour at this stage to show how the difficulties raised by Boso on behalf of certain critics of the Christian faith are to be met. His whole book constitutes his answer, and as we read it we are obliged to remember that its argument had a contemporary reference, a word for the times, without which no theology can be theology.

4

To complete this analysis of, and commentary upon, the introductory chapters of Bk. I, account must be taken of certain other matters which St. Anselm raises. Since these prove to be integral to his systematic discussion, they will be embodied in the detailed examination of it.

In I.7 the rights of the Devil over man are investigated and the traditional view which had been held for eleven centuries is refuted.[10] The attribution of the sufferings of Christ to His human nature and not to the impassible Divine nature is the subject of I.8, and is but a preliminary treatment of the relation of the two natures in Christ, to be dealt with in so much greater detail in regard to the sinlessness of Jesus Christ.[11] St. Anselm, also, in I.9 and I.10, embarks upon a theme to which he recurs frequently throughout the rest of the work—the relation of Christ's Death to the Will of God, and the implications of that relation for Christ's freedom in choosing to die. Though he deals with certain aspects of the problem at considerable length, these will best be understood in connection with his later extensive account.[12]

From this setting of the stage by St. Anselm we are led straight into the systematic treatment of the subject: *Cur Deus Homo*.

PART B

St. Anselm's analysis of the redemptive activity of God in Jesus Christ, the God-man, is preceded, by way of preparation, by a lengthy argument intended to establish the theorem that apart from God man could not have saved himself. This argument forms the bulk of Bk. I. The exact relation of this argument to his assertions about the redemption accomplished in Jesus Christ constitutes a logical and theological problem of the first magnitude in determining what we might call the order of St. Anselm's thought, namely, whether he actually argues from sin to grace. That problem, however, must wait until we have examined the steps and method of his argumentation concerning man's condition previous to his redemption. Immediately, then, we shall discuss St. Anselm's treatment of (1) God's purpose for man; (2) the nature of sin; and (3) God's reaction to sin, in terms of the famous disjunction—either punishment or satisfaction. Finally (4), we shall examine Bk. I, c. 25, in relation to previous chapters of Bk. I and to Bk. II.

1. GOD'S PURPOSE FOR MAN (*Quod Deus de homine proposuerat*) [13]

One of the chief reasons, in St. Anselm's judgment, for God's initiating the salvation of man [14] is that thereby God may prevent His purpose in creating man from being brought to nought by man's sin. This theme, while presupposed throughout Bk. I, is clearly defined only in Bk. II, where in the opening chapter he gives a concise statement of what that purpose is which will be frustrated apart from salvation. God created man with a rational nature which was upright, in order that he might be happy in enjoying God. The rest of the chapter is an explication of this opening sentence. Man is created rational in order that he may discern between right and wrong, good and evil, greater good and lesser good; and that, discerning between these moral alternatives, he may choose one and avoid the other, love one and hate the other. In choosing the *summum bonum* which St. Anselm later equates with God, man chooses it for itself and not because of any extraneous consideration. In addition, therefore, to the power of moral discernment, God imparts to the rational nature of man the will to follow that which he loves. It is in fulfilling his rational nature and choosing and following the right and the good that man achieves the happiness of the enjoyment of God.

(1.1) Now it is obvious that here we have a Christian anthropology *in parvo*, and its merits are clear.

(1.1.1) Rationality is conceived of as implying not merely the ability to distinguish true from false propositions, or valid from invalid inferences, but also the power to draw moral distinctions. St. Anselm is not saying merely that a being who is rational may also have the power of ethical discernment, as he might have the ability to appreciate aesthetic objects, but more, that a being who does not have ethical discernment is to that extent not rational. Ethical discernment is integral to any definition of rationality, as the ground for the very existence of rationality.

(1.1.2) But rationality is understood as expressing itself through the affective and conative modes of consciousness as well as through the cognitive. Rational natures desire and will ethical ends, and it is in reference to these ethical ends that their rationality has its specific expression. Such an integrative psychology of morals avoids the error to which Kant was driven, by his rigorous distinction between reason and feeling, of saying that reason wills ends which it cannot desire. It is in line with Hebrew psychology, which regards man as a unity and not as a dualism, and by its affirmation that God imparts the will to follow that which is discerned to be right it eliminates the fallacy of all Platonic ethics, that point the way but give no power to move along it. *Video meliora proboque; deteriora sequor* is the stultification of all Platonic rationalism in ethics, and a mistake corrected by St. Anselm in his linking of the pursuit of good ends and desire for them with the intellectual processes of discernment.

(1.1.3) St. Anselm, further, interprets the end of rational nature in self-transcending terms. Rational nature has been created for this purpose that, by discerning desiring and following the good, it may come to enjoy God. Rationality, in short, is religious in significance, and man's relation to God is consequently viewed as a total response of the human personality. Mind, will and affections are all brought into play in that highest blessedness of rational man which is his enjoyment of his Creator. St. Anselm's equation of the *summum bonum* with God implies, on the one hand, that for him all ethics are ultimately religious in character and, on the other hand, that God does not stand beyond the categories of morality—a view of St. Anselm's which is not always remembered by the critics of his soteriology.

(1.1.4) St. Anselm's assertion that rational nature is created by God to love the *summum bonum* for itself, and on no other grounds, brings out the non-utilitarian character of the opening sentence of I.1. The blessedness of enjoying God, which was His purpose in creating man, is not to be regarded as a pleasant consequence, which is to be anticipated if he discerns, loves and follows the right and the good, and above all the *summum bonum*, and which may operate as an additional incentive to virtue.   In fact, this blessedness is *itself* right discerning, loving and following the *summum bonum*.   Incidentally, it may be noted that St. Anselm uses this term to designate God, and not, as do so many philosophers, to refer to the noblest condition of man (cf. Kant).

(1.1.5) The *Monologion*, cc. 68, 69,[15] forms a very apt commentary to the analysis of rationality given in the *Cur Deus Homo*. There St. Anselm uses the strongest terms possible to emphasise the fact that man was endowed with rationality for the purpose of remembering, understanding and loving the *summum bonum*. His devotion to the highest Good, which is also the supreme Reality, is a pursuit which is for him unending, and it fills the whole of his living.   The degree of his success in this pursuit determines the quality of his life, its happiness or unhappiness. In other words, love of God is the most natural expression of man's rationality, and, as such, it integrates the whole of his personality in all its modes, for it is no mere *amor intellectualis*.

(1.2) We must, at this early stage, draw attention to a technique of argumentation which St. Anselm employs in this chapter (II.1) and which might well be called "the denial of impossible alternatives".   He uses it at least five times—to deny the possibilities that God might have created man rational but without moral discernment, or without love for and choice of the Good, or without the will to follow the good—indicating that had God created man without any of these capacities He would have created man with a rational nature in vain, or to no purpose (*frustra*).   Now, since it is conceivable—and indeed has been held by a long and distinguished line of philosophers to be so—that rationality, as such, does not entail capacities of moral discernment, moral decision and virtue, it has to be made plain why these alternatives are logically impossible for St. Anselm.   They are so on two grounds: .

(1.2.1) First, his definition of the *purpose* for which God created rational natures, namely, that they might enjoy Him, entails those capacities in man which make such enjoyment possible, and negates such human incapacities as would prevent his enjoyment of his Creator. The true character of St. Anselm's argument in I.1 thus emerges: God is the *summum bonum*. God's purpose in creating man was that he might enjoy Him. Therefore man must be endowed with a rational nature capable of the highest moral insight, affection and endeavour, in order that he may fulfil that purpose. The "impossible alternatives" conflict with the third proposition in this argument, and must therefore be denied.

(1.2.2) Secondly, St. Anselm thinks not so much of the logical incompatibility of the "impossible alternatives" with God's purpose for man as of the "unfittingness" of a situation in which God's Will should be frustrated. These "impossible alternatives" are religiously as well as logically unacceptable. The apprehension of the "unfittingness", which he does not at this stage attempt to define, St. Anselm seems to regard as being in some way intuitive. It would cease to be so only if he were to advance some fuller analysis of the relation of pure rationality to moral discernment, etc., instead of postulating a definitive axiom.

(1.3) While it has been stated above [16] that for St. Anselm the definition of rationality necessarily includes the ethical references which he specified, it is worthy of notice that his statements are not unequivocal. The opening sentence of I.1, "*Rationalem naturam a Deo factam esse justam . . . dubitari non debet*", might be translated to mean either of two things which are not logically equivalent.

(1.3.1) Thus the sentence may mean: "God created man with rational nature and also created him upright." In this case, man's rationality could have been employed by him for several purposes, not all morally praiseworthy but all equally rational. However, God created this rational nature also upright, so that man would fulfil His purpose for him. Such an interpretation is admittedly counter to what has been said above in (1.1.1), but would be more in line with accepted notions of rationality.

(1.3.2) On the other hand, the sentence may be read in the light of the next sentences and given the sense that "the rational nature with which God endowed man at creation was upright *qua* rational, and its rationality would express itself in purposes, choices and actions which did justice to that fact of its origin"; that is, the rationality which was created by God in man was such as would be self-frustrating in amorality or immorality. While the former interpretation is not exegetically impossible, the latter I should regard as the more probable, not only because of its agreement with the sequel, but also because it is presupposed, as we shall see, in St. Anselm's description of sin as the failure of man to subordinate the *whole* of his *rational* will or heart to God, his Creator—a description which sees man's nature as one whole, and not as loosely aggregated parts.

(1.4) It remains to investigate the *form* which the God-endowed power to discern the right and to follow it will take in man's actual behaviour, namely, the subordination of the whole of man's rational will to the Will of God.

(1.4.1) Such subordination is presented by St. Anselm as being an obligation, a debt, a *debitum*, which we owe to God and which God requires of us; in fulfilling it we do God an honour which is pleasing to Him.[17] It is a task which calls forth the fullest effort of heart and will.

(1.4.2) St. Anselm conceives of all our duties as being subsumed under, or as being instances of, this sole responsibility. C. D. Broad would call St. Anselm an "ethical monist" in the sense that he regards all right actions as fulfilling this our duty to God. Alternatively, for St. Anselm, the only thing in man which is unconditionally good is the will which obeys the Will of God; the will, that is, which wills that end for itself, and for no other reason. This introduction of the notion of "the Will of God" establishes, with greater precision than does II.1, the ends which are willed by the good will. II.1 presented the general idea that the rational nature of man, when created upright, discerns and follows the *summum bonum*; here, in I.22, God is presented as having a will for definite situations, with which man must align himself. It might not be unfair to indicate the distinction between the two presentations by saying that II.1 pictures the *summum bonum* in the quasi-Platonic terms of the attraction of the best in man by God, whereas I.11 is more in line with the

Hebraic-Christian conception of God as an active being, Who has a quite specific interest in and will for the situations in which men have to act.

(1.4.3) It must also be pointed out that for St. Anselm the notions of "ought" and "owing a debt" are the same, so that the propositions: "the rational nature *ought* to subject its will to the Will of God", and "the rational nature *owes* God *the debt* of subjecting its will to the Will of God", are logically equivalent. This equivalence is of supreme importance in the understanding of St. Anselm's soteriology, but it is most frequently ignored. For, while etymologically the two notions of "ought" and "owing a debt" are identical, in modern thought they have become quite separate; very few modern analyses of the concept "oughtness" ever take account of the debt implication contained in it. Thus, when we today say that "we ought to obey the Will of God", and continue that "we owe God the debt of obeying His Will", or that "obedience to God's Will is a debt that we owe to Him", we should generally understand that we had added something to the first proposition, in stating the other two, and had not merely repeated it in alternative forms. But not so for St. Anselm: the first proposition would contain no more and no less than the other two. Our reason for maintaining a difference between the first proposition and the other two would be this, that in the first no ground is given for the "oughtness" of our obedience to God's Will, whereas in the other two the "oughtness" is grounded in the fact that such obedience is a debt that we owe to God. That is, whereas we nowadays might seek other grounds for our obedience to God, suggesting that the debtor-creditor category is inadequate to describe the relation of creature to Creator, St. Anselm finds the sole reason for such obedience in the fact of man's owing God that debt, or, more accurately still, St. Anselm conceives such obedience to be *ipso facto* the debt that we owe. Therefore, when St. Anselm develops the notion of debt in the chapters succeeding I.11, in his investigation of human sin and of salvation, he must not be interpreted in economic rather than in moral or religious terms. In St. Anselm moral or religious oughtness is never reducible to economic indebtedness, and all criticisms of his entire theory, such as that of A. M. Fairbairn,[18] which assume that it is a "commercial drama" rest on a completely false premise.

2. THE NATURE OF SIN (*Quid sit peccare*)[19]

It is in terms of this previous description of man's obligation as a rational nature to obey God's Will, which is his just debt to God, that St. Anselm proceeds to define sin as non-payment of this debt. As he had previously regarded moral rectitude and enjoyment of God as a total response of the human personality to God—mind, will and affections all being involved—so now, by implication, sin is conceived as the orientation of the total personality away from God. It is a radical alienation of man from that Person, Whom, by virtue of his creation and of the very essence of his being, he ought to love and follow after. There is no question of a sinless intellect being betrayed by lustful flesh; both intellect and body express the rebellion of the will which refuses to pay the debt due to the God Who created them for obedience. While, therefore, in the sequel to I.11, St. Anselm speaks almost invariably of sin as failure to pay a debt, it must always be remembered that the failure is of a quite specific nature —the failure of the whole man to subject his will to the Will of God, the failure of a creature to give to his Creator what He desired from him.

Other aspects of the nature of sin as outlined by St. Anselm may be observed, for they amplify the basic conception:

(2.1) St. Anselm offers an alternative description of the nature of sin when he says, at I.15, that sin is a disturbance of "the order and beauty of the universe" (*ordo et pulchritudo universitatis*). This description introduces no new notions, though, on a first reading, it would appear that St. Anselm shows a certain sympathy with idealistic philosophical or aesthetic views of the nature of sin, and that this "order and beauty" are something apart from God. In fact, however, "the order and beauty" signify nothing more than the course of behaviour which God prescribes or wills for natural entities or rational beings. In the case of rational beings this course is obedience to God, and it is violated when man refuses to subject himself to God's direction.

(2.2) St. Anselm accepts the view that man's disobedience to

God is the cause of man's death, and there is no doubt that the death he intends is physical as well as spiritual or moral death,[20] and it is eternal.[21] This fact is substantiated by reference to his treatment of the non-necessity of Christ's physical and spiritual Death.[22] St. Anselm, then, would be in complete disagreement with all traditional formal logicians, who have shown an inveterate weakness for the proposition, "All men are mortal", as the Major Premise in their syllogisms. The attribute of "mortality", in St. Anselm's judgment, would not appear in any definition of man as such—though neither, of course, would that of immortality. The exact ground which St. Anselm offers for this view is not absolutely clear. In his following words in II.11, where he goes on to affirm that "corruptibility" and "incorruptibility" are not relevant to the definition of man, the reason he gives is that neither affects the *essentia* of man; man is man, whether corruptible or incorruptible. A fair analogy would be the relation between the definition of a line and the attributes of being straight or curved. A line must be straight or curved or partly both, but the definition of a line does not necessarily include any reference to these forms in which a line may exist. A line is a line, whether straight or curved. When, however, we do use the terms "corruptible" and "incorruptible", St. Anselm proceeds, we signify that these facts are the source of man's misery on the one hand, and his happiness on the other. These terms may be regarded as shorthand statements of the facts that men who are corruptible experience misery on that account, and those who are incorruptible happiness.

This direct relation between disobedience and death St. Anselm does not return to discuss after he has given his account of the Atonement that is made by Jesus Christ for the disobedience of man. Physical death remains even after men have been accredited by God with the merits which their Saviour won for them. This difficulty is not peculiar to St. Anselm, however, for it occurs to any student of the soteriology of St. Paul. St. Anselm does not labour the sin-death relationship—a fact which some, as we shall see, regard as the gravest defect of this theory—for he is more concerned with the effects of sin upon God than upon man, and, consequently, the dishonour done to God is for him the dominating feature of the sin-situation.

(2.3) We shall not delay long to indicate what St. Anselm says on man's relation to the Devil as a result of his sinning. He denies that, by his sinning, man becomes the property of the Devil: even in his sin he remains God's. He does admit that in his sin and as a result of it, God allows the Devil to harass him. It is generally agreed that in a few swift strokes St. Anselm destroys a view of the control of the Devil over man in his sin which had been held from the second century until the twelfth. The fact is commented upon by almost all the writers on St. Anselm's theory of the Atonement.[23]

(I.7 is the chapter in which this theme is discussed, and it is composed of a single speech attributed to Boso. There is no textual evidence to suggest that such attribution is wrong. When, however, we look closely at the speech, we discover that it consists of a comparatively brief introduction, which reflects the traditional view of the power and property rights of the Devil over sinners, and of a much longer refutation of that view. Since Boso's rôle up to this point in the book, and in fact throughout, is to raise objections and "Anselm's" to answer them, it would not be incorrect to divide the speech, assigning the introduction to Boso and the refutation to "Anselm". Moreover, there is a natural point at which the transition could take place, namely, at p. 56, l. 2; "*non video quam vim habeat*" then becomes the beginning of "Anselm's" answering speech.)

(2.4) St. Anselm affirms that man is culpable for his sin on the ground that he sinned in the first instance of his own free will.[24] His present state of impotence to pay that greater debt under which he now stands to God, by reason of his having failed to obey God and pay his original debt,[25] is therefore blameworthy, and provides no excuse for his continued wrongdoing. St. Anselm, in the passage in I.24 where he deals with this theme, holds that *this* present condition of man's impotence, his inability to do what God wills, is the state of guilt (*culpa*). Man's present sin has thus a double character—as failure here and now to pay the debt owed to God, a debt greatly increased by reason of that first sin, and as guilt in consequence of previous non-payment of debt. It is significant that St. Anselm raises the problem presented to all who endeavour to describe the Fall-situation in terms of a coherent system, namely, of how it is that man should, on the one hand, before the Fall receive the power not to sin, and should, on the other hand, at the Fall give way to sin. It is not a valid solution to this problem to help St. Anselm out by saying that while man received the power to sin, he did not receive the power to use the power, for not only does such a solution involve an infinite regress, but also it fails to realise that in this case the power to use the power would be identical with the power itself, so that the regress need never have been begun.

(2.5) In conjunction with St. Anselm's affirmation about the responsibility of man (which includes representatively all men subsequent to Adam) for his inability to obey God, we must take his further acceptance of the doctrine of original sin, in one of its forms, namely, that sin is propagated throughout mankind in the process of natural generation.[26] St. Anselm is here seeking to indicate the universality of sin among men, or the necessity of sin, as well as man's solidarity in his sin, and he employs the form of the doctrine popularised by St. Augustine to this end. It should be observed that this account of the origin of sin is not greatly emphasised in this work,[27] in relation to man's sin, though, as will be shown later, the subject is of great importance in relation to the sinlessness of Jesus Christ.[28] What is important for St. Anselm is the facts which the doctrine states, and which no soteriology of any value can afford to deny or neglect. It may well be that St. Anselm's insistence on the spontaneous character of sin, which is a recurrent theme in his analysis of it, was felt by him to be irreconcilable with the cruder Augustinian form of the doctrine of original sin.

(2.6) Since most of the critics of St. Anselm have much to say concerning his conception of sin, it will enable us to bring out the fuller implications of this conception if we examine their charges. Though T. H. Hughes[29] maintains that "most writers find [St. Anselm's] defective view of sin as the main blemish in his Theory", in fact the writers on the subject would appear to be far from the agreement which he suggests.

(2.6.1) R. C. Moberly,[30] quoting "*non est aliud peccare quam Deo non reddere debitum*",[31] makes three criticisms of this statement ("definition" is his word) of the nature of sin. "It makes sin in its essence quantitative, and, as quantitative, external to the self of the sinner, and measurable, as if it had a self in itself." [32]

(2.6.1.1) Moberly's criticisms reflect his own general theory about the relation of Atonement to personality, for he finds the notion of personality absent from St. Anselm. But while this notion is a product, in a way, of the recent advance of the science of psychology—and we cannot therefore criticise St. Anselm for being born out of due season—it is not entirely true to say that his view of sin is consequently impersonal, or that for him it lies in the deed and not in the personality. On the contrary, for St. Anselm sin is an intensely personal thing: it is the failure of the creature to make that response of will, intelligence and affection which he ought, by reason of his very creatureliness, to make to his Creator. "When Anselm speaks of sin as robbing God of honour, it is his way of saying that when we sin we wrong a person, and an infinitely great person, not merely a law or a principle." [33] St. Anselm's whole analysis of the results of man's failure to give God the honour due to Him shows that he thinks of the sinner not as if he were a series of bad deeds but as if he were a person who, because of his own sinful nature, cannot do deeds acceptable in God's sight. In fact, Moberly tries to press too far the distinction between the "I" and his deeds: if it is true that sin lies not in the deed as deed, it is a false abstraction to think of sin as residing in an "I" which is not doing this deed or that. Moberly admits as much when he says that sin lies "in the 'I' as doer of the deed", though he seems unaware of this implication of the admission. Against Moberly we must, therefore, conclude that St. Anselm does primarily conceive of sin in a personal fashion.

(2.6.1.2) It has, however, to be conceded to Moberly that St. Anselm speaks of sin abstractedly, for example, in the title of I.21. But in doing so, he does no more than St. Paul, who spoke of the wages of sin being death, or any other Christian writer who affirms, say, that the sin of mankind was responsible for the Death of Our Lord. In every age the Christian Church has thought of sin as if it were an aggregate, or a mass, or even as quasi-personal, and, in fact, in the history of Christian theology understanding of the nature of sin has been at its poorest and shallowest when theologians preferred to speak of *sins* rather than of *sin*. Here St. Anselm seems to be on very good ground; the problem for Christian theology is not merely that there should be sins of individual sinners—though that is problem enough in itself— but rather that there should be sin, repeating itself throughout the world and in every generation of history, ever inventing new methods of expressing itself, new ways of defying God by dis-obedience to His Supreme Will. In short, the Church has very often regarded sin as if it were some sort of self in itself, and so Moberly's charge is really a general one, even if it is correct. When this point is made, however, it is still very difficult to see how Moberly reaches his conclusion from the premises he gives. He wants to deduce it from the facts that sin is quantitative and measurable, according to St. Anselm, but these are the very characteristics that cannot be attributed to anything that is a self. Moberly may have one or the other, but not both. It is note-worthy that in the remainder of his treatment of St. Anselm's view of sin he nowhere returns to this fallacious piece of reasoning, confining himself to the criticisms of the idea that sin is measur-able and quantitative.

(2.6.1.3) While it is true that St. Anselm speaks of sin as a failure to pay a debt owed to God, it is unfair to take such a statement out of the context of his general treatment of the nature of the debt owed, and of the sin involved in the non-payment. Far too much has been made by unsympathetic critics of St. Anselm of the commercial and economic implications of the word "debt".[34] The primary significance of the term is religious and moral: a *debitum* is something I ought to do, an obligation I ought to fulfil, as well as something I owe. When it is affirmed that St. Anselm defines sin as a failure to pay a debt, in justice to him we must comprehend within that definition all that he intended, and not be content with a caricature of an analogy with financial em-barrassment.

(2.6.1.4) Nor do I find it easy to follow the intention of Moberly's assertion that for St. Anselm sin is "quantitative and measurable". In one sense no one denies that sin is quantitative. Some sins are greater than others: the collective sin of a society or of a class or of a nation is greater than the aggregate of the sins of all the individual members, as Reinhold Niebuhr has so comprehensively shown, and anyone who confesses his manifold and great sins before Almighty God is using quantitative language. In fact, such language is unavoidable, and no one troubles to avoid it unless he has an axe to grind. But we may deal with Moberly's criticism in a different way. It is easy to see that he has only deduced the "quantitative" (in some bad sense) character of St. Anselm's conception of sin from his misconception of sin, as if it were for St. Anselm a financial debt which could be counted up. Once that notion is shown to be a misconception Moberly's deduction collapses, as does his suggestion that for St. Anselm sin is "measurable". In any case, the point which St. Anselm makes later—one should have said unmistakably—is that sin, even the tiniest sin, is immeasurable, for it ought not to be committed, even if by it this universe and many others were to be saved from annihilation.[35] In fact, St. Anselm's fundamental contention in this work is that sin is such a grave thing that we have nothing by which we can adequately measure it. As Denney says, "St. Anselm is right in saying that we ought not to commit the slightest sin for worlds, which is only another way of saying that even the slightest sin involves a responsibility for which there is no material measure." [36] It is therefore impossible to avoid the judgment that Moberly's criticisms of St. Anselm are quite unsatisfactory, and that they spring from a failure to sift out what exactly St. Anselm's views were.

(2.6.2) G. B. Stevens [37] would accept much of Moberly's verdict on St. Anselm and go still further. He regards St. Anselm's theory as being a feudal theory, and his conception of sin as no more than "an enormous affront, a shocking insult to the heavenly Majesty".[38] In a series of rhetorical questions he suggests that St. Anselm fails to appreciate the unreasonableness of sin ("its real ethical character"! [39]), its nature as an offence against inherent truth and right. He continues by saying that on this theory "sin is high treason and not moral corruption . . .; it is indeed a great fault but it is hardly a moral fact", and so on in the same vein until he concludes that "it would be difficult to name any prominent treatise on atonement whose conception of sin is so essentially unethical and superficial".[40] These are strong words, but gravely inaccurate. Whether the theory is predominantly feudal is a matter to which we shall soon return,[41] but in any case St. Anselm was not the first to think of God as the Heavenly King, the Ruler of the Universe, and any religion or theology which regards God as King is bound to regard sin as an offence against Him. Stevens' statements at this point read rather like those of a more than ordinarily irreverent free-thinker. Further, his own conception of sin, while perhaps ethical, is no more than ethical. There is a good deal more to sin than un-reasonableness, in any sense of that almost meaninglessly vague term. Nor is sin simply an offence against inherent truth and right, whatever these are when separated from the Personality of God. On these terms St. Anselm's theory is not ethical, and one is glad that it is not. It is rather religio-ethical: sin is active disobedience to God's Will for His creatures, a violation of His government of the world, and a contempt for the glory which is His due. Finally, it is only to be conjectured that for Stevens St. Anselm's view of sin is superficial because it is at variance with his own quite inadequate view; he suggests no other good reason. In fact, Stevens' criticisms of St. Anselm tell us more about Stevens' own theology than they do about St. Anselm's.

(2.6.3) T. H. Hughes [42] is the latest of those who attack St. Anselm's conception of sin. Towards the end of his discussion he quotes both Moberly and Stevens in a manner which vaguely suggests that he is in agreement with the quotations from them. Having already dealt with the originals, we may dismiss the quotations. In the earlier part of his discussion, however, Hughes makes statements which the reader can only guess are intended as veiled criticisms of St. Anselm. He writes, for example, "Sin is more than a commercial matter, more also than a moral fault or a breach of the law. It is more even than a crime against society. . . . Sin is, in the ultimate, a religious term, rather than a moral or a social one. It holds in the realm of personal relations, and is really a matter between man and God, for in the end it is against God that sin is committed." [43] All this is perfectly true, but quite irrelevant if calculated, by implication, as a criticism of St. Anselm. As we have already shown, for him sin is no commercial matter; here Hughes falls into the error of Fairbairn,

Moberly and the rest. It is never for him simply "a moral fault" or "a crime against society", but always a failure of the creature to make that response of total personality which he owes to his Creator. His concept is religious through and through.

3. GOD'S REACTION TO MAN'S SIN (*Aut poena aut satisfactio*)

It is to be remembered that in this section we are discussing St. Anselm's thought on this subject within the self-imposed limits stated in the *Praefatio*, namely, of examining man's sinful state and of God's reaction to it, apart from the full knowledge of God and His purpose which can be derived from the revelation of God in Jesus Christ. Nor must we commit the error of supposing that the views set forth represent St. Anselm's complete account of God's reaction to sin. The God Who will in this part of our examination be found to *demand* either satisfaction or punishment is the same God Who, according to the later chapters of Book II, will Himself *make* the satisfaction, thus showing forth His compassion and love for us.

God's reaction to man's sin St. Anselm states in the famous disjunction: either man makes satisfaction to God for the sin committed, or God will punish man for it. Let us deal with the two arms of the disjunction in that order.

(3.1) *Aut Satisfactio*

The full consequence of man's sin we can properly estimate only when we pass to the discussion of God's reaction to sin. The natural transition to that discussion is to indicate the immediate result of sin to man himself. In a word, the result is that wherever man as a rational creature owed to God the single debt of continual obedience to God's Will, he now as a result of his sin owes, in addition to that continuing debt, the debt of paying God further honour for the injury done Him by disobedience. To enforce this contention St. Anselm employs an analogy from what is taken to be the practice of the private (as distinct from the public) law of his times. If, in private life, I injure the health of another person, then I am obliged not only to restore that person to full health, but, by some additional action or gift, to make amends for the harm I have done him. Such a gift is proportionate to the injury done — *secundum exhonorationis factam molestiam*. The nature of the gift depends upon the private pleasure of the person to whom the injury has been done. It is this additional gift or action which constitutes the satisfaction proper. So, when man sins against God the situation cannot be put right unless, first, the original debt owed by every creature to God is paid by complete obedience of will and mind and heart, and, secondly, the additional debt incurred by the act of disobedience is paid through some amends being made. It is this second payment which St. Anselm strictly regards as the satisfaction due to God for sin. He himself says, "Thus, therefore, everyone who sins ought to (re)pay the honour which he has stolen from God (by sinning); and this is the satisfaction which every sinner ought to pay." [44] But this second payment in itself is not sufficient to rectify the situation. Accordingly, St. Anselm seems very often to suggest that it is the total payment—of the original and the additional debts—which is the satisfaction.

(3.1.1) Such being the nature of satisfaction, the question next arises of whether anyone can make the satisfaction to God which He demands. The negative answer which St. Anselm gives rests upon four grounds: the first is a rejection of certain specific actions with which man might try to make amends; the second is the enormity of the debt which man is required to pay off as a result of his sin; the third is a certain principle involved in satisfaction which man is completely unable to achieve; and the fourth is man's original sin and his consequent inability to conquer the Devil.

(3.1.1.1) First, since man, as God's creature, owes to God the total allegiance of his will, and, in fact his whole self, even in his unfallen state, according to I.20, there is nothing remaining for him to offer to God, once he has fallen, to make satisfaction for his sin. Boso suggests that he might offer God the round of duties prescribed by the penitential system of the contemporary Church—for example, repentance, contrition of heart, humility, fastings, and all manner of bodily labours, etc. But since the fulfilment of these duties is required of man quite apart from his having sinned, such fulfilment in no way reduces the additional debt which man has incurred by sinning. Man therefore finds

that he has nothing to offer God by way of satisfaction for the
dishonour he has done to God. By a single stroke St. Anselm
here destroys what had obviously become a misconception of the
early medieval penitential exercises, namely, that of themselves,
apart from the Work of Christ, they achieved forgiveness for the
sinner. He thus strikes a blow for evangelical theology, for justification by God's grace in Christ as against justification by works,
the importance of which has not been fully realised.

(3.1.1.2) Secondly, man's inability to make amends to God for
his sin is seen to be due to the greatness of even one single sin
against God. Sin, as the defiance of the Will of God, should it
involve but the slightest glance that God has forbidden, is heinous.
It is at this point [45] that St. Anselm's famous line to Boso appears:
"*Nondum considerasti quanti ponderis sit peccatum.*" Boso has not
fully appreciated the extreme seriousness of sin if he is suggesting
that it could be removed by some evidence of remorse or regret
over its having occurred. One sin against God is a mighty crime,
for we are always in God's sight, and He always instructs us not
to sin.[46] If any deeper reason is to be found for St. Anselm's view,
it is to be sought in two directions. On the one hand, his reason
could be found in his general emphasis upon God's demand for
total obedience from His creatures. Any sin, however great or
small, is a violation of that obedience, and, consequently, evidences
opposition on the part of the creature to his Creator. St. Paul's
view that to break the Law at a single point is to break the whole
Law is a comparable notion. On the other hand, the reason
could be found conceivably in the legal standards of St. Anselm's
day, according to which the gravity of the crime varied in direct
proportion to the dignity of the person injured. So great is the
dignity of God that any sin is exceedingly great. Of these two
possible reasons, it seems that the first is preferable, not only
because it is more in line with what St. Anselm has to say elsewhere,[47] but also because it is obvious that St. Anselm's insight is
here religious rather than legal: he is more concerned with disobedience to God's Will than with dishonour.

(3.1.1.3) In I.21 [48] St. Anselm enunciates a principle for the
determination of the degree of satisfaction required to restore
to God the honour of which He has been robbed by man's sin,

a principle which proves to be of supreme importance for his argument in II.6 concerning the God-man. Throughout I.21 St. Anselm has been illustrating to Boso the heinousness of what might happen to be even the slightest sin against God. At I.21, p. 89, ll. 1 ff., St. Anselm has made it plain, as is seen from Boso's reply, that even if some sinful action is to save the whole universe and everything that is not God from annihilation, nevertheless it ought not to be done. Even an infinity of universes to be saved would not affect the issue. These things, therefore—the whole universe, all that is not God, and an infinity of universes—constitute the objects *for the sake of which* even the slightest sin is not to be committed. In this context St. Anselm asserts that if, in fact, we do commit sin, satisfaction will not be complete unless it exceeds this totality, for the sake of which we should not have been willing to commit it in the first instance. This view is interesting for several reasons:

First, while it is agreed that the argument set out above is essentially part of that discussed in (3.1.1.2), it is nevertheless important to distinguish the two; while the former draws attention to the seriousness of sin, as violation of the Will of God which is constantly operative for His creatures, the present argument finds that seriousness in the massive considerations which can never under any circumstances justify it. These two different grounds for the heinousness of sin lead virtually to two different, but of course not unrelated, interpretations of the satisfaction due to God for the sin committed by man. On the one hand, the satisfaction is determined by the general principle that satisfaction is proportionate to the offence committed (the offence in this case acquiring its extent from the nature of God and the continual demands He makes on His creatures). In other words, an offence against an infinite God is an infinite offence. On the other hand, the satisfaction required is asserted to be commensurate with all the actual and possible factors for the sake of which the offence must not be committed. In both cases the issue is identical: man cannot make the satisfaction.

Secondly, the account here given of the satisfaction which man would need to make to God for his sin places St. Anselm's conception beyond the realm of commercial transaction between equals. The situation which St. Anselm is endeavouring to describe is without exact analogy in private or public law; it arises from the unique relation in which God, the Creator, stands to man, His creature. Even if it is said that the analogy consists in the use of the term "satisfaction", it must immediately be plain that the analogy has been broken through completely in the use to which it is put.[49]

Thirdly, St. Anselm must be safeguarded against a possible misapprehension. From the fact that even the slightest sin requires more than an infinity of universes to be offered to God before He will be satisfied, it must not be concluded that no sins are more heinous than others, or that God is less dishonoured by some than by others. Such a conclusion would be morally deplorable, and it arises only if we obscure St. Anselm's purpose in this chapter (I.21), which is to show that for no sin (however great or small) can man make the satisfaction which God requires. Without denying the difference between coveting your neighbour's ass and murdering his brother, St. Anselm does intend to make it plain that there are no simple sins which God easily condones without compromising His honour, and from the effects of which we can readily escape with a little penance and a few good works.

Fourthly, some explanation ought perhaps to be offered for what seems to be a hiatus in St. Anselm's thought, the gap between the statement that sin should not be committed, no matter how weighty the considerations entertained in its favour, and the conclusion that the satisfaction required by God is in excess of all that ought not to induce us to sin (i.e. preservation of the universe, all that is not God, an infinity of universes). The explanation would appear to be as follows: St. Anselm balances sin against these "weighty considerations", and sees that they are not weighty enough to justify its being committed. Alternatively, they are not equal in value to it. If, then, we do actually commit sin, we must offer to God by way of atonement for it something which is at least equal to it: i.e. not only these "weighty considerations" ("all that is not God" turns out in II.6 to be that in which St. Anselm is most interested) but something extra which will complete the balance. In other words, our satisfaction will have to be something greater than that for the sake of which we ought not to have committed the sin.

(3.1.1.4) Finally, since man in sinning allowed himself to succumb to the will of the Devil in contempt for God's purpose for him, he can make proper satisfaction to God only if he conquers the Devil and so honours God. But because in the Fall man in sinning gave way to the Devil, and so, having been potentially immortal, received from God the punishment of mortality, he must, further, in order to achieve the proper satisfaction, effect the victory over the Devil in a specific way, namely, by sinlessly undergoing the affliction of death. But man, who is conceived and born in sin, cannot die sinlessly. Consequently, he is unable to vanquish the Devil in the fashion required and to furnish God with the satisfaction which He demands. St. Anselm's argumentation [50] concerning the sinless death by which man is required to conquer the Devil is succinct to the point of obscurity, and indeed is only to be understood fully in the light of what he has later to say on the Death of Christ, Who is Himself the Sinless One. In the meantime it should be observed that even if it is true that the Death of Christ, as Sinless, involves the conquest of the Devil, it does not necessarily follow that the sinless death of man (as distinct from that of the God-man) would be a victory over the Devil. In fact, the value of Christ's Death [51] arises from the *Person* of Jesus Christ, and not solely from His sinlessness, so that the argument given in I.22 (ll. 20-23) is not by itself valid.

(3.1.1.5) It is necessary at this point to draw attention to what we might call a "secondary ground" for the necessity of salvation. The primary ground is to be found in God's purpose for rational creatures; in creating rational beings it is His Will for them that they should serve Him and give Him honour by obeying His commandments, and so achieve their highest blessedness. By their sin they have temporarily frustrated God's great destiny for them, and so to achieve His purpose for them satisfaction must be made to Him. The "secondary ground" for the necessity of salvation [52] is that God has resolved to substitute men for the fallen angels. But the men who are to be raised to this glory must be righteous in God's sight, and this they can be only if and when they have made to God adequate satisfaction for the sins that they have committed against Him. Once again St. Anselm affirms [53] that it would be unfitting for God to grant man full blessedness until such satisfaction had been made. This argument is in the spirit of the times and it need not delay us further.

(3.2) The Concept of Satisfaction

This occupies such a central position within the *Cur Deus Homo,* and so much research has been devoted to the subject, that it is essential to deal with the main issues connected with it at this stage of our examination of St. Anselm's work, for the interpretation given to this concept will inevitably determine our views of the use which he makes of it as the argument develops. Historical and critical research has quarried the mine almost to the point of exhaustion, and in that field the minor duty of correlating the findings is all that remains to be done. On the other hand, the task of theological integration and interpretation has not been satisfactorily followed through, with consequent grave injustice to the reputation of St. Anselm. Research has concentrated particularly on two problems: the first—what is the origin and history of the notion of *satisfactio*? and the second— to what extent does St. Anselm accept or alter the meaning of this notion, having taken it over from his predecessors? [54]

(3.2.1) In the treatment of the first of these problems the chief point at issue is that of determining how far the idea of satisfaction has been influenced in its formulation by purely secular factors (such as Roman public and private law, and the Teutonic practice of Wergild) and how far by the ecclesiastical doctrine of penance and the actual penitential systems. The first step towards such determination is suggested by Franks,[55] namely, an assessment of the part played by Tertullian in introducing the idea into theological thought, and in coupling it with that of "merit". The latter had already appeared in Hermas,[56] but Tertullian systematised it, showing how God Who is the great Law-Giver regards as meritorious actions which His Will does not make obligatory.[57] It is in relation to sins committed after baptism that the question of satisfaction arises.[58] In the *De Poenitentia* Tertullian is obviously endeavouring to correct certain evil practices which have grown up in the Church, through a misunderstanding of the forgiveness of sins offered in Baptism. Some people, being assured that their sins were forgiven when

they were baptised, are making that fact an excuse for unrestricted
licence. These offenders are urged to practise repentance in
order to placate God, the Law-Giver Who has been offended by
their evildoing.[59] For God has determined that penitence is the
price to be paid for the re-purchase of forgiveness [60] and of freedom from the punishment of His anger. This penitence, for which
the Confession makes ample provision by way of disciplinary
fasting, groaning, weeping and mourning,[61] is the satisfaction
by which God is appeased.

There are two ways in which we may interpret the influence
of Roman law upon Tertullian's account of satisfaction, and these
two interpretations disagree as to whether the satisfaction is penal
or not. On the one hand, Schultz, collaborating with his colleague
Merkel, claims that in Roman private law satisfaction is the
making of compensation, other than by direct payment (*solvere*),
to an injured person for damage done to him or to his property,
and it must be performed in a manner acceptable to the latter.
Satisfaction, in this sense, is not the acceptance of one form of
punishment for another. If we apply this interpretation to Tertullian's concept, the *satisfactio* becomes a sub-species of merit,
an action by which an abundance of merit is established to cancel
the sin, and to win the forgiveness of God. God may either
punish the sinner outright for his sins, or He may pardon him
after being placated by his penitential actions, but He does not
do both at once. On the other hand, according to Roman public
law [62] the satisfaction was itself the penalty required by the law.
If this view is taken as the basis of our interpretation of Tertullian
it follows that in making satisfaction for his sins the sinner is
undergoing temporal punishment. His penitential actions, repre-
senting his own judgment upon his sin, discharge the eternal
punishment,[63] and so win him God's forgiveness. They may not
constitute punishment equivalent to God's, but they are certainly
penal in nature. In this case the *venia* comes through the *poena*,
even though it is not the *poena* of *De Poenitentia*, c. 12, with its
storehouse of everlasting fire.

The truth is that the influence of both of these elements in
Roman law is to be traced in Tertullian's view of satisfaction.
Franks, who follows Schultz almost uncritically, has to admit
that the penitential actions have a painful and penal quality, but

‧nevertheless he fails both to charge Schultz's analysis with inadequacy for that reason and to recognise that public as well as private legal practice is relevant to the whole case. Satisfaction in Tertullian, then, is both meritorious and penal, and his well-known saying, "Every sin is discharged either by pardon or by punishment, by pardon as a consequence of chastisement, by punishment as a consequence of damnation",[64] does not invalidate this conclusion, if Tertullian's argument after the passage quoted is properly understood. For while the disjunction *aut venia aut poena* seems at first to suggest that punishment and forgiveness are never applied together, the exclusiveness of the disjunction is broken down in what follows. Forgiveness is said to come through chastisement, which is painful, and the punishment referred to is eternal damnation, which does not preclude God's punishing temporally those to whom He offers forgiveness through chastisement. Therefore, while it is to be admitted that for Tertullian satisfaction is not a substitute punishment of sin extracted by an outraged God, nevertheless, as Harnack says, it is permissible to call it a "compensating penalty".[65]

On this conclusion concerning the influence of Roman law, in its two forms, upon Tertullian's presentation of the idea of satisfaction two comments may be made. First, the qualified nature of the conclusion makes it plain that Tertullian's presentation has not been *determined* by either one or the other of the influences that are discernably at work. The reverse is rather the case, that he has made free use of contemporary legal concepts in order to formulate and clarify a system of thought which is essentially theological in its origin and in its nature. It is this system which determines the use which he will make of these contemporary concepts, and we err if we assume that the concepts exactly prescribe the content of the system. No matter how accurately we are able to define the use of the concept of satisfaction in either private or public Roman law, it is still not conclusively proved that Tertullian used the concept in precisely that form. This aspect of the matter simply does not come over the horizon of such legalists as Schultz and Merkel, who seem to be quite content to settle Tertullian's use of the concept of satisfaction on the basis of "an exhaustive list of passages from Roman legal authorities",[66] though Franks should have known better.

Secondly, sufficient consideration has not been given to c. 9 of the *De Poenitentia*, where Tertullian refers to what is obviously an elaborate and well-established system of Confession. The theological foundation of this system is some such idea as that of satisfaction, and the stage of elaborateness such a system had reached by the end of the second century or the beginning of the third plainly shows that it is no recent innovation. It was this practice of Confession, later to develop into the sacrament of Penance, which, I suggest, formed the dominant idea of Tertullian's thought concerning satisfaction, and to it the legal notions derived from the contemporary systems were subordinated. The dominance of the one and the subordination of the others explain the difficulty which is encountered by those who endeavour to regard Tertullian's idea of satisfaction as a theological transcript of a legal term of fixed connotation, which remains unchanged in the process. Such critics have, in fact, committed "the naturalistic fallacy" or "the fallacy of origins": the fallacy, that is, of assuming that the nature of an entity has been adequately defined once its origins have been stated, and that such an entity is no more than its origins. It is a fallacy still common enough among ethical evolutionists, anthropologists and sociologists to be a contemporary danger, but it belongs more properly to the nineteenth century.

Though the examination of Tertullian's employment of the term *satisfactio* enables us to determine what might be called the academic origin of the notion, nevertheless he was writing some eight hundred years before St. Anselm, and he cannot be regarded as exerting any great influence upon the latter. In fact, the two theologians differ so much in other respects that it would be improper to name Tertullian as a primary source of Anselmic theology. For that reason, any close linking of the two would be both unhistorical and unwarranted by the content of their writings. Such additional evidence of the idea of satisfaction as we can gather from the writings of Cyprian, Hilary and Ambrose, and even of St. Augustine, does not fill out the picture given by Tertullian to any great extent. The twin ideas of satisfaction as meritorious and quasi-penal persist, neither at any time excluding the other. It has consequently become customary to look upon the penitential system of the early Middle Ages as the

background of St. Anselm's idea of satisfaction. Certain altera-
tions and developments, taking place gradually over centuries,
of the system of the Confession, to which Tertullian bore witness,
yield the medieval sacrament of Penance. For example, the
fastings and mournings, etc., which formed a necessary part of
the penitential discipline of the Confession, and by which satisfaction was made to God, have been materialised and depersonal-
ised, so that the sinner may either make payments or hire others
to fast or sing psalms in his stead. It appears that this system of
commutations or redemptions was well organised by St. Anselm's
time, though not without frequent objection from the official
Church. We saw previously how Tertullian had allowed a certain
penal character to satisfaction, in so far as the sinner by punishing himself anticipated God's punishment of him. This notion
is not entirely absent from the early medieval penance system
either, for we find such sentences as *poenitere est enim poenam
tenere*,[67] but in actual practice the commutation was so painless
for the sinner that it would be frivolous to regard the *satisfactio*
as *poena* in any real sense. Once again, the question of secular
influence, whether of the Irish system of commutations or of the
Teutonic Wergild, is raised, particularly by Cremer but also by
Loofs,[68] Harnack and Franks. Their conclusions seem to be
fairly uniform: that while no doubt these extra-ecclesiastical
practices must have had some influence upon the development
of the system of Penance, it is impossible to prove that this influence is all-determinative. This conclusion is completely in line
with that suggested above concerning the relation of Tertullian
to the Roman law, and the reason for it is similar. The Church
had a long tradition of theology about penitence, and this tradition determined the kind of use its exponents made of contemporary ideas. So long as that tradition and the theological concepts associated with it remained dominant, the secular influence
could be only secondary.

(3.2.2) We are now ready to consider the second question which
we set ourselves: how far does St. Anselm accept or alter the
notion of *satisfactio* as it comes to him out of eight centuries of
usage, in the Church's theology and practice? Or, alternatively,
how is St. Anselm's use of the term related, by way of similarity

and difference, to that of his predecessors? Certain answers come immediately to mind. For example, it is clear that St. Anselm has taken over the idea that God expects moral obedience as a debt due to Him by His creatures, and that failure to obey places the sinner in a state of debt. Faced with this situation, God may, according to His good pleasure, choose one or other of two alternatives. He may punish the sinner, or He may receive from him some satisfaction which atones for the dishonour done to Him —*aut poena aut satisfactio*. At that point the differences between St. Anselm and his predecessors begin to appear. As we shall see later, no great case can be made out for the view that St. Anselm regards *satisfactio* as "compensating penalty".

He does not in his reference, at I.20, to the contemporary penitential disciplines suggest that these are in any way penal, and even when he treats of the Death of Christ (e.g. at II.11), though emphasising the difficult and painful character of that Death, he does not regard it as a penal substitution. It should be noted, too, that the link between satisfaction and penance— so close both in Tertullian and in the penitential system—is entirely absent from St. Anselm's conception. In fact, at I.20, his main contention is that penitence is *not* satisfaction. In his discussion of the Death of Christ there is no suggestion that the satisfaction offered by the God-man is "vicarious penitence".

It is, therefore, undeniable that St. Anselm by employing the concept of satisfaction is necessarily committed to certain interpretations of the relations holding between God and man, and of the nature of sin, but it is equally plain that St. Anselm builds the concept and the interpretations implied by it into a fabric of thought which differs essentially from that of his predecessors, either in the field of theology proper or in that of penitential practice. The meaning of the word as it appears in Anselmic soteriology is to be discovered, therefore, not by a historical analysis of previous uses of it, but by an examination of the place which it occupies within his scheme. For in a very real sense he builds up his own interpretation of it as the work proceeds, so that in the end we have an entirely new conception. This purpose he achieves particularly by the association of satisfaction with the Death of Christ—an original departure in the usage of the term—and, as a consequence, in this new reference the word acquires significance, implications and shades of thought which are not to be found—nor should one expect to find them—in its previous history. This kind of occurrence is frequently taking place in the history of theological language and usage. It happened when the words "ransom" and "propitiation" were applied to the Death of Christ by the earliest writers; in the new reference these words were "baptised" into a new meaning, which had certainly associations with the old in that the same words were still used, but in which these associations were radically transformed. A similar occurrence is taking place in modern theology, with such words as "crisis", "existential" and "dimension", to mention an obvious few. For that reason I should say that most of the historical and critical analysis of the notion of *satisfactio*, as it appears in writers prior to St. Anselm, has been downright misleading, for it has created the impression that St. Anselm is bound in his employment of the notion by the interpretations placed upon it by his predecessors.

This conclusion enables us to deal briefly with a matter of which much has been made by the critics of St. Anselm, namely, that his thought is determined by extra-religious, secular considerations, such as the practices of Roman law and the Teutonic Wergild. It is suggested that these influences may be direct or indirect. In the first case, St. Anselm is said to be affected by the practices because he lived in a world in which they were customary. In the second, he is said to have been influenced by them through their prior influence on such writers as Tertullian or on the exponents of the Penance system. The answer previously given as to the inconclusive character of the charge that Roman law affected Tertullian, and the Wergild the Penance system, is here immediately applicable, and the charge of direct influence of these secular practices upon St. Anselm must be dropped.

A fortiori and for the same reasons the charge of indirect influence cannot be maintained. Not only did St. Anselm sit very loose to interpretations of satisfaction accepted by his predecessors but, further, he had certain theological concepts—such as the justice, righteousness, honour and love of God, and, most important of all, the *aseitas* of God—which predetermined the meaning which subordinate terms would have within his system. It is possible, of course, to make a counter-assertion to this analysis which I have given of the situation, by saying that it is really only a matter of private and arbitrary choice whether we hold that these dominant theological ideas of St. Anselm determined the form in which he presented that of satisfaction, or that it is his idea of satisfaction that dominated and dictated the others. That it is not a matter of private choice is seen, I should reply, from the fact that the latter alternative is arguable only on the assumption that St. Anselm adopted a previously fixed conception of satisfaction to which the rest of his theology was made to conform. Once we demonstrate that St. Anselm's interpretation of satisfaction is not reducible to its antecedents, then that assumption is disproved. On the other hand, when we establish the position that the Anselmic idea of satisfaction can be understood only in terms of the general Anselmic theology and soteriology, then the former becomes the only possible alternative. To put the situation differently, St. Anselm's procedure in the *Cur Deus Homo* is not: Given an *a priori* idea of satisfaction, God must be so-and-so and do such-and-such in order to save fallen mankind; but rather: Given that God's attributes are mercy, justice, righteousness, omnipotence, love and (if we may for the present call it an attribute) *aseitas*, then He will save mankind in a manner which is not only conformable to these attributes but, in fact, is more completely expressive of them than any other event in the whole history of the relations of God and man, namely, by means of a satisfaction offered by Himself. It is in the description of God's act of salvation in the *Deus-homo* and not in the setting of Roman law or Teutonic Wergild that the notion of satisfaction finds its proper place.

It is their equivocation on the relation of St. Anselm to his predecessors, their concern with, and even their criticism of, the extreme views on this subject (for example, those associated with Cremer), coupled with their failure to give the notion of satisfaction its own peculiar and rightful basis in St. Anselm's theology, which I find to be the fundamentally unsatisfactory characteristic of those who have dealt extensively with these topics. The errors to which this equivocation leads may be seen from illustrations of criticisms made of St. Anselm by selected writers:

(3.2.3) Ritschl's [69] technique of criticism is to elicit what he calls "features in Anselm's theory which are incompatible". His starting-point is a rigid distinction which, he claims, exists in St. Anselm between the glory of God and the justice of God. When relations between God and man are determined by the glory of God, then God is presented as the superior, the Sovereign in a moral universe Whose subjects must maintain the order and beauty of that universe by obeying His Will and glorifying Him; whereas, when the idea of the idea of the justice of God is regulative, God and man are regarded as equals on the analogy of the sphere of private rights, where relations are fixed by contracts between persons of co-ordinate status. These two views of the relations between God and man are inconsistent, says Ritschl. Introducing without explanation the term "honour of God" to replace that of "glory of God", he pursues the inconsistency further. He admits that the equality of God and man implied by the private-right analogy is "modified" by the idea of honour: for it is God's honour which has to be satisfied, and for which reparation has to be made by the offending sinner. But, he continues, this modification serves only to emphasise the equality of God and man; here he gives as his reason the fact that in private law such compensations can be offered and received only by those who are not subordinate one to the other. Therefore, either St. Anselm should adhere to the notion of the glory of God and insist that, for the sake of moral order in the universe, God should punish all sinners and allow no satisfaction—for satisfaction holds only between equals—or he should lay exclusive emphasis upon the possibility of satisfaction, made even by a third party, by mutual arrangement between the injured and the offender. Ritschl would force St. Anselm's disjunction *aut poena aut satisfactio* upon the author himself, and demand that he make his choice, for he cannot have both, even in the form of a disjunction![70]

This statement is the case for the alleged incompatibility of the glory or honour of God with the justice of God, as St. Anselm describes these attributes. It would be difficult to imagine anything more confused or better designed to misrepresent St. Anselm. It is important because of the popularity which this kind of criticism has enjoyed, and also relevant to our immediate purpose, but certain initial inaccuracies may be observed. The glory of God as distinct from the honour of God is by no means as clear a concept in St. Anselm's thought as Ritschl insinuates. In fact, the phrase "the dignity of God" appears fairly frequently and should have been considered by Ritschl along with the others. Again, the relation between the justice of God and the honour of God is not antithetic but complementary. The position is that God's justice requires that His honour should be satisfied (as is so clearly suggested in I.13) and there is no evidence whatsoever for Ritschl's suggestion that God's honour requires one thing and His justice another, or for his contention that St. Anselm's compromise, the alleged modification of the attribute of God's glory by that of His justice, introduces actual tensions in his system of thought. The absence of such evidence, and he does not offer any, disposes of his case. What Ritschl has really failed to see is that after all analogy is only analogy, and that no analogy, particularly on its negative side, should be pressed to its extreme limits. The purpose of the analogy referred to by Ritschl [71] was to show that, just as in our dealings with a fellow-man we require to make some compensation, over and above exact payment, for the fact of having done the injury to him, so, in our relation to God, we must not only pay the debt we did not pay when we sinned but also make amends for having sinned. In fact, in the light of I.21,[72] what St. Anselm could be construed as saying is this: *a fortiori*, when I sin against God I ought to make the very greatest amends possible for the dishonour which I have done to Him. Equality between God and man is very distant from Anselm's thought and speech, either directly or by implication; indeed, such an imputation stultifies the whole argument of the *Cur Deus Homo*. Besides, it is grossly unwarrantable to bring in the charge by literal interpretation of the detail of an analogy. The truth is that, whether St. Anselm is thinking more particularly of the justice or of the glory of God in relation to man, he never loses sight of the fact that God and man are unequal. If there is a fundamental contradiction in St. Anselm's thought it is not to be found in this quarter.

If there is no textual or other basis for Ritschl's criticism of St. Anselm, namely, that there is an "incompatibility between the glory or honour of God and the justice of God", why should Ritschl have been so anxious to hold that there is? The answer is to be found in the motive which prompted our own enquiry, that of discovering how overemphasis on the historical antecedents of certain elements in St. Anselm's thought led to distorted presentation of his views. Ritschl rightly recognises that there are traces in St. Anselm of the influence of both public and private law—though, as we have seen, they are no more than traces, and though he does not state his case sufficiently clearly by indicating whether he is thinking of Roman law or Teutonic law, or which aspects of these legal systems he has in mind. He, again rightly, recognises that these two systems of law as vaguely described by him are incompatible in certain respects. His next step is the false one. On the assumption that St. Anselm takes over without modification the two incompatible systems, he concludes that the incompatibilities persist into the *Cur Deus Homo*. He even tries to insist that St. Anselm should have followed the practice of public law more rigorously than he did. What he does not appreciate is that St. Anselm uses concepts which have affinity with legal practice of one kind or another, in the interests of his general theory, steadfastly refusing to allow previous usage to determine his own interpretation. Had Ritschl followed up his own suggestion concerning the modification of the private law conception of reparation by the idea of God's glory, he would have reached a position similar to that which has been outlined above. Instead, however, he prefers to affirm that the modification serves, in some way which he does not make clear, to illustrate the incompatibility for which he is arguing.

(3.2.4) Franks,[73] in a strain similar to that of Ritschl, affirms a fundamental antinomy in St. Anselm's theory, on the basis of the analogy used by St. Anselm in I.11, though he gives different reasons from those put forward by Ritschl. On grounds, first, of St. Anselm's assertion that after injury to some person we must make amends for the wrongdoing by an action or gift which pleases him, and, secondly, of the fact that in private law "the measure of satisfaction is simply the good pleasure of the offended person", he concludes that for St. Anselm there is no absolute necessity for man to make satisfaction to God. Absolute necessity has to be imported from public law of the Teutonic variety, in accordance with which the *princeps* is obliged to enforce all compensations for injuries done and so maintain public peace. This absolute necessity, so runs Franks' comment, has to be imported in order to remove the laxity of arrangements made by private law. On the analogy of the *princeps* God is conceived as being necessarily bound to remove anything that disturbs the peace and order of His realm. Franks is here making a criticism hinted at by Ritschl,[74] though he makes it much more lucidly than the latter and gives it a somewhat different form.

In answer to Franks it must be said that close examination of the *ipsissima verba* of the text would have prevented the fallacious interpretation of St. Anselm which he here attempts. St. Anselm states quite plainly that restitution of the health of the injured party and compensation for the fact of the injury done are both obligatory. He speaks in the same terms of moral necessity concerning both, and for St. Anselm moral necessity is absolute. Whether in fact, according to private law, the payment of compensation as distinct from restitution is absolutely necessary is beside the point. It is plain that in I.11, which is St. Anselm's opening discussion of satisfaction, he regards the payment of the compensation as being in no way arbitrary: it is morally, and not simply legally, obligatory on the offender to perform it, and therefore necessary. He offers that affirmation as being ethically self-evident, and attempts to give no explanation either from private or from public law to account for why it should be so. It is idle criticism to say that because St. Anselm's illustration is somewhat similar to situations which occur in private law, therefore St. Anselm is fettered to the detail of that law and obliged to regard satisfaction as non-absolute. There is, then, no need to say that St. Anselm has to pass over from private law to the analogy of public law to prove the necessity of satisfaction, because, on the one hand, St. Anselm exhibits no anxiety to *prove* the necessity of satisfaction—he states it as a fact of moral experience and, *a fortiori*, of our relationship to God—and, on the other hand, he emphasises the necessity of satisfaction without *passing over* to public law at all; the necessity he regards as inherent in any situation where injury is done to some person in private life. In fact, I should affirm that St. Anselm throughout his discussion of satisfaction is considering more particularly the *moral* rather than the *legal* aspect of any analogies he uses, a point which Franks, Ritschl and Mozley all miss.

Franks, it will be recalled, reached his conclusion about the non-necessity of satisfaction from the premise that "the *measure* of satisfaction is simply the good pleasure of the offended person". This premise is as false as the conclusion which he draws from it. St. Anselm states, one would have thought unambiguously, that the compensation must be in proportion to, or in accordance with, the extent of the injury done. The actual form, however, of the compensation will be determined by the pleasure of the person injured. Thus, given that an injured person has already received restitution for injury, it is judged that g_1, g_2, g_3, g_4 are all equal compensation for the injury (all being additional, of course, to the restitution). The good pleasure of the injured person is the sole criterion of whether g_1, say, is to be preferred to any of the other three. It is, therefore, quite erroneous to hold that "the measure" of the compensation is simply "the good pleasure of the offended person": the measure of the compensation is solely the gravity of the offence committed. This fact is borne out by the order in which St. Anselm has arranged the sentence dealing with this topic: "*Ita qui honorem alicuius violat, non sufficit honorem reddere, si non secundum exhonorationis factam molestiam aliquid, quod placeat illi, quem exhonoravit, restituat.*" [75] By placing the *non secundum . . . molestiam* before the *aliquid* St. Anselm draws attention to the importance of the wrong committed as the determinant of the degree of reparation to be made. Had the pleasure of the injured party been the sole measure of the compensation in St. Anselm's opinion, then the phrase *secundum . . . molestiam* would have followed *quod placeat illi*.

In any case, when St. Anselm comes to deal with the measure of satisfaction to be offered to God by the man who has sinned against Him (I.20,21), then the matter is put beyond doubt. He plainly affirms that the satisfaction to be made to God must be commensurate with the offence committed,[76] and throughout I.21 he indicates that by satisfaction he means the payment of honour beyond the debt which is ordinarily expected by the Creator from His creature. The notion of "proportionate compensation" is not, however, there the entirely "new principle" which Franks claims it to be,[77] for even on Franks' own interpre-

tation of the compensation which St. Anselm suggests is to be
made to the injured person, the pleasure to be given him must be
in proportion to the wrong done to him; and, so by analogy, the
satisfaction to be made to God must be proportionate to the
gravity of the dishonour that we have done to Him. The whole
issue is not one of linguistic or syntactical nicety. For if it can be
shown, as I believe it has, that St. Anselm, on the one hand,
regards the payment of some definable compensation in addition
to restitution as absolutely necessary, and, on the other hand,
affirms that such compensation is determined in degree by a
retrospective consideration of the gravity of the offence given, and
only in form by the hedonic consequences produced by it, then
it follows by analogy that satisfaction is not some arbitrary offering
which God may or may not demand of sinners according to His
private pleasure but is on the contrary an absolutely necessary
obligation upon all sinners.

Our examination of the relevant criticisms made by Franks has,
therefore, yielded results similar to those reached in discussing
Ritschl, namely, that he interprets Anselmic notions too uncritically
in terms of their historical antecedents and parallels, and that such
interpretation has not only had insufficient support in the text
of the *Cur Deus Homo* but has actually produced misrepresenta-
tions of such texts as have been employed. They have both failed
to realise that our first responsibility is to interpret St. Anselm
by St. Anselm, and that the *Cur Deus Homo* is autonomous in its
logic. A true appreciation of these facts would have saved them
from some of their more extreme inaccuracies, a closer scrutiny
of the Anselmic text and method from the others. It must finally
be said in favour of them both that they did not go to the absurd
lengths reached by Harnack,[78] who wrote of St. Anselm's "mytho-
logical conception of God as the mighty private man, who is
incensed at the injury done to his honour and will not forego his
wrath till he has received an at least adequately great equivalent".
Nowhere does God appear in the *Cur Deus Homo* as God of
wrath; He is the Creator, the Lord of all, while satisfaction is
as much associated with His justice as with His honour, and has no
arbitrariness to it. Harnack's account is crude caricature, based
more upon a refusal to see in St. Anselm anything but the legal concepts of his day than upon any profound knowledge of his theology.

(3.3) *Aut Poena*

If the proper satisfaction is not made for sin, then in St. Anselm's opinion there is only one alternative, namely, that God should punish the sinner. That this is the sole alternative St. Anselm emphasises by indicating the impossibility of God's forgiving (by which, as we shall see in the sequel, he means "condoning") sin, and the incongruity of the non-punishment of sin. The double emphasis is made by means of an equation which he supplies at I.12, l. 11. To forgive sin (without satisfaction being made for it) is equivalent to not punishing it. St. Anselm develops his argument by examining both sides of the equation, beginning with the incongruity of the non-punishment of sin. His reasons for the necessity of punishment (if no satisfaction has been made) are explicit:

(3.3.1) First, if the sin is unpunished, the sinful and the sinless should receive the same treatment from God; secondly, this impropriety is underlined by the affirmation that the righteousness of man is under a law whereby God makes retribution proportionate to the extent of righteousness or unrighteousness which men achieve. Consequently, if sin is not punished, and if no satisfaction is made to God for it, then it is subject to no law whatever and becomes freer even than righteousness, which is quite unfitting. St. Anselm's meaning here is: Whereas righteousness is subject to the law of obeying God's Will on every occasion and to the general restraints placed upon the members of a moral society, and is in a certain sense unfree, on the other hand unrighteousness would, on the premises of the present argument, be free from any such law of obedience, and from these restraints, as well as from the moral sanctions imposed by God, sanctions which St. Anselm believes to be essential to the order of the universe. Thirdly, if unrighteousness goes free and unpunished, then it becomes like God, Who is Himself subject to no law; this is the height of incongruity. In fact, however, we shall discover soon that St. Anselm modifies this rather extreme statement concerning God's freedom in the next few speeches in I.12. Boso rather expertly indicates the conclusions which follow from an unqualified assertion of this kind, and St. Anselm, in modifying what he has said at I.12, ll. 29-30, virtually rejects his third reason above-mentioned.

Before leaving these three reasons which St. Anselm gives for the necessity of punishment of sin if no satisfaction is made to God, three comments may be made.

(3.3.1.1) First, the nature of St. Anselm's argument in each of the three cases is identical. He indicates a consequence which will follow if sin is unpunished; this consequence, he says, is seen to be unfitting when considered in relation to God, and it is therefore rejected. It is obvious that each of the three arguments, then, depends upon a prior notion of what is proper or improper in God; the nature of this prior notion seems to be self-evident to St. Anselm and Boso at this stage of the argument. But when we come to the next stage of the discussion of the impossibility of forgiveness we discover that very different conclusions are drawn from it by St. Anselm and by Boso. In fact, the real distinction between this present discussion of the necessity of punishment and the next concerning the impossibility of forgiveness is that between the *conveniens* and the *necessarium*.[79]

(3.3.1.2) Secondly, these arguments are mingled with the appeal to the fitting in God, as we have seen, and references to God's moral government of the universe, which will be stultified if certain events take place. This theme is so common throughout the whole of the Old and New Testaments that it is idle to look anywhere else than there for St. Anselm's source. Any suggestion that St. Anselm is here describing God simply as if He were the civil ruler of a medieval state is both unscholarly and amusing.

(3.3.1.3) Thirdly, these three arguments constitute only preliminary bouts in St. Anselm's tackling of the problem. They demonstrate the necessity of punishment, through the exposition of the impropriety of non-punishment, and they would carry weight perhaps with believers but not with unbelievers, who seek the *necessarium*. In the argument to which we now turn St. Anselm's aim is to demonstrate the impossibility of forgiveness without punishment and apart from satisfaction. He thus brings us closer to the heart of the problem, and, judging by the space which he devotes to it, the argument is regarded by him as of great importance.

(3.3.2) St. Anselm's equation was: "To forgive sin is equivalent to not punishing it." [80]   It remains for him to deal with the first side of the equation.   The general ground for the rejection of forgiveness as a possible manner in which God may deal with sin is that such forgiveness would conflict with God's government of the moral order.   The exact nature of this conflict is the subject of a very interesting dialogue between St. Anselm and Boso.

Boso's arguments for the necessity of forgiveness are twofold. On the one hand, since God commands us to forgive others,[81] it would be self-contradictory for Him to demand of us what is improper in Himself.   On the other hand, since God is so free that He is subject to no law,[82] since He is so kind that nothing kinder can be imagined, since, finally, nothing is right or proper except if He wills it, then it seems curious that He should not will or be permitted to forgive wrongdoing.

St. Anselm's replies are as follows: First, God instructs us to forgive those who have wronged us, lest we should treat them with vengeance.[83]   Vengeance is God's prerogative, and we dare not trespass upon it.   Those earthly rulers who take measure of vengeance do so as the instruments of God's vengeance.   It is plain that St. Anselm has here avoided the real issue raised by Boso, who, presumably, has also in mind some such passage as Lk. vi. 35-36, where the ground for our being merciful is the very fact which St. Anselm here chooses to neglect, namely, that God is merciful, or the parable of the unmerciful servant,[84] where the implication is that being greatly forgiven by God we must also forgive those who have sinned against us.

Secondly, St. Anselm argues [85] that God's freedom in will and action is bounded by considerations, internal and essential to His own nature, of good order and propriety, as St. Anselm calls them. God is not free in the sense that He may will what is not right, or undertake some deed of kindness which is contrary to His dignity (or "worthiness"), or lie.   Right is not right because God wills it, nor could right become wrong if God chose that it should be so.   God would have to cease to be God; He would have to change His nature entirely in order to will what is not right and true.   If we do say: "If God wills xy, then xy is right," we must add that this assertion can only be made of things which are worthy of God's willing, of things which God can will without contradicting His own nature or violating His own moral ordering of the universe according to His Will and Nature. Very succinctly, however, St. Anselm concludes that since it is impossible for God to exercise His liberty, His Will, His kindness except within the limits of what is just and right, He cannot forgive the sinner without punishing him. St. Anselm tries to elaborate on this position by his contention [86] that the punishment of the sinner is just and the non-punishment unjust, because the one ministers to the honour of God and the other detracts from it. In short, it is the fact that non-punishment or forgiveness of sins is intolerable in a morally ordered universe that forms the ground for its rejection.

Before we pass to the discussion of this important argument of St. Anselm's, let us indicate its logical form, which is as follows:

To forgive sins violates the moral ordering of the universe. Whatever violates the moral ordering of the universe does not minister to God's honour. Whatever does not minister to God's honour is unjust. Whatever is unjust is a contradiction of God's nature. A contradiction of God's nature is something which God is not free to permit.

Therefore God is not free to forgive sins.

The full significance of St. Anselm's argument may be indicated in the following terms:

(3.3.2.1) First, St. Anselm's analysis of the nature of God's liberty is an important contribution to theological thought, though, as Schmitt states,[87] the argument is adumbrated in St. Augustine, *De Symbolo*, c. 1, n. 2. To understand that God's attributes co-exist in Him under the limiting conditions which each imposes upon the others, to recognise, too, that these attributes form an integrated unity and not a loose aggregate, is a corrective both to false interpretations of the Divine nature, which conceive of it as unlimited in its liberty, and to the theological textbook treatment of the Divine attributes, which does not appreciate the necessity of considering their interactions upon each other. However much we disagree with St. Anselm's statement in I.13, l. 17, that "highest justice is none other than God Himself", we can find no fault with the theological insight which has prompted the statement, namely, that God's attributes are essential to Himself, not accidents which He can change at will but elements in His very Being which cannot be changed without causing substantial change in the very nature of God. St. Anselm in a few lines states a position which no voluntarism, even though it springs from an emphasis upon the transcendence of God, can ever finally deny, namely, that God wills right because it is right, and that He would need to cease to have the nature which we know Him to have in order to will what was wrong; alternatively, that whatever the transcendence of God may mean, no definition of the concept implies God's superiority to human moral categories.

It would seem that voluntarism of the kind popularised by some Barthians trying to be more Barthian than Barth has gained its strength from the false assumption that it forms the only alternative to a type of Platonism which regards values (or "Ideas") as more ultimate than God, and sets them over against Him as the supreme realities which limit His Being and activity. St. Anselm, however, implicitly demonstrates that there is a third way, a live option to voluntarism and Platonism: it is that the moral notions are neither more ultimate than God's nature, nor are they willed to be what they are, as it were, arbitrarily by Him. On the contrary, they are co-eternal with Him, existing integrally to His very Being. Therefore, to ask whether God wills the right because it is right, or whether the right is right because God wills it, is to ask questions which by reason of their false premises do not admit of a true answer; the false premise is in the one case that the right is logically or ontologically prior to God, and in the other that right is arbitrarily made right by God's volition. The correct description of the situation which these two questions are seeking is that God wills the right because he is God and, righteousness being essential to His being, He cannot will otherwise. For St. Anselm, therefore, moral concepts are personalised in the nature of God, a view which is literally stated at I.13, l. 19, but which is reflected also in his identification of God with the *summum bonum*.[88]

(3.3.2.2) When we grant the validity of St. Anselm's starting-point in the discussion of the possibility of God forgiving sins without enforcing punishment or demanding satisfaction, we are not thereby committed to his conclusion—that God is not free to forgive sins. While it is true that God is not free to will anything which violates His essential nature, it remains to be proved that forgiveness of sins belongs to that class. It is self-evident that God is not free to lie, for lying obviously contradicts God's nature as Truth. But forgiveness of sins does not *prima facie* conflict with God's nature for, as Boso in raising the whole problem indicates,[89] forgiveness of sins seems to follow from the kindness of God, than Whom nothing kinder can be imagined. Two features of St. Anselm's reply stand out. On the one hand, he does not seriously return to Boso's association of the forgiveness of sins with the kindness of God. Neglecting that association entirely, he sets forgiveness of sins against the justice of God and argues for the contradiction at that point. It may be said severely that St. Anselm is avoiding the issue, or that he prefers not to raise the question of the possibility of an internal contradiction in the very nature of God Himself, between His kindness and His justice. Perhaps a more accurate account of the matter is that St. Anselm in this portion of his work is confining himself within the self-imposed limits set down in the *Praefatio*, and that he can see God's kindness or mercy only in the redemption achieved for men by the God-man, and only His justice in His dealings with men apart from that redemption. The kindness of God, from which Boso argues, would, then, have no place in a discussion conducted within the terms of *ratio justitiae*.[90] It could, however, justifiably be asked whether St. Anselm, by this exclusion of the kindness of God, does not render his whole discussion in the major part of Bk. I rather artificial, and whether his statement that justice is none other than God Himself[91] should not have led him on to say that love is none other than God Himself.

On the other hand—to come now to the second feature of St. Anselm's reply to Boso—while his treatment of the problem of whether right is right because God wills it is valid, his discussion of the rightness of God's forgiving sins is guilty of an *ignoratio elenchi*. Despite the sorites [92] in which St. Anselm seeks to prove that forgiveness of sins is a violation of the principles of justice and rectitude, he does not succeed in demonstrating that forgiveness of sins is in the same case as, say, lying. The sorites is, in fact, scarcely syllogistic at all, in so far as for St. Anselm anything which violates God's moral ordering of the universe *ipso facto* does not minister to God's honour, and *eo ipso* violates the prin-

ciples of justice.   There is no real logical sequence from one stage
to the other, so that they could easily be set down in reverse order
without affecting the general argument in any way whatsoever.
"To violate the principles of justice", "to dishonour God", "to
violate God's moral ordering of the universe", are for St. Anselm
equivalent phrases.   To Boso's assertion [93] that forgiveness of
sins is perfectly proper in a God than Whom nothing kinder can
be imagined St. Anselm, in effect, responds with the assertion
that forgiveness of sins is not proper in a God Who is Himself
justice.   I.13 does not advance the argument beyond the general
position reached at I.12, p. 70, ll. 27-30; it merely restates that
counter-assertion in terms that appear to be more self-evident to
Boso.

It might be said that we have now disposed of St. Anselm's
reply to Boso by showing that he produced no genuine argument
to show that forgiveness of sins is unjust, but before such a conclusion is categorically stated it is necessary to mention certain
considerations which compel us to qualify it.   An advocate for St.
Anselm might say that St. Anselm cannot be expected to *demonstrate* the manner in which forgiveness of sins conflicts with God's
justice and he might add that for St. Anselm the conflict is self-
evident, as is the conflict between God's truthfulness and lying.
The notion of self-evidence is at any time fraught with difficulty
but its significance in the present situation is plain.   To know the
nature of God's truthfulness is to know the impossibility of God's
lying: that is the ground upon which St. Anselm would exclude
God's lying, rather than its contradiction of God's own command-
ment not to bear false witness.   Similarly, to know the nature of
God's justice *is* to realise that He would not allow in Himself
anything which contradicted His justice, which St. Anselm would
obviously define in such a way as to include the sustention of the
moral order, and the implementation of the moral sanctions.   If
then we want to quarrel with St. Anselm's views on the impossibility of God's forgiving sins (always, be it remembered, under
the double condition of the sin not being punished and of no
satisfaction being made), we must concentrate not so much upon
the logic of his arguments as upon his theological conception of
justice in God, upon which the arguments rest, and particularly
upon whether His justice is to be defined, partly at least, in terms

of bringing punishment upon sin. It is just there that forgiveness of sins presents *to us* a different problem from lying, in that, whereas inability to lie or, to put it positively, an eternal adherence to truth, or self-consistency, is obviously involved in the definition of truthfulness, the punishment of sin is not *for many of us* necessarily a part of the definition of God's justice. The qualification involved in the phrases *"to us"* and *"for many of us"* is most important because clearly justice has come to have a different connotation for the modern mind from that which St. Anselm accepted. We tend to include in it such ideas as impartiality, integrity, equality, disinterestedness, ideas coloured in meaning by the political, social and economic usage of our time. The problem is therefore fundamentally one of self-evidence and definition, rather than of validity of argument.

(3.3.2.3) The fact that St. Anselm takes such care with Boso's questions assures us that he was not insensitive to what is now known as the "Liberal" view of the Death of Christ. It is interesting that Boso's questions anticipate accurately the kind of objection which was later to be raised by those who disagreed with the so-called "objective" account of the Atonement and also argued that it was God's nature to forgive anyway—"c'est son métier". When we cleave through the sorites and the equivalent statements in which St. Anselm clothes his thoughts we find that essentially his antagonism to the "Liberal" view of the Death of Christ is implied in the two demands which he here makes of any adequate doctrine of the Atonement. First, it must not be such as to conflict with God's moral ordering of the universe, that is, it must take full cognisance of the gravity of sin, and of the consequences which must necessarily follow upon sin in an order in which moral values are both significant and operative. Boso's presentation of the "Liberal" case brings him into such conflict as he himself in the end admits. St. Anselm appears here to have laid his finger on a most important feature of any complete soteriology, for however much we emphasise the kindness of God we cannot escape the fact of God's judgment, a fact more real to us even than to those who knew only the Law. Secondly, any adequate doctrine of Atonement must come to terms with the justice of God and not simply treat it as if it were removed by

God's love or mercy. Even although St. Anselm has limited his discussion in Bk. I almost exclusively to the *ratio justitiae*, nevertheless he describes one attribute of God's nature which he nowhere rejects in Bk. II and which, moreover, is recognised by all but the adherents of some sentimental varieties of theology as an incontrovertible attribute of God. We may quarrel with the precise connotation which St. Anselm gives to the term—and in quarrelling we must be completely sure that we are not substituting some sociological or economic concept for one which ought to be strictly theological—nevertheless, on the one hand, the attribute remains even when God is known as a God of love, and, on the other hand, the fact upon which he seeks to base his whole delineation of justice, namely, the necessity of God's moral ordering of the universe, cannot easily be refuted.

(3.3.3) As St. Anselm refers on two other occasions in Bk. I to this theme of the possibility of God forgiving sin, it is necessary for us now to consider them, for while they do not alter the original thesis of I.12,13, they throw added light upon his general position.

(3.3.3.1) Boso [94] finds difficulty this time in the sentence in the Lord's Prayer "Forgive us our debts", and states the difficulty in the form of a disjunction. Either we have already paid God the honour which is due, and made satisfaction for our sin, in which case it would be unnecessary for us to pay for forgiveness, or we have not made the necessary satisfaction for our sin, in which case to pray for forgiveness would be to ask God to do something unbecoming. It may be observed that in dealing with the first part of this disjunction Boso makes a rather obscure statement: "Surely God is not so unjust as to demand a second time what has been paid." [95]   This statement is to be related, by a suppressed statement, to that which has preceded it: "For if we have paid that which we owe, why do we pray that (God) should forgive it?" [96]   This last-quoted sentence indicates that having paid the debt and being free of any demand that God may make upon us for it, we no longer stand in need of forgiveness. If, however, we thereafter still require to pray God to forgive our sins, we imply that God is still demanding payment of the debt, which *ex hypothesi* we have just paid; in other words, God is demanding payment of our debt to Him twice over.

St. Anselm's reply to Boso [97] is simple and direct, namely, that the supplication for the forgiveness is still a part of the payment of the debt; in other words, the payment of the debt is not completed until that supplication has been made. St. Anselm adds that Boso will understand better the answer given to him when he has listened to St. Anselm's exposition of the reasons for Christ's Death. In the light of what has gone before, it *is* difficult to see what St. Anselm has accomplished by his reply to Boso, and, in fact, it would appear that Boso's question is still unanswered. In the preceding speeches of I.19 St. Anselm and Boso have both been talking about the punishment which man must endure if he does not make the satisfaction required by God, and about the blessedness which will be his if he makes satisfaction. On these terms, Boso's dilemma remains unsolved, and St. Anselm's answer is no answer. The prayer for forgiveness demanded by God is a second payment and, therefore, unjustly expected of man. But in Bk. II the solution of Boso's problem presents itself. The satisfaction for man's sin is not offered by man but by the God-man through the special merits of His Death. That offering does not, of itself, redeem all men and erase their sins. They must appropriate "the benefits of His death", and they do so by some such prayer as Boso quotes.[98] If, therefore, we paraphrase *solutio* (payment) as "all that is required by God before forgiveness can be completed", then St. Anselm's statement at I.19 [99] is correct: the prayer for forgiveness is actually part of the payment as a result of which forgiveness comes to the sinner. Harnack [100] is particularly critical of this reply made by St. Anselm to Boso, describing it as "the vitiated conception of our prayer to God for forgiveness, that it is a part of our satisfaction and that it can never in itself effect forgiveness". Harnack here commits the error of ignoring St. Anselm's plain injunction to us to read his reply in the light of what he has later to say on the Death of Christ; when so read, it bears none of the vitiation suggested by Harnack. As for the latter part of Harnack's criticism, it must be said that what he regards as a fault in St. Anselm is actually a correct statement of the situation. For the Christian, the prayer for forgiveness does not "of itself effect forgiveness", if thereby we mean that it is a necessary and sufficient ground of forgiveness, apart from the saving work of God in Jesus Christ. The Christian believes that his prayer is but the last in a long series of much mightier events, which began with "the Lamb slain before the foundation of the world".

(3.3.3.2) At I.24, ll. 13 ff., St. Anselm works towards a conclusion which, while it is fundamentally a restatement of his view expressed at I.12, p. 70, ll. 27-30, gives that view in sharper and even harsher terms; further, it is prefaced by a different series of assertions. The conclusion [101] is that forgiveness is a form of mercy which is contrary to God's justice, and because it would involve Him in self-contradiction it is impossible for Him. Once again, God is conceived of as being one with His justice,[102] and consequently what conflicts with His justice is regarded as conflicting with God's nature as a whole, and therefore as an impossible course of action for God. On this occasion forgiveness is linked not with the kindness of God (*benignitas* [103]) but with the mercy (*misericordia*) of God, which, whatever other forms it may take, does not take that of forgiving sins, no satisfaction being made.

St. Anselm prepares for his conclusion by a consideration of two possible *objects* which a merciful God might be conceived of as achieving by forgiving sins, both of which considerations lead to untenable conclusions. The first alternative is that God should absolve man from payment of the debt under which he stands because of his having sinned against God, a debt which he ought spontaneously to pay but which because of its enormity he cannot. The second is that God should set man free from the punishment which He was about to inflict upon him, namely, that of taking from him, against his will, the blessedness which would have been his had he obeyed God's Law. The first alternative is rejected on the ground that it is equivalent to God's absolving man from a debt which God could never have received from him in any case, and constitutes a mockery (*derisio*) of God. The mockery consists in the fact that God is forced into a certain line of action not by His own Will but by man's failure. The second alternative is unsatisfactory because by relaxing punishment of guilty sinners, whose inability to make recompense to God is their own responsibility, God raises man to blessedness because of his sin.[104]

From I. 24, p. 93, l. 30, to I.24, p. 94, l. 7, St. Anselm emphasises his now common principle that the final blessedness of enjoying

God in glory will not be given to any who have not paid to God the full debt that is owed to Him, or who have not made adequate satisfaction to God for their sin. At this point [105] Boso's despair concerning God's mercy reaches its nadir, as he realises that there is for man no escape from God's justice. St. Anselm, in trying to relieve that despair, draws a distinction which is significant but which he does not develop, namely, between God's general mercy (which we might translate as "Providence"), which He shows when He saves men and beasts, and that final mercy by which He raises man to eternal blessedness. This final mercy is, however, shown only to those who have been completely forgiven, and such forgiveness is only for those who have made adequate satisfaction for all their sins. Once again we have the notion of forgiveness which St. Anselm introduced at I.19, p. 86, ll. 6 ff., that forgiveness is indissolubly related to satisfaction.

If we review St. Anselm's discussion of the forgiveness of sins throughout Bk. I,[106] we find that there are two distinct interpretations to be given of the term. On the one hand he equates it with the non-punishment of sin, *no* recompense being made to God for it, and in this sense it is strongly condemned on the grounds already examined. On the other hand he equates it with the non-punishment of sin, when the sinner pays the debt which he has incurred by sinning. Under these circumstances, God recognises that His honour has been upheld and the moral order of the universe safeguarded. He consequently absolves the sinner from all responsibility for past sin. In fact, it could be said that there are for St. Anselm two species of forgiveness of sin, the one possible and the other impossible for God, according to whether the necessary satisfaction has or has not been made. It is a great pity that St. Anselm did not use different words for these two senses (he uses *dimittere* throughout), for they are two quite different conceptions of forgiveness. The reader would then be spared the deception of thinking that the statements of I.24 contradict those of I.19. It will be important to remember [107] that St. Anselm regards the latter sense as a genuine form of forgiveness, and not simply as an alternative to forgiveness or the remission of sins without punishment. In other words, St. Anselm's full theory will be that it is through satisfaction that forgiveness takes place.

(3.3.4) It will be discovered from a close examination of sorites given in (3.3.2) and of our comments given in (3.3.2.2) upon St. Anselm's equivalent phrases "to violate the principles of justice", "to dishonour God", etc., that whereas in I.12 and I.13 St. Anselm deals fully with the assertion that the non-punishment or forgiveness of sin is a violation of God's honour, he has not examined the obverse of that assertion, namely, that the punishment of sin ministers to the honour of God. This question is dealt with in I.14 and the allied problem, of whether, in fact, it is a real possibility that God's honour can be in any way impugned, is discussed in I.15.

(3.3.4.1) The problem, as stated by Boso in his customary artless way, is this: while it may be conclusively demonstrated that the sinner, by making satisfaction to God for the sin that he has committed, restores God's lost honour, it is by no means obvious that the punishment of the sinner either itself does honour to God, or in doing so restores to God the honour that He lost through man's sinning. The problem could be illustrated from ordinary law. A poor man robs his neighbour's garden, eating the fruit and vegetables he has stolen, and he is apprehended. Being unable to pay from his possessions the equivalent of the things stolen, and to make the additional payment required to make amends for the fact of having stolen, for the dishonour done, he is physically punished or incarcerated. Such punishment cannot make good the neighbour's loss. Similarly, it is possible that by man's sinning God lost something which could not be restored by man's punishment. Accordingly, Boso contends, St. Anselm must show, on the one hand, that the punishment of the sinner redounds to the honour of God, and, on the other hand, what is the nature of the honour thus accomplished.

St. Anselm's reply takes the form of a general assertion that it is impossible for God to lose His honour. The grounds for the general assertion in this particular case are that either man gives spontaneously to God the honour that is due to Him, by obeying God's Will or by making adequate satisfaction should he actually sin, or God puts him in subjection and receives the honour from him against his will, thus forcibly demonstrating that He is Lord. What exactly it is that God wrests from man, St. Anselm demonstrates by means of a strange and rather strained analogy. Just as man in sinning took from God what was His, so God by punishing man takes from man what is his, i.e. what it was in his power to have had he not sinned, namely, his eternal bliss. In this way, man repays to God, even though against his will, what is his own. What God takes redounds to His honour, in the very fact that it is taken away. Thus God proves that the sinner and all that is his are in subjection to Himself.

Since Boso at the beginning of the next chapter says [108] of the above argument: "*Placet quod dicis,*" we must pause to discover whether St. Anselm has properly met Boso's difficulty. It would appear not, for the following reasons: First, it is quite false to equate what is man's with what it is in his power to have if he sins not, i.e. his eternal bliss. Obviously, that bliss is precisely what man does *not* have. St. Anselm pictures God as taking from man a reward which in the very nature of the case, because of his sin, man could not possibly have received. Secondly, it might be said that St. Anselm appreciates the relevance of Boso's question, whether honour can be done to God by His punishing the sinner. Honour can be done to God only by His receiving some payment—that is a general principle throughout the whole of the *Cur Deus Homo*; consequently, God must hypothetically give man something, so that man can make repayment. The result is a highly artificial argument. Thirdly, it is difficult to see just why St. Anselm should be trying to maintain such an impossible position, especially in the light of I.20, where he argues so emphatically that the sinner has nothing with which to make repayment to God. In fact, the theme of this chapter (I.14) flatly contradicts the whole contention of Bk. I, that man is completely unable to make satisfaction for his sin. Fourthly, St. Anselm unjustifiably makes a great deal of the fact that God wrests submission from man, whereas actually, as St. Anselm has described the situation, God does not. The sinner continues to sin; his heart is still turned against God, for it is against his will that he gives God the hypothetical gift; he does not submit to God, and the dishonour continues. In a word, the whole discussion is unfortunate.

(3.3.4.2) Boso (perhaps sensing the inadequacy of this previous argument) raises yet another awkward problem.[109] If it is contended that God continually endeavours to safeguard His honour, why then does he allow anyone to infringe it, even in the slightest degree? Boso's question rests on a conclusion accurately drawn from the earlier chapters of Bk. I. Throughout, God is described as One Who at every turn in his relations with the sinner jealously protects His honour. If the sinner does not make satisfaction for his sin, then God will defend His honour by punishing him. The proper amount of satisfaction to be made to God, could the sinner accomplish it, is in direct relation to the immensity of the dishonour done. Even the righteous man who obeys the Will of God as a rational creature does so to maintain the honour of God. How then, says Boso, does it come about that a God so continually concerned with His honour should ever allow anyone to violate it?

In answering Boso's question, St. Anselm gives virtually two replies. First, he maintains that nothing can be added to or taken away from God's honour, so far as He is concerned (*quantum ad illum pertinet*).[110] His honour, like Himself, is incorruptible and immutable. That fact is the sheet anchor of the discussion. Secondly, St. Anselm, realising that the first answer in itself is a setting aside of the problem which Boso raised, endeavours "to save the appearances". In spite of the unchangeable character of God's honour, human beings *seem* to increase that honour, when they obey God's Will and submit to Him, and to diminish it when they disobey Him. God's Will for the universe is that it should exhibit strict order and beauty by each creature fulfilling the function for which God created it. The sinner, as far as he is concerned, disturbs that order, but only under the permissive Will of God, Whose supreme wisdom turns the perversity to order and beauty. While St. Anselm does not go so far as to say that sin and evil themselves have a place within the pattern of the order and beauty of the universe, he does say that satisfaction for sin and punishment of sin have such a place, for God in many ways brings good out of evil. If it were not made plain that God conforms human perversity to His general plan for the universe, then two undesirable conclusions, or "impossible alternatives", would follow: first, the perversity would be allowed to persist as a continual violation of the order of the universe, and constitute a deformity of it; secondly, God would appear to fail in His moral government of the world. These two results are unfitting, and therefore impossible. St. Anselm combines both his replies in his conclusion: God, as far as He is concerned, can be honoured or dishonoured by no one; any human being, as far as he is concerned, only appears to do so, when he either submits His Will to God's or withdraws such submission.

This chapter (I.15) is particularly interesting, not only because of its place within the *Cur Deus Homo*, but also because it represents St. Anselm's attempt to deal with a perennial problem of all types of theism.[111] The problem is fundamentally the problem of evil—though it is not raised in the form with which St. Augustine, according to *The Confessions*, concerned himself in his immediately pre-Christian days, the form *unde malum*? For St. Augustine the problem was: how it is that evil exists in a world which has been created by a good God? Nor is the problem raised in the form which is the usual corollary to that just mentioned: how is it that an omnipotent God allows evil, which is a denial of His whole nature, to persist in a universe where His Will is law? St. Anselm's difficulty is more akin to the latter form of the problem, and it is: how is human sin to be reconciled with the immutability of God's honour, and with God's moral government of the universe? His answer may be commented upon in the following terms:

First, there would seem to be a fundamental incompatibility between the general conclusions which St. Anselm is here seeking to establish and the dominant theme of the whole of the *Cur Deus Homo*; namely, of asserting, on the one hand, that any loss of honour to God through man's sin is a mere appearance, and that in itself God's honour remains unchanged; and, on the other hand, that the gravity of human sin, even if the smallest sin, consists in the fact that it robs God of honour due to Him from His creatures, and that adequate satisfaction must be made to atone for the dishonour. There is no way out of this incompatibility by saying that St. Anselm does admit that dishonour is done to God by violation of the order and beauty of the universe, for the purpose of I.15 is to demonstrate that though this appears to be so, in actual fact God's essential honour is in no way affected. In short, the introduction of the theme of I.15 threatens to cut the nerve of the whole argument of the book.

Secondly, it is extremely doubtful whether any analysis of

human sin which regards it as an appearance, a "seeming to be so", is truly Christian. Sin has to be regarded as real, not only as far as man is concerned, but also as far as God is concerned. Sin creates a relation of estrangement between God as He is in Himself and man as he is in himself. To suggest that this relation is illusory in any way is to weaken the whole conception of sin.

Thirdly, St. Anselm reaches his conclusion that God's honour only seems to be violated by employing a distinction, the relevance of which would have to be questioned; namely, between God's honour as it is in Himself, and as it is expressed in the order and beauty of the universe. The distinction is admittedly valid. God's honour existed before the world was created and there were human beings to fulfil or defy His Will; and that honour expresses itself now and maintains itself in a world well ordered morally— though that is but one of its many forms of expression. But it is the use which St. Anselm makes of the distinction which is to be questioned. He wants us to believe that by defying God's Will in the universe, and thus disturbing its harmony, we do not dishonour God as He is in Himself. From the legitimate beliefs that the honour of God can be—indeed is—expressed in other situations than in a morally well ordered world, and that a disturbance of that order is not a violation of *all* methods in which God's honour may be expressed, he seems to conclude that it is, therefore, not a real violation of God's honour. God's honour is involved, even though perhaps not so completely, in any situation in which He lays His imperative upon a human being, as truly as it is in some loftier situation in which we might conceive of Him as entering into relations with angels. A human refusal to obey that imperative is dishonourable to God, as He is in Himself, and does not simply seem to be so.

Fourthly, of course, it is rather obvious that it is the conception of the immutability of God's honour which is the distorting factor in the whole of St. Anselm's argument. The theory of the immutability of God has had an influence on theology disproportionate to the truth of many of the popular interpretations of it. The theory is too often cast in the mould of Platonic or Aristotelian thought, which antithesises the visible as changeable and corruptible, and the invisible as unchanging and eternal. In Hebrew-Christian thought the immutability of God is construed in terms of self-consistency, which permits of the kind of change which might be expected in One Who is a living God, Who enters continually into historical relations with His people, giving Himself supremely to them in a historical Person, and Who as a moral God reacts to their words and deeds. Changelessness of the kind with which St. Anselm's conception shows certain affinity is a metaphysical rather than a religious category, as is seen also in the further Platonism of distinguishing God's honour as it is in itself, and as it appears in the world of phenomena. St. Anselm is not, however, wedded to this conception, for he soon shows in the sequel that his sympathies with Greek metaphysics are not so profound as those with the Christian doctrine of God.

Fifthly, even if we do allow St. Anselm his premises, his distinction and his Platonic background as in this chapter (I.15), we nevertheless discover that his difficulties are not resolved. It is, for example, no easy task to determine the function of the *voluntas permittens*,[112] the permissive Will. The term, when first read, suggests that the sin of the sinner, since it is a human action, can only be done by the strength which God supplies to all His creatures to keep them in life; but God would wrongly be said to will the sin of the sinner. The conclusion is evaded by means of the notion of the permissive Will. St. Anselm, partly at least, conveys this intention by his use of the phrase, for he is seeking to preserve God's sovereignty within the moral order and to protect His goodness from all question, and cannot, therefore, inpute the sins of evil men to God. The permissive Will solves his problem, superficially, at least. However, St. Anselm uses the notion in a rather strange way, which suggests that he has more in mind than we have just stated. His general theme in the preceding sentence [113] is that, whether a man or an angel obeys or disobeys God, he is still subject to God's Will and government; by changing from obedience to disobedience he but flees from under the Will which commands to the Will that punishes. But he makes the transition under the Will of God that permits it. St. Anselm, then, conceives of three possible modes of the Divine Will—imperative, punitive and permissive. The permissive Will is not simply that which allows a man to sin, without denying him the physical strength to do the action, but is also that by which a man who has disobeyed God finds himself passing under the shadow of God's punishment. In this sense the permissive Will is the punitive Will in the process of going into operation.

The notion of the permissive Will in its former sense raises the question of whether St. Anselm is prepared to allow that sin does disturb the order and beauty of the universe. At I.15, p. 73, ll. 6-9, he affirms that he who dishonours God disturbs this order and beauty. The addition of the phrase *quantum in se est*—which might be variously translated as "as far as he is concerned" (i.e. from a human point of view, we must say that God is dishonoured, though from God's side we know that this is impossible), or as "as far as in him lies" (i.e. as far as he has the power to go, he dishonours God, but God immediately intervenes and prevents total or permanent disordering of the universe)—does not alter the admission that sin introduces disharmony in God's world. Even though, by means of satisfaction or punishment, God restores order, there has been disorder; and even if God brings good out of evil, evil still does not become good. St. Anselm fails to understand that he is trying to maintain more than anyone could be reasonably expected to maintain; namely, both the absence of deformity in the moral order and beauty of the world, and the almightiness of God's moral government. He seems to feel that the latter depends upon the establishment of the former, hence his elaborate arguments to prove the former. Few dogmatic theologians would accept the dependence of the latter on the complete demonstration of the former, or would be prepared to argue for the former at all.

<h2 style="text-align:center">4</h2>

At the beginning of I.25,[114] in answer to Boso's pessimism about the possibility of man's salvation because of his inability to make satisfaction to God, St. Anselm replies that such pessimism is a challenge to those who deny that Christ is necessary to man's salvation. By means of a series of startlingly swift jumps he proceeds to show to Boso why mankind must of necessity be saved by Christ. There are three possible fates that may attend sinful man: he may be saved by Christ; he may be saved in some other way; he may not be saved at all. Even unbelievers are prepared to admit that the last possibility is false, so that the choice lies between the first two. St. Anselm, however, affirms, as already proved, that if salvation does not come through Christ, then it does not come at all; this he regards as disproving the second possibility, and as establishing the first. The premise upon which even unbelievers would not join issue, namely, that God's purposes would be frustrated if some men were not raised to ultimate blessedness, is repeated as giving strength to the whole argument, and as, therefore, proving the case against the unbeliever completely. Wherefore, either satisfaction can be made to God outside the manner indicated in the Christian faith—which, in fact, no argument can ever prove—or that faith must be accepted, as a logical necessity. Boso then pleads that the convincing logic which has demonstrated man's inability to make satisfaction to God may be extended to the proof of all the subject-matter of Catholic belief concerning Jesus Christ and the salvation which He wrought for mankind.

(4.1) The latter half of this chapter [115]—with its recapitulation of the general conclusion of Bk. I, namely, that man by reason of his sin has put himself in so great a debt to God that he cannot possibly pay it himself, and with its plea from Boso that St. Anselm should demonstrate with logical sequence the necessity of the kind of salvation which the Christian faith affirms in Jesus Christ—is much as we should expect it to be. Not so the former half of the chapter, which presents the following difficulties.

(4.1.1) St. Anselm suggests that the argument of Bk. I has proved not only the impossibility of man's saving himself but also the necessity of salvation by Jesus Christ. It is by no means the case that the proof of the first position carries with it the proof of the second. If it did, we should quite rightly expect St. Anselm to make more use of this fact than he does in Bk. I. If it did, too, the continuity between Bk. I and Bk. II would have been more sustained than it is. In fact, St. Anselm does not develop his argument in Bk. II from this point at all. He begins *de novo*, using only the general conclusion of Bk. I, that man's payment of debt to God by himself is a moral and logical impossibility.

(4.1.2) It is premature for St. Anselm to introduce reference to the "value" of the salvation which Christ accomplishes before he has described *Who* Christ is. In Bk. II the value of Christ's Death is proportionate to His Person. Until it is actually demonstrated that the payment made by Christ is very different from that which any other person could make, then the believer is justified in questioning both the possibility and the necessity of salvation by Christ, precisely because he does not know how it is accomplished.[116]

(4.2) In view of these rather obvious difficulties, it must be contended that St. Anselm has introduced this section [117] not in the interests of logical consistency, or even for the sake of rounding off the conclusions of Bk. I, but rather for dramatic purposes. In an almost perverted and roguish way he indicates the course which his argument must take if it is to accomplish the task which Boso gave him, that of demonstrating the necessity of the God-man for the salvation of mankind. There is no doubt that I.25, p. 95, ll. 18-19, contains the theme of Bk. II, namely, the description of the way in which the Death of Christ makes human salvation possible, and the sin of man makes Christ's Death necessary. To that subject we now turn.

CHAPTER THREE

DEUS-HOMO: CHRISTOLOGY

ST. ANSELM'S frequent use of the name *Deus-homo*, which Schmitt hyphenates in II.6 ff., suggests that the English translations of the title of the work, *Cur Deus Homo*, require revision in order to be brought more into line with the central theme of the book. The translations given are: "Why was God made man?" [1] and "Why God became man?" [2] Both assume that a question mark is to be found in the title, whereas Schmitt omits the question mark. In view of the fact that from II.6 onwards St. Anselm is seeking to demonstrate why the God-man is required for the only salvation possible for man, in the light of his inordinate debt to God because of his sin, it would be wise to retain this emphasis in the translation of the title, and to suggest, literally, "Why there should be a God-man", or, in paraphrase, "The reason for the God-man". His whole argument develops around the theme of the God-man, the unity of His Person, the necessity of His two natures, and the value of His Death as atonement for the sins of mankind.

1

St. Anselm prefaces his discussion of the God-man with an examination in II.5 of Boso's suggestion that, since God seems to save us of necessity lest His purposes for man should be frustrated and He Himself be involved in inconsistency, salvation is not of His free grace. Since his argument at II.17 (in Schmitt's division of the chapters) is an amplification of his views given in II.5, it may be included in the discussion. At II.5 St. Anselm gives two answers to Boso's suggestion: first, that while God is admittedly under the necessity of accomplishing the salvation of man, that necessity arises out of God's gracious decision to create man and to bring him to perfection; and, secondly, that God knows no necessity except that imposed upon Him by His own nature and attributes. These answers are obviously connected, but they are distinguishable and call for separate treatment.

117

(1.1) St. Anselm prepares [3] for his first answer by saying that there are two kinds of necessity operative in the conferring of benefits: in one case, the benefactor against his will does the kindness, and, in the other, the benefactor of his own free will submits himself to the necessity, or, as we should say, freely undertakes the responsibility, of conferring the benefit. From the moment of his undertaking the responsibility, in the latter case, the necessity is laid upon him of fulfilling the responsibility. That kind of necessity, which springs from no external compulsion, is not properly called "necessity" at all: rather is it grace. And the thanks of the beneficiary are due to the benefactor. It is noticeable that St. Anselm throughout the chapter plays on the double meaning of the word *gratia* as "thanks" and "grace". He agrees with Boso, who initiates the ambiguity in his speech at the beginning of the chapter, saying that it is only a benefaction done of grace that deserves thanks. St. Anselm illustrates his answer with two examples: that of the necessity of honouring a promise freely made, and that of the discipline of the religious life, even though the votary freely elects to live that kind of life. *A fortiori*, even though God by His creation of man and by His promises to him imposes upon Himself the responsibility and, in that sense, necessity of honouring these promises and completing His creation, nevertheless, the creation, the promises and their fulfilment all stem from God's grace. St. Anselm's point is well made and it is worth making. But it is significant that, in his application of the principle illustrated in the two examples to God's grace in conferring benefits, he omits the word "necessity" altogether, which indicates his unwillingness to regard the second type of necessity mentioned at the beginning of his argument as strictly necessity at all. This unwillingness is shortly to reappear.

(1.2) For he introduces what I have called his second reply to Boso with the statement that "God does nothing by necessity". [4] Here he clearly has in mind not the second type of necessity already noticed in II.5, but the first, which, in II.17,[5] he says is always of two kinds: either coercion or prevention. God is not subject to either of those nor is He subject to any impossibility, for both necessity and impossibility are dependent upon His Will. St. Anselm cannot, however, avoid the use of the word "necessity", for as soon as he continues with the argument he says that when, as it were, from the necessity of avoiding inconsistency, God does something, this necessity is that of maintaining His own integrity. This integrity He derived from no other but Himself (*a se*). Consequently, the necessity which it imposes upon Him, the necessity of consistency, is not properly so-called —again the embarrassment over the word "necessity". It is, in other words, the necessity of self-determination. So an unchangingly good God will necessarily bring to perfection that which He has begun in man, and He will do so of His own free grace.

While it is true, therefore, that St. Anselm experiences difficulty in deciding whether to assign necessity to God's actions or volitions, it cannot be said that there is any confusion in his mind on the matter, or that there is any self-contradiction in his statements when they are put in their proper context. Necessity of coercion or prevention is denied of God; the necessity imposed upon Him by His own nature and attributes is affirmed. It is, moreover, most important to draw attention to the phrase *a se* which St. Anselm has used, for it is destined to play a major rôle in the development of his position.[6] For the present we record that the phrase is linked with the idea of God's self-determination in His activity in accordance with His essential nature. The phrase is the root of the word *aseitas*, which, while not actually used by St. Anselm himself, is a neat expression for a concept which is of complex connotation. It is significant, too, that St. Anselm introduces the conception at the climax of his argument as if it represented his mature judgment on the question of the application of the idea of necessity to God's actions.

(1.3) To the question of whether God ever acts under necessity, St. Anselm provides in II.17, also, a somewhat different answer from those mentioned in II.5, in spite of the similarities at the points already mentioned in (1.2). Dealing, first of all, with the question of whether it can truly be said that "God cannot do" certain things, he interprets the sentence not as the denial of any power in God but as the affirmation that God has in Him a certain power or strength which nothing outside of Himself can subdue; that is, nothing can compel Him to do that which it is said He cannot do. An ordinary situation illustrates the point. Thus, when it is said that "this man cannot be conquered", we do not assign any weakness to him, but rather mean that there is in him some power which no one else can conquer. So when the statement is made that it is necessary for God to do this or not to do that, the intention is, says St. Anselm, that nothing has the power to compel Him to do this or prevent Him from doing that.[7] When it is said that it is necessary that God should speak the truth and not lie, what is meant is that so great is God's steadfastness in the truth that nothing can constrain Him not to speak the truth.

It is possible to write off this discussion as an early Scholastic analysis of the nature of necessity in God, or as an elaborate attempt on St. Anselm's part to extricate himself from a rather too nice problem of his own choosing. In fact, however, it is more accurate to see in his discussion a very true account of the nature and operation of the God of the Christian revelation. For St. Anselm is drawing attention to what might be called the dynamic quality of God's nature. His God is a moral God in action. It is not sufficient, in his opinion, to say simply that God is identical with truth, or consistency, or righteousness. It must, in addition, be said that God *in His actions* conforms His Will to the dictates of truth, consistency and righteousness, even though these have in Himself the source both of their being and meaning. From this conformity of His Will He will allow nothing whatsoever to turn Him aside. While, therefore, the two arguments of II.5 present to us the kind of constraint which is placed upon God by His promises to man and by His own nature, at II.16 St. Anselm brings out God's reaction to that constraint as the reaction of a moral will which refuses to be deflected from its steadfastness and integrity by any contrary influence. Such then is the proper setting for the arguments which St. Anselm offers in relation to the nature and value of the Death of Our Lord: the setting of a wholly moral God, Who initiates salvation freely of His own Grace, and Who in bringing that salvation to completion willingly submits Himself to the necessities of consistency, truth and righteousness. Any interpretation of St. Anselm's soteriology which contradicts that position has failed to that extent to understand the truly Christian character of his thoughts about God and the Atonement.

Turning now to St. Anselm's actual treatment of the Person of Jesus Christ, we find that his argument unfolds itself in a series of definite statements on the following themes: the extent of the satisfaction due to be made to God for man's sin; the Divinity or the Deity of the Person who alone can make such satisfaction; the humanity of the Person; the compresence of these two natures in one Person; and the sinlessness of this Person, Who is the God-man.

2

Broadly stated, the task which St. Anselm is set in Bk. II is to make clear who the Person is Who is able to repay to God the debt which man has incurred by his sin, and how, in fact He achieves this end. The argument by which he establishes the Person of the Mediator is stated in II.6, with brevity out of all proportion to the central position which it occupies in St. Anselm's thought. The steps of the argument are fairly precise: they set forth the qualifications of Him Who is to be capable of offering to God the adequate satisfaction for man's sin.

Due satisfaction can be made to God only if he who undertakes the task is able to provide something which exceeds in value all that exists apart from God, *omne quod praeter Deum est*.[8] The consideration of this condition need not now detain us, for it is a reaffirmation of a view enunciated at I.21, and previously discussed.[9] It is noteworthy that St. Anselm uses this proposition as the starting-point of what is the central argument of his book, even though he did not elaborate it to any great degree in I.21. It will be recalled that, after maintaining that not even the slightest sin should be contemplated, though its commission would preserve the whole universe, all that is not God and an infinity of universes, St. Anselm affirms the principle that, consequently, the satisfaction to be made to God for sin must exceed all that for the sake of which it ought not to be committed.

3

Next, in order to establish the Deity of this Person who is to repay to God's honour the satisfaction necessary for man's sin, St. Anselm stipulates two conditions which the Person must

I

fulfil. On the one hand, he must be able to pay of his own (*de suo*) what exceeds all that is beneath God.[10] This stipulation is not so arbitrary as may at first appear, for if the Mediator could not give "of his own", then *he* would be beholden to the person from whom he had to obtain what he paid; and a regress would then be set up. In addition, beneath St. Anselm's discussion of satisfaction in Bk. I there is the general assumption that the Person who makes the satisfaction must offer a *personal* gift to God of obedience and worship, and this assumption rules out any possibility of his giving something which is not his own. On the other hand, the Person making the adequate satisfaction to God for man's sin must be greater than all that is not God, i.e. He must be God Himself. That is, so great is the debt incurred by man for his sin—a debt measured for the purposes of the present argument, in terms of that for the sake of which the sin ought not to be committed—that none other than God Himself is in a position to pay it. What, in fact, St. Anselm is asserting now is that it is the *Person* of Him Who makes the satisfaction which gives to His offering the great value that it has. His intention is not only that no one less than God Himself is in possession of physical objects, such as an infinity of universes, that might be greater than all that is not God, and so none other than God can make that immense offering, but, further, and more important still, none but God has the uprightness of will, the purity of heart and the truthfulness of mind which are essential in anyone seeking to make satisfaction for sinful men. It is advisable to emphasise this contention of St. Anselm's at this stage, for he later rests the merits of Christ upon His Person, having thus early prepared for that kind of exposition of the nature and significance of the Death of the God-man.

4

Having established the Deity of the Person capable of making the satisfaction necessary for man's sin against God, St. Anselm proceeds to argue for His humanity. He does so most fully in II.8, where he offers three grounds for his view. St. Anselm does not make it clear here whether the *homo* of the *Deus-homo* is man as such, Humanity in general, or, on the other hand, a particular man. At II.18, p. 102, ll. 26,27, he speaks of God assuming human nature, but as the chapter develops it becomes plain that he is not thinking of the abstract universal, but of something more particular. The "concrete universal" of a later logic is perhaps closest to St. Anselm's intention. The view of the efficacy of the Death of Christ which he gives us later in Bk. II, moreover, depends upon the particularity of the manhood of Jesus Christ. There is confirmation of this conclusion in *Epistola de Incarnatione Verbi*, c. 11, where St. Anselm, after arguing in the early sections of the chapter for the Chalcedonian view that the Word did not take a human *persona* as well as a human *natura*, concludes with the words: "But since the Word is God and that man assumed by the Word is man, it is true to say that the same person is God and man; but by the name 'God' is to be understood the Word, and by the name 'man' is to be understood the Son of the Virgin." St. Anselm's purpose here is to make it plain that the manhood which the Word assumed was not general manhood—the Word was not made *quilibet homo* (p. 29, l. 9)—but this particular man, announced by the angel (l. 10) and born in this precise way.

His first ground for asserting the humanity of the Mediator is that, as it is *man* who has committed sin, so it must be man who makes good to God for the dishonour done Him. Since Adam and Eve have propagated the sin that exists among mankind and are not themselves able to make satisfaction, therefore someone born of them must achieve what they cannot. The Ancient and Modern translation [11] of II.8, p. 103, ll. 3-5, includes an error which both ignores the Latin text and contradicts the whole sense of the passage in which it appears: ". . . *ita nullus nisi vel ipsi vel qui de illis nascitur, pro peccato hominum satisfacere debet*" is translated thus: "(Now since from Adam and Eve sin was propagated among all men) therefore, neither of these two, nor anyone born of them, could atone for the sin of man." If the Ancient and Modern translation were accepted, then St. Anselm would be contradicting himself when in the next sentence he asserts that someone of the descendants of Adam and Eve should make the satisfaction, which they cannot make because of their sin. While the Ancient and Modern translation is patently incorrect, it draws attention to a difficulty which St. Anselm later faces,[12] the sinlessness of Jesus. If it is the case that sin is propagated among all men (*in omnes homines*),[13] then anyone born of the line of Adam and Eve seems to fall beneath the universal curse. It must be said in St. Anselm's favour that he is not insensitive to the problem, though the suggestion is that he has rendered the problem doubly difficult for himself by interpreting "original sin" in terms of physical propagation. But, again, that kind of interpretation has only begun to lose its general popularity in orthodoxy in recent times. We cannot blame St. Anselm for not living in the twentieth century.

His general theme St. Anselm develops in a sentence [14] which seems to lend weight to the criticism made by Gustav Aulén in *Christus Victor*,[15] namely that St. Anselm does not treat Atonement as the work of God from start to finish. "Just as Adam and the whole race would have stood by itself without the support of any other creature had he not sinned, so it is fitting that the same race after the fall should rise and remain upright through itself." This is the second ground for the necessity of the *human* nature of the Person Who makes due satisfaction to God for man's sin. The previous argument rested on the identity that must exist between the person who committed the sin and the Person Who makes the satisfaction, whereas now St. Anselm is establishing identity of means—and *per se* is the key phrase—in what looks like an analogical argument. As *by himself* would man have stood, so *by himself* shall man rise. A full consideration of this criticism of II.8 must be postponed until we deal with Aulén's general attack on St. Anselm. But we may for the present note that St. Anselm does not regard the relation between the manner in which man would have stood had he not fallen, and that in which he is finally raised up after the Fall, as a necessary logical connection. It is important to observe that, whereas he uses the phrase "*necesse est*" when speaking of the identity of the Person making satisfaction with the humanity which sinned, he now uses the verb "*oportet*". The similarity is fitting rather than necessary.[16] St. Anselm must not be conceived of as providing us with an analogical argument which would convince the unbeliever, so much as drawing an analogy between the means by which man would have remained sinless had he not succumbed to temptation, and the means by which he is to be redeemed. In a word, we have here an analogical description in faith—*analogia fidei* would not be an inept characterisation of the position—and not analogical argument.

The third method by which St. Anselm endeavours to establish the humanity of the Mediator is one with which we are already familiar—that of the "impossible alternatives".[17] At II.8, p. 103, ll. 14-18, St. Anselm uses this method in two connections. In the earlier part of the speech (ll. 10 ff.) he has argued that because God created human nature in Adam alone, therefore He clearly demonstrated that it was His intention to accomplish His purposes for the human race through Adam; that is, it is God's Will that man should recover his proper status by the action of a member of Adam's race. Now, if some being other than one descended from the line of Adam is the means by which satisfaction is made for man, then not only will God be frustrated in His purpose declared in Adam's creation but, further, man will not come to the true dignity of his destiny. The two conclusions represent the "impossible alternatives" in the present argument. Therefore, St. Anselm implies, God's Will must be fulfilled, and man must rise to his true dignity through some member of his own race. The Mediator must be a descendant of Adam.

It will be readily seen that there are two premises which St. Anselm accepts as self-evident for the purpose of this argument. The first is that by creating human nature in Adam alone, God indicates His intention that man shall be redeemed through Adam's descendant. The second is that man would not achieve his true destiny if someone other than man were responsible for his redemption. In regard to the latter, we can say that man would come under the bondage of this other being, and his final state would be worse than his first, for he would be yet further away from giving God his total allegiance and obedience. With regard to the first premise, it may be pointed out that it belongs to the class of postulates which even those who do not accept the necessity of the Atonement are prepared to accept.

The rest of II.8 is taken up with what now appears to be a very artificial demonstration of the Virgin Birth. There being four ways in which God can make a human being—by a man and a woman, which is the normal method within the created order; by neither man nor woman, as in the creation of Adam; by man without woman, as in the making of Eve; and, finally, by woman without man—and the first three having been already employed by God, it remained for Him to demonstrate His ability to accomplish the fourth.   This He did in the Virgin Birth.   This ingenious argument is supported by another of the analogical inferences discussed recently above: as through a woman and a virgin evil was introduced into human life, so it is fitting [18] that the Person Who is to be the source of human good should be made of a woman and a virgin.   St. Anselm, towards the end of the chapter, places *Deus-homo* and *virgo-mulier* in juxtaposition.   That St. Anselm does not himself believe that these inferences will carry the conviction borne by strict logical inference is evidenced by his description of them as *picturae*,[19] and by his use of the verb *pinge*.[20]

5

In setting forth in detail St. Anselm's views on the subject that the Person making satisfaction for man's sin must be a member of the human race, we have gone ahead of the actual section of the *Cur Deus Homo* where St. Anselm argues that that single Person should be both *Deus* and *homo*.   It was necessary to do so because St. Anselm's argument for the *Deus-homo* presupposes what he had to say on the humanity of the Mediator.   We now retrace our steps to examine St. Anselm's arguments, as given in II.6, p. 101, ll. 16-19, and II.7, p. 102, ll. 11-21, for the necessity of the existence of the God-man, i.e. for the existence *in one Person* of the Deity and the humanity which have been proved to be the essential qualifications of anyone who seeks to make satisfaction for man's sin; and, thereafter, to discuss his views on the necessity of the Incarnation of the *Word*, or the Second Person of the Trinity, rather than either of the other two Persons, as stated in II.9, where he refers us also to the *Epistola de Incarnatione Verbi*.

(5.1) The *Unity* of the Person of the Mediator is maintained in the following terms:

(5.1.1) At II.6, p. 101, ll. 16-19, God is asserted to be the only One Who is in a position to pay the enormous debt under which man stands by reason of his sin against his Creator. On the other hand, man is the guilty person and he is the one who ought to pay. God alone can; man must. Therefore, satisfaction has to be made by One Who is *Deus-homo*.

(5.1.2) At II.7, p. 102, ll. 11-21, St. Anselm comes to the heart of the problem, and argues for the necessity of the *same* Person being God and man. The previous discussion, given in (5.1.1), is amplified from the statement that unless the same Person is God and man, then the satisfaction necessary will not be made, for the following reason. Let us assume, he argues, that the Person Who is God is not also man; i.e. that one and the same Person is not both God and man. Then the Person Who is God is under no obligation to make any satisfaction; God has committed no sin, and there is none greater than Himself to Whom He owes any kind of honour or obedience. On the other hand, the person who is man, while he is certainly under the gravest obligation to make amends for his sin, is by reason of his very sinfulness impotent to do so. If, then, there is no identity of person of God and man in the Mediator, God's purpose of redemption will be frustrated. Accordingly, the Person Who is to make the satisfaction must unite in Himself the Deity which possesses the ability to pay the enormous debt and the humanity which owes the debt; that is, He must be perfect God and perfect man, both natures existing inviolate in One Person. There will be allowed no changing of the human nature into the Divine, or the Divine into the human, and no fusing of them into a third which is not wholly either, for in each of these three instances God's purpose of salvation would be frustrated. St. Anselm is here obviously confessing his allegiance to Chalcedon and its four adverbs, but is basing his confession on grounds characteristic of his own theology. It is, incidentally, very interesting that R. Hooker, in his *Ecclesiastical Polity*,[21] in a few lines states a completely Anselmic soteriology.

(5.1.3) Since this discussion of the necessity for the two natures to reside in one Person is crucial in the development of St. Anselm's theme, we must look at it closely.

(5.1.3.1.) By establishing in this way the unity of the Person of the

Deus-homo, St. Anselm seeks to bring together the warp and the woof from which the texture of his theory of the Atonement is to be woven. His rejection of the possibility of satisfaction being made through two separate persons—one, God, and the other, man—indicates that for him the unity is no logical fiction, as it appears to be in some treatments of the two natures and the One Person; elaborate discussions of *enhypostasia* often give this impression. It is essential to his whole scheme of salvation that the nature which has the power to make the satisfaction should be united through one Person with the nature which bears the responsibility for the sin. Otherwise, redemption for man would remain an impossibility. More precisely still, the Person Who makes the satisfaction, in virtue of His Divine nature, is the same Person who bears responsibility for sin, through His human nature. It is therefore absurd that Harnack [22] should say in a derogatory fashion that "Anselm . . . continues to use the two-nature doctrine as a hallowed tradition". On the contrary, St. Anselm, so far from treating the doctrine as a tradition, accepted simply on that ground, quite unmistakably holds it to be a central feature of his whole scheme, without which it would be meaningless.

(5.1.3.2.) If we examine St. Anselm's statements about God's and man's relation to the satisfaction required for man's sin, we see that they are really twofold. On the one hand, he says that God alone can make adequate satisfaction for sin, and man alone ought to make it. On the other hand, he says that God ought not to make satisfaction for sin, and man cannot. It is noteworthy that St. Anselm, quite without hesitation, and for obvious reasons, uses the first statement in the argument for the necessity of the *Deus-homo* for human salvation; the one Person can and ought. Had St. Anselm followed the line of his second statement, he would have reached a very different conclusion, in fact, precisely the opposite of that which he intended, namely, the impossibility of salvation by the *Deus-homo*. The one Person ought not (*quâ* Divine) and cannot (*quâ* human). Of course, St. Anselm's reply could be that, in His mercy, God has elected that the former alternative should occur—a God-man, able to make amends and assuming responsibility for sin. Such a reply would constitute, however, a departure from demonstration by logical principles, in the rationalistic sense of this phrase, and an admission that from the point of view of reason alone the possibility and the impossibility of salvation by the *Deus-homo* are equally valid. So, it might even be said, his whole argument has broken down at its centre. This conclusion has, however, to be modified in the light of two considerations. On the one hand, as his work develops St. Anselm shows that the reason for the occurrence of one alternative rather than the other is discoverable not in its greater rationality (in the rationalist sense again) but in the nature of God; and, on the other, we must wait until St. Anselm has demonstrated why there had to be a God-man before we can make judgment as to what he really means by "rational proof".[23]

(5.2) At II.9, St. Anselm shows that he is aware of the incompleteness of his argument as he has so far developed it. He has stated the case for God's becoming man, or assuming human nature, but it remains to be demonstrated which of the three Persons of the Trinity becomes incarnate. He tries to pass over the issue with a brief reference to the *Epistola de Incarnatione Verbi*, but Boso insists on a brief rehearsal, at least, of the reason why the Son had to undertake this particular work. St. Anselm's proof in reply to Boso's request consists of two *reductio ad absurdum* arguments and two arguments for the more fitting (*convenientius*) situation. The *reductio ad absurdum* arguments are: first, the Incarnation of either of the other two Persons of the Trinity would entail the existence of two Sons, the Eternal Son and the Son born of the Virgin, and the inferiority in dignity of the latter to the former—which is impossible if the Persons of the Trinity are all equal; secondly, particularly if the Father were incarnate, then the Father would be the grandson of the human parents of the Virgin, and the Eternal Son, being the Son of the Father Who had thus assumed humanity, would be the grandson of the Virgin —which, in St. Anselm's opinion, produces the absurdity of two grandsons in the Trinity! Without delaying over one rejoinder to, at least, part of this fantastic logomachy, namely, that the result would be not two grandsons, but a grandson and a great-grandson, we may say that in Christian dogmatics the Doctrine of the Trinity rests logically and epistemologically on the Doctrine of the Incarnation. Christians believe in the Doctrine of the

Trinity, because it is only in these terms that they can understand the true nature of the revelation of God in Jesus Christ. They do not *first* believe in the Doctrine of the Trinity, and find themselves subsequently faced with the very difficult task of proving which of the Three Persons will become incarnate. Cullmann's strictures on the methodology of dogmatic theologians who follow the Trinitarian, as distinct from a more Christocentric, exposition of the subject-matter of the Christian faith, are relevant to St. Anselm's treatment at this point.

(5.3) Since St. Anselm, at II.9, p. 105, ll. 7-9, explicitly refers to his letter on the subject of the Incarnation of the Word, we may amplify his short statement in the *Cur Deus Homo* from his views given at length in that work. The letter consists of a lengthy commentary upon, and criticism of, a statement which Schmitt rightly assigned to Roscelin.[24] "If," says Roscelin, "the three Persons in the Deity are only one thing and not three things, each separately self-existent, like three angels or three spirits, in such a way, however, that they are entirely identical in will and power; then, the Father and the Holy Spirit are incarnate with the Son." [25]   Before dealing specifically with these statements by Roscelin, St. Anselm in c. 1 enunciates the principle of *credo ut intelligam* and then goes on to state some of the logical and epistemological views of those contemporary dialecticians who have so presumptuously tried to dispose of Christian beliefs without first committing themselves to God in the obedience of faith; e.g. that universals are noises and have no objective reality; that colour and matter are indistinguishable, as also are human wisdom and spirit; that reason, which ought to be the supreme judge of everything in human existence, is so confused with material imagery that it cannot differentiate itself from the latter, nor can it rightly discern those things which it ought to contemplate in isolation from all else.   With such dialecticians St. Anselm adopts the *a fortiori* argument; if they cannot discriminate the common humanity in all men, how improbable is it that they shall discern one God in three Persons.   If they cannot differentiate between a horse and its colour, how much more difficult will it be for them to distinguish between one God and the intra-Trinitarian relationships.

Two comments on St. Anselm's treatment of these contemporary dialecticians might be made. First, since it is generally agreed that St. Anselm and Abelard constitute our main sources for the views of Roscelin,[26] this passage [27] from St. Anselm's *Epistola de Incarnatione Verbi* is of great importance. But it must be used with the greatest of care. For, while St. Anselm refers to Roscelin's views on p. 4, he does not say that the views expounded on pp. 9-10 are necessarily all of them held by Roscelin. Carré's treatment of this passage is therefore unsatisfactory for this reason that he implies, by his mention of the charge of Tritheism brought by St. Anselm against Roscelin, immediately after quoting the "contemporary dialecticians" passage,[28] that the views of the latter were also held by Roscelin. We may put the situation thus: the *Epistola* does not enable us to say *which* of the logical and epistemological views set down by St. Anselm in his statement of opinions of contemporary philosophers were held by Roscelin, and which were not.

Secondly, in the *Epistola* we do not receive any precise account of the way in which the "Nominalist" theory of universals, or the denial of the distinction between substance and attribute, affects the Doctrine of the Trinity, or, more accurately, the intra-Trinitarian relationships. After c. 1, p. 9, l. 22, St. Anselm never again uses the phrase *flatus vocis*, and only rarely (e.g. at c. 2, p. 13, l. 22, and c. 4, p. 17, l. 3, does he use the word *nomen* from which, as is well known, the term "Nominalist" is derived), and then not as a definition of a universal. St. Anselm rather confines himself to the examination of the quotation from Roscelin and indicates only in a general way, and by implication, the inadequacies of Nominalist logic as an instrument of orthodox Trinitarian statement. In other words, his purpose is to draw out the implications (heretical, as he claims) of Roscelin's position as stated in the quotation, and not to query its logical presuppositions. The conclusion could then be drawn that the views of the "contemporary dialecticians" constitute an illustrative interpolation, which we must not try to integrate too closely with the main argument of the letter.

When St. Anselm comes to deal critically with the quotation from Roscelin [29] he adopts two lines. He accuses Roscelin of Tritheism, and proceeds thereafter to set forth an orthodox account of the relations between Nature and Persons within the Trinity. It is within this latter account that the passage occurs (c. 10) which forms the immediate link with the *Cur Deus Homo*, II.9. The interest, for our purpose, of the comparison of these two passages from the separate works lies in the study of the two different ways by which St. Anselm approaches what is virtually the same argument. Let us then examine the approach which he makes in the *Epistola de Incarnatione Verbi* to the question of the necessity for the Incarnation of the *Word* rather than of either of the other two Persons of the Trinity.

St. Anselm's criticism of Roscelin in c. 2 is that he is committed to Tritheism. Roscelin's stated case is as follows: if the three Persons in the Godhead are one thing and not three things, then the Father and the Holy Spirit are incarnate with the Son. St. Anselm assumes that Roscelin has gone on to say: since it is generally agreed by all Christians that the Father and the Holy Spirit are not incarnate with the Son, then it is not true that the three Persons are one thing and not three things, i.e. the three Persons are three things, like three angels or three spirits. The implied argument is a hypothetical syllogism with the denial of the consequent validating the denial of the antecedent. Of course, St. Anselm would know independently that Roscelin favoured Tritheism, for in the *Epistola ad Fulconem* [30] he says: "I hear . . . that Roscelin says . . . that three Gods could be truthfully postulated if tradition allowed."

A subsidiary criticism which St. Anselm makes of Roscelin, in c. 3, on the basis of the quotation from the latter, is that Roscelin interprets the proposition: "The three Persons are one thing or substance" in what St. Anselm calls a Sabellian fashion. That is, by his attack Roscelin refutes Sabellianism, but not orthodox Trinitarianism. Roscelin seems to assume, suggests St. Anselm, that if, say, Father and Son are one thing, whatever is true of the Father is *ipso facto* true of the Son, and whatever can be affirmed of the Son cannot be denied of the Father. If the Father is Begetter and Unbegotten, these properties must be predicated of the Son. In the same way, if the Son is incarnate, then so also is the Father and likewise the Holy Spirit. On St. Anselm's interpretation of the situation, Roscelin regards, for the purpose of his arguments, the three Persons as being in fact one Person.[31]

Of course, the question could be put with regard to St. Anselm's interpretation of Roscelin, whether he does not affectively reduce the latter's account of Trinitarianism not to Sabellianism (which is quite definite in its retention of *three* Persons) but to what we should now call Unitarianism or to an undifferentiated monotheism.

Still referring continually to the quotation from Roscelin, St. Anselm proceeds [32] to show how orthodox Trinitarianism differs from Tritheism on the one hand and the so-called Sabellianism on the other; to argue that human nature was taken up into the Son *quâ* Person of the Godhead and not into the essential unity of the Godhead, which the Son shares with the other two Persons,[33] and to demonstrate why it was that the Son was most appropriately incarnated.[34]

(While dealing with these main topics he discusses other issues, e.g. the omnipresence and omnipotence of God [35]; God as *summum bonum* [36]; the Nile, its source, the river, the Lake (or Delta) as a *vestigium Trinitatis*,[37] and so on.)

In this statement of orthodox Trinitarianism St. Anselm follows fairly orthodox lines, and the implied reply to Roscelin is that he does not truly understand or distinguish properly the way in which the three Persons are one and three at the same time. Father, Son and Holy Spirit are not several but one as regards substance,[38] each being substantially God, or as regards the nature of God.[39]   But they are three in respect of their Persons,[40] or personal properties,[41] i.e. *generatio, filiatio, processus.*   Within each Person it is legitimate, therefore, to distinguish between that which is common, *communis,*[42] to Him and the other two Persons, and that which is predicable only of that Person.   It is because Incarnation falls within the latter member of this distinction in regard to the Second Person of the Trinity that it is unwarrantable to predicate Incarnation of the other two Persons.   Incarnation is not a *commune,* a common property of the three Persons of the Godhead; it does not belong to the substance of Deity; it is a *proprium* of the Son.   So, at c. 9, St. Anselm can argue that at the Incarnation the Son assumed humanity not into "the unity of His nature, but into the unity of His Person".[43]   Incarnation is a personal work of the Son, not a substantial work of the Godhead, and not, therefore, to be attributed to the Father or the Holy Spirit.   When God assumed humanity, the nature of God and the nature of man did not become one and the same; rather was it the Second Person of the Godhead and the person of man which were identified. St. Anselm uses this statement for a *reductio ad absurdum*,[44] showing that if the three Persons are incarnate then the three Persons becoming identical with (the person of) the same man become identical with each other. Therefore, if one Person of the Godhead is incarnate no other can be.

At c. 10 St. Anselm sets himself the task of showing why it is the Son Who should most fittingly be incarnate, and here we make our link with the *Cur Deus Homo*, II.9. The similarity of the two sets of arguments is striking: they are of the same kind and they occur in the same order, two *reductio ad absurdum* arguments and two of the *convenientius* type. Of the *reductio ad absurdum* arguments, the first differs from its counterpart in the *Cur Deus Homo* in that here St. Anselm thinks not of either of the other two Persons being incarnate but of the Holy Spirit explicitly. The resultant inequality of origin of the two Sons is mentioned in both works. The second argument about the two grandsons in the Trinity is the same in both works. It should be said of the argument in the *Epistola* that it gives the impression of dealing more carefully with the consequences that follow when the other two Persons are *each* conceived of as being incarnate. The first *convenientius* argument is the same in both, while the second is much fuller in the *Epistola*, mainly because St. Anselm wishes to emphasise that man's own will was the author of the sin that led him to do dishonour to the "Image of God". He Who was the true Image of the Father most fittingly should restore man. He Who was the Truth could alone cure falsity.[45]

A comparison of the *Epistola* with the *Cur Deus Homo*, and particularly of the points at which these fairly identical arguments occur, yields the following conclusions:

First, the similarity in meaning of the two titles might lead us at first to expect that St. Anselm was dealing with the same theme in the two writings. By this time it is obvious that this is not the case. In the *Epistola* he tries to answer the question of why the Word only is incarnate, and not the other two Persons. He does not touch the problem of why there should be an Incarnation at all, beyond saying that it is a *proprium* of the Second Person. In the *Epistola* there is a limiting of the range of the *credo ut intelligam* principle; that is, he assumes, and does not seek to give a rational proof of, the fact of the Incarnation, whereas he does apply the principle to the dependent problem, given the fact of the Incarnation, of why the Son should be the Person Who is incarnated. In the *Cur Deus Homo*, on the contrary, the central issue is the necessity for an Incarnation. In this work St. Anselm merely cites the argument given in the *Epistola* for the necessity of the Incarnation taking place in the Person of the Son—and then at a period somewhat late in his analysis, having already spoken frequently about the Incarnation of the Son, as if it were assumed that the Son was the proper Person to become incarnate. To put the matter briefly and in Barth's symbolism: in the *Epistola* the fact of the Incarnation belongs to the *a b c d*, and the Incarnation of the *Son* is the *x*; whereas in the *Cur Deus Homo* the fact of the Incarnation is the *x*, and the Incarnation of the Son falls within the *a b c d*.

Secondly, c. 10 of the *Epistola*, on the necessity for the Incarnation of the *Word*, occupies a central place in the development of the thought of that letter. Up to that point St. Anselm has shown only that if any one Person is incarnate, then it is impossible that either of the other two should also be incarnate.[46] But this necessity for the Son's Incarnation is a central issue, though St. Anselm does not seem to realise it, in the *Cur Deus Homo*. Why is the Son the Person most fitted to the subject Who offers the satisfaction which man cannot offer? The question, then, of the necessity for the *Son's* Incarnation takes on a somewhat different form within the context of the *Cur Deus Homo*, which renders the citation of the answers given in the *Epistola* quite inadequate. The failure of St. Anselm to deal with this question, too, in terms of satisfaction, the key concept of the *Cur Deus Homo*, constitutes a grave defect in St. Anselm's execution of his argument.

Thirdly, had St. Anselm given us an exposition of this kind, he would have corrected an error, not only in his account given in the *Epistola* of the intra-Trinitarian relationships and of the "personal properties" of the Persons of the Trinity, but in most orthodox Trinitarian statements on these subjects. This error consists in separating too rigidly the *opera ad intra Trinitatis* from the *opera ad extra*. It is generally agreed that Christians know that God is Trinity in Unity and Unity in Trinity from God's revelation of Himself in Jesus Christ. That revelation is, as Karl Barth would say, the ground of the Doctrine of the Trinity. From that ground, Christians go on to speak of the work of the First Person in Creation, and of the Third in Sanctification, making full use of the knowledge of God as revealed in the created order and in the spiritual life of the Church and its members. In this way the statement of the *opera ad extra Trinitatis* develops. But, and here the error arises, when discussion of the *opera ad intra Trinitatis* begins, many dogmatic theologians seem to think that they must turn their backs on the *opera ad extra* and give an altogether separate account of the *opera ad intra*. The result is —as can be seen so clearly in St. Anselm, or in the more modern setting in Heppe [47]—that the most abstract terms are used for the differentiation of the three Persons; to the Father, the property of *generatio* or *paternitas* is attributed; to the Son, *filiatio*; and to the Spirit, *processio*. Each of these properties is a relational property, and as such tells us nothing about the Person Himself. It simply says that He stands in a certain relation to one or both of the other two Persons. It would be wiser, then, not to pretend that these "personal properties" define the Persons, but rather to describe the Persons in terms of the *opera ad extra*, and to confess greater agnosticism concerning the intra-Trinitarian relationships. The problem which St. Anselm sets himself in the *Epistola de Incarnatione Verbi* may seem artificial, but his handling of it is even more artificial than it need be because of his keeping the whole examination on the intra-Trinitarian plane. The problem of the *Cur Deus Homo* is not artificial at all, just because it begins from the situation of God and man in relationship. That situation must always be our starting-point for the investigation of God as He is in Himself, and it must save us from the excesses of too detailed intra-Trinitarian theology.

6

We return now to St. Anselm's treatment of the Person of the *Deus-homo*. In the speech, II.7, p. 102, ll. 11-21, St. Anselm, in using the phrases *verus homo* and *perfectus homo*, raises a problem which has always been of great interest in Christology, and which on examination throws more light on his position at this stage of the work. The problem is that of whether St. Anselm holds that it was *sinful* humanity that was present in the *Deus-homo*. The sinlessness of Jesus Christ is a topic of such importance that it will merit treatment independent of the immediate issues raised in II.7, taking account, also, of views stated in II.10 and II.16. The evidence arranges itself in a fairly definite way, thus:

(6.1) At first the question of the sinlessness of Jesus Christ might appear to be answered outright by St. Anselm's use of the phrase *perfectus homo*, but in fact the meaning of the phrase is to be interpreted, on the one hand, by the other phrase mentioned above, *verus homo*, which clearly shows that St. Anselm intends by "perfect man" one who is true man or very man, and not that "new man" to whom he later refers at the beginning of II.8; and, on the other hand, by his reference [48] to the fact that in one Person no violence is done to the completeness of both natures, in the light of which "perfect man" would mean "complete man".

(6.2) The citation of the phrases *verus homo* and *perfectus homo* leaving the sinlessness of Jesus Christ still open, we may prepare for the discussion of II.10 and II.16 by considering how St. Anselm's own logic would lead to two seemingly contradictory positions.

(6.2.1) On the one hand, in II.6-8, as St. Anselm continually affirms that the *homo* in the *Deus-homo* is the nature which ought to make satisfaction, because of its responsibility for the sin, and as St. Anselm's whole position rests on the contention that this sinful and impotent nature is united in one Person with the divinely competent nature, it would appear to be conclusive that the human nature which belongs to the God-man is a sinful human nature. This conclusion could be said to be confirmed independently by two considerations: first, by St. Anselm's emphasis on the fact that the person to make the satisfaction must be born of Adam's race, and stand beneath the curse of sin and evil which Adam propagated; and, secondly, by the fact that had it been sinless humanity that was joined with Deity in the Person of the God-man, then that humanity would be under no debt to God and under no necessity to make satisfaction. St. Anselm might, on this analysis of his thought, be regarded as placing himself within that Patristic tradition which affirmed that "what God did not take He did not redeem". Further, it will be recalled that, as already indicated,[49] it was not manhood in general that was united with Deity in the Person of the God-man, but a concrete instance of it, which embodies all the definitional characteristics of manhood. St. Anselm, it might be said, could avoid affirming that Jesus Christ had the sinful nature of man only by holding either that sinfulness did not pertain to the essential being of man as set down in the definition of man, or that in some way the Word, in assuming complete human nature, avoids the sinfulness which is characteristic of man in his fallen state. As we shall see later, it is the latter alternative which St. Anselm finally adopts.

(6.2.2) On the other hand, if the human nature joined with the Divine nature in the *Deus-homo* were sinful, then that nature would be under an infinite debt to God for its own sinfulness. A single sin against God is so grave—a glance which God forbids must not be made even if the salvation of the entire universe is at stake—that it requires greater satisfaction than any man can possibly make. Such satisfaction as the human nature in Jesus Christ could offer through being joined with the Divine nature would therefore be required to atone for its own sin, and would not be available for the rest of mankind. St. Anselm's later argument (particularly at II.19) demonstrates that the salvation of Christ's sinful brethren depends upon the merits achieved by the *Deus-homo*. A sinful *homo* in the *Deus-homo* would negate such a possibility. These considerations seem to lie at the back of the statements in II.16, p. 117, ll. 1-3, that the God-man cannot be the reconciler of sinners unless He Himself is sinless, and that He is derived sinlessly from the sinful human mass. While, therefore, one part of St. Anselm's logic seems to demand that the human nature taken by the Second Person of the Trinity should be sinful, another part of it demands a sinless *homo* in the *Deus-homo*. It remains now to examine St. Anselm's arguments for the second alternative, which is his choice of the two offered by his own logic.

(6.3) St. Anselm's explicit case for the sinlessness of Jesus

Christ consists of three main contentions: first, that it is necessitated by the Person of Jesus Christ,[50] secondly, that Jesus Christ was unable to sin,[51] and thirdly, that the assumption of a sinless human nature from the *massa peccatrix* is a Divine mystery.[52] St. Anselm's discussion of these contentions shows both his own concern about the contradiction within his logic—or, perhaps more accurately, the contradiction in the situation itself which tends to defy the logic of his dogmatic—and his anxiety to establish the position which is so important for the development of his argument on the nature of the Death of the *Deus-homo*.

(6.3.1) Despite St. Anselm's earlier emphasis, in II.7, that the two natures in the God-man do not intermingle to produce a third nature, which is a mixture of both, at II.10 and 13, and II.17, he presents a view which is very similar to the Lutheran *communicatio idiomatum*. There could be no sin in the man who was to effect salvation, because he would be God. The unity of the Person of Jesus Christ is the medium through which the sinlessness of the human nature is guaranteed. That one Person could not be sinful as regards His human nature and sinless as regards His divine nature. As one Person, Who is God primarily, even though He is also man, He is sinless. The sinlessness of the human nature derives, then, from the Person of Jesus Christ. In II.10, p. 106, ll. 13 and 15, the *ille homo* and the *iste* refer not to the human nature of the God-man but demonstratively to this Man, Who is the God-man. So, at II.10, p. 108, ll. 11-12, St. Anselm is asserting that the human nature possesses sinlessness, because the Person, Who is Jesus Christ, is sinlessly Divine. From II.10, we can say then that the sinlessness of the human nature is mediated from the Divine through the Person. This type of transference belongs to the *genus idiomaticum* of the Lutheran description.

At II.16 a difficult point of interpretation arises, namely, whether St. Anselm does not go beyond the affirmation of the *genus idiomaticum* to the *genus majesticum*, that is, to the view that certain Divine attributes are predicable of the human nature (in addition to being predicable of the *Person* of Jesus Christ). In II.16 he is discussing the question of whether Jesus Christ is ignorant or omniscient, and, on the ground that His ignorance would hinder the work of salvation which God intends through Him, he concludes that He has the omniscience of God Himself. The implication of this conclusion is that the human mind of Jesus Christ has none of the defects of the ordinary human intelligence, but is, rather, endowed with the attributes of the mind of the Divine nature. While it is true that the problem of the nature of the knowledge possessed by the Incarnate Lord has never been solved—Dr. Leonard Hodgson holds that it is our greatest contemporary Christological problem—and while also it is possible that it is a problem which can only be reverently stated and never solved, it does seem that St. Anselm settles the problem outright by saying that the *Deus-homo* has no ordinary human intelligence, or that His human intelligence has Divine attributes. In the light of I.16—though St. Anselm is not there specifically examining the sinlessness of Jesus Christ—we might be justified in making an analogical inference, and in saying that in St. Anselm's judgment the goodness of the human nature of Christ is a derivative of the goodness of His Divine nature. If this description of St. Anselm's argument is correct, then H. R. Mackintosh's statement [53] that "The Lutherans . . . became responsible for what was really a theological innovation, by definitely teaching that Divine attributes may be predicated of the human nature" of Jesus Christ, is not entirely true. Indeed, St. Anselm's statements, in later chapters, that the merits of the Death of Christ derive their infinite value for mankind from the fact that the Divine nature communicates its worth to the human nature, demonstrate that St. Anselm held to "a real transference of properties from one side to the other" which Mackintosh regards as a Lutheran innovation.

Two comments must be made upon the Anselmic form of the *communicatio idiomatum*. First, the transference of properties is not total. To sinlessness we may add omnipotence and wisdom [54] but not immortality.[55] The *Deus-homo* chooses a mortal human nature because that property is necessary to the means by which God has willed to save mankind. This principle is for St. Anselm determinative of the degree to which the *communicatio idiomatum* takes place. Secondly, in spite of affirming this *communicatio*, St. Anselm does not confound the two natures. Not only does the *communicatio* itself depend on their remaining distinct, but the whole trend of his later analysis of the Death of Christ becomes meaningless if one nature passes over into the other. St. Anselm is not culpable either of Eutycheanism or of Docetism.

This fact, that there occurs in St. Anselm a foreshadowing of the Lutheran *communicatio idiomatum* in its fullest form, is of great importance for the history of Christology. In St. Anselm this theory rests upon what is effectively an enhypostatic interpretation of the Chalcedonian symbol rather than an anhypostatic. The Person of Jesus Christ is the subject of the human nature and its attributes and not only of the Divine nature and its attributes, as we have already clearly indicated from the *Cur Deus Homo*. Just because the human nature is enhypostasised in the *Persona* of the *Verbum* the *communicatio* can take place. The importance of this Anselmic portion is threefold.

First, it indicates fairly clearly how the Latin Church had developed an enhypostatic tradition in Christology, comparable with that represented by Leontius of Byzantium and John the Damascene, even though it had no word exactly corresponding to ἐνυπόστατος, and how it used that tradition to preserve the humanity of Jesus Christ and to avoid the pitfalls of Apollinarianism. Whatever else we may say of St. Anselm, we cannot accuse him, as we can so often the Greeks, of minimising the humanity of Jesus Christ or of being anti-historical in his view of the Incarnation. The entrance of the Word into history, into the human scene, is the great fact with which he has to come to terms.

Secondly, the existence, side by side, of an enhypostatic position with a *communicatio idiomatum* theory in St. Anselm is itself evidence for the views that the Lutheran theory was not an innovation but was rather the re-emergence of a quite orthodox tradition stemming from Chalcedon itself, and that this theory was not invented to support a doctrine of the Sacraments. Too often in popular presentations of Lutheran theology the doctrine of the Sacraments is regarded as the logically prior feature of that theology, and as necessitating a certain interpretation of the Person of Jesus Christ. The reverse is the case: Lutheran Christology, which, as we have seen, belongs to a quite orthodox tradition, is the ground for his doctrine of the Sacraments.

Thirdly, St. Anselm's thought on the subject of the one Person and the two natures provides us with a *multum in parvo* of the history of orthodox post-Chalcedonian Christology—particularly if we supplement the statements in the *Cur Deus Homo* with those made in c. 11 of the *Epistola de Incarnatione Verbi*. In this latter place St. Anselm outlines what we call the anhypostatic position [56]: "When the Word was made flesh, He assumed another nature, but not another person," for in the Incarnation he retained the Divine Person.[57] This anhypostatic tradition is not the last word, however, for it becomes the basis for the enhypostatic theory, which evolves a *communicatio idiomatum* position. The human nature, which has been stated to be without a *persona*, and therefore impersonal, is in the Incarnation enhypostatised in the *Persona* of the Word made flesh. The one Person is both God and man.[58] Accordingly, not only is it possible to speak of this one Person in terms of Deity and humanity,[59] but, further, the same collection of properties (*collectio proprietatum*), since it belongs to the Word and the human nature which He has assumed, may be alternatively predicated of each in turn.[60] In other words, because of the unity of the Person of Jesus Christ, transference of properties takes place between the natures. The *Epistola de Incarnatione Verbi*, then, provides us with substantially the same account of the relation of the Person to the two natures as does the *Cur Deus Homo*, and with a picture of the development from Chalcedon to Lutheran Christology.

(6.3.2) In II.10 we have St. Anselm's lengthiest discussion of the sinlessness of Jesus Christ, and here he tries to answer two questions raised by Boso. The first is: could Jesus Christ sin? The second is: if He could not sin, then is His righteousness necessary or praiseworthy? In both cases St. Anselm raises the question by means of an argument of his own, and the form and content of his argument prescribe also the limits of his reply to the fundamental issues. The two issues are closely connected, because the establishment of the necessity of Christ's sinlessness would appear to contradict the generally accepted view that Christ's righteousness merits the highest praise that man can give Him; involuntary virtue in every other instance is unpraiseworthy.

(6.3.2.1) Could Christ sin? Boso's intention is to establish the affirmative answer to the question, namely, *peccare potuit*. At

the outset he asserts that he will abandon the accepted premise
of the discussion on the Death of Christ, namely that, the fact
of the Incarnation being set aside, the necessity of the existence
of such a Person, both God and man, can be rationally demonstrated—a premise which is soon reasserted at II.10, p. 107,
ll. 10,11—and he proceeds to refer to an event in the life of Jesus
Christ. Our Lord is quoted in St. John's Gospel, viii. 55, as
saying: "If I should say, 'I know (the Father) not,' I shall be a
liar like unto you." Boso points out that it is quite conceivable
that Jesus Christ could say the words, "I know (the Father) not,"
by themselves, out of the context of the other words in St. John
viii. 55. Not only is this situation conceivable by us but, according to the actual text, Jesus Christ did Himself conceive of that
possibility, as is shown by the opening words, "If I should say".
Since, therefore, Jesus Christ thought of lying as a real possibility for Him, and since lying is an instance of sinning, it is
difficult to avoid the conclusion: *peccare potuit*.

Before proceeding to St. Anselm's treatment of Boso's statement we may draw attention to certain features of it. First, it is
an argument for the possibility rather than for the actuality of
Christ's sinning. Boso, that is, would agree with St. Anselm that
Christ was sinless; he would, at this stage, disagree on whether
this sinlessness was maintained in spite of an ability to sin or was
due to an inherent inability to sin. The temptations of Our Lord
might have provided Boso with a better illustration than that
which he employs, to make a strong case. As it is, his illustration
almost completely obscures the issue. Secondly, he has in fact
offered us two arguments for the *posse peccare* position, neither of
which is valid. On the one hand, he is saying that anyone can
imagine Christ saying "I know not the Father," and in doing so
can imagine Christ lying. Here Boso has committed the simple
fallacy of confusing the conceivable and the possible, a confusion
which frequently occurs in everyday life. A centaur is a conceivable object of the imagination for the layman, but the student
of human and animal anatomy and physiology knows that it is
impossible for such a being to exist. For centuries the existence
of the Antipodes was inconceivable, but advances in astronomy
and geography soon demonstrated not only the possibility but
the actuality of the Antipodes. In other words, to the untutored

the difference between the conceivable and the possible, between the inconceivable and the impossible, are scarcely, if ever, accurately defined. It falls to the expert in each field of knowledge to demonstrate the limits of the possible, and the impossibility of much that is popularly conceivable. Therefore, in Boso's illustration, it is conceivable to anyone who does not know Christ that he could lie, but for anyone who has a close acquaintance this conceivable becomes impossible, or, at least, its conceivability does not imply its possibility. On the other hand, to come to the second argument which Boso submits, Christ Himself envisaged the possibility of lying, when He spoke the words of St. John viii. 55. A reading of the rest of the verse would have saved Boso the folly of submitting such an argument at all, for Our Lord merely states the possibility of His lying to deny it outright. "But I *do* know Him, and keep His saying." What Boso has regarded as an instance of Christ's conceiving of Himself as possibly sinning is in fact a circumlocution to make perfectly clear that Christ could not possibly sin by lying about His knowledge of the Father.

The substance of St. Anselm's reply to Boso is that the possibility of Christ's sinning depends on His volition. St. Anselm prepares the way for his answer by a series of short statements [61] on the relation of *potestas* to *voluntas*. *Omnis potestas sequitur voluntatem* is his opening sentence. *Potestas* is usually translated as "power", but such a translation loses the close Latin connection between the noun *potestas* and the verb *potest* (*peccare*) which had been the subject of Boso's previous speech. The English translation "power" actually causes a breach in the continuity of St. Anselm's speech with that of Boso's which is not present in the Latin. Even so, however, it is important to notice that when using *potestas* in the Latin St. Anselm is not arguing for abstract possibilities but is, in fact, saying that the question of whether anyone is able to do this or that depends upon whether he wills to do it. *Potestas* is therefore better translated as "ability" than as "power". All ability, that is, to initiate action, says St. Anselm, is a consequence of volition, and this ability exists only in so far as the will initiating the action is free. For example, I have the ability to speak or walk, if my decision to do so is a free volition. On the other hand, I may be compelled to do certain things, in which case I am under necessity, and the ability to deal with me in this way resides in an agent other than myself, who is free. The affirmation that a person can do or not do a given action rests on a prior consideration of whether he is free to will it. The question of Christ's ability to sin must therefore be discussed at a deeper level than Boso's examination, namely, at the level of Christ's volition. At that level it becomes immediately clear that Christ cannot will to sin. *Peccare non potuit quia non potuit velle peccare.* His conclusion is that we may say *peccare potuit*, so long as we preface the statement with the words, *si vellet*, if He should will it, but that it is much truer to say *peccare non potuit*, since we know that He could not will to sin.

Two possible views might be taken of St. Anselm's answer to Boso. On the one hand, we might say that he has added very little to the solution of the problem which Boso raised. Boso, in holding that Jesus Christ was able to sin, also virtually held that Jesus Christ was able to will to sin—sinning being in most cases an act of volition. To this view of Boso's position St. Anselm has set up an unargued, categorical negation of it, by saying that Jesus Christ cannot will to sin. Boso could quite easily accept the fact emphasised by St. Anselm, that ability to do anything is a consequence of an act of volition, and still cite his example; thus "it is conceivable that Christ could *will* to say: 'I know not the Father'". In other words, the fundamental problem remains, whether you describe it as that of whether Christ could sin, or as that of whether He could *will* to sin. On the other hand, it is possible to take a more charitable and no less correct view of St. Anselm's purpose. By relating man's ability to do this or that to the volition which expresses itself in action, St. Anselm is drawing attention to the inner aspect of all overt behaviour, and, by distinguishing ability from necessity, is indicating that actions are to be judged not by their outward appearance but by the will from which they proceed. When, therefore, he discusses the possibility of Christ's sinning, in terms of His will to sin, St. Anselm implies that Christ, being Who He is, cannot possibly sin. As St. Anselm presents his case, it could seem that he regards Christ's inability to sin as self-evident. Now such a view is not so arbitrary as it might at first appear to be, because there are, in fact, no grounds beyond Himself upon which His sinlessness could be based. He is limited in this, as in so many other respects, by His own nature. In brief, there are some actions which are not open possibilities for a Person such as Jesus Christ. To do them He would have to cease to be Who He is. St. Anselm, we could say therefore, has argued at this point for a position which is theologically very sound.

(6.3.2.2) Boso's second question arises in regard to the sinlessness of the God-man Whose existence St. Anselm has established —Boso mentioning that they are now reverting to their original assumption that Jesus Christ had not existed. If Christ could not sin, is He righteous of necessity, and His righteousness therefore unpraiseworthy? Boso's statement of his case is that of a rather immature student of moral philosophy. He is drawing out the implications of St. Anselm's answer to his own previous statement on the *posse peccare*. If it be true, as St. Anselm holds, that Christ's sinlessness is based on His inability to will to sin, then two consequences follow: first, He is virtuous of necessity (*ex necessitate*); secondly, His virtue is not in the least meritorious. God assigns moral worth to the actions of men and angels only because, being created in such a way that sin was a real possibility to them, they elected of their own free will to be virtuous. To have moral value at all, an action must be consciously willed in preference to some other action which constituted a genuine alternative at the time of choice. Action of this kind is the expression of a free will. Wherever a righteous action is done without the wrong action being in any way a possible alternative, there you have action according to necessity.

In answering Boso St. Anselm first of all employs a *reductio ad absurdum*. If Boso's position is correct, then it is impossible to praise God. Secondly, since it is undeniable that God is to be praised, St. Anselm uses that fact, which Boso cannot truthfully deny, to prove why it is that the angels are to be praised, and what is the nature of Christ's sinlessness. Whatever God has, He has *a se* (from Himself); His righteousness is an expression of His own nature. As he says in another connection,[62] God is not constrained or forbidden to do anything by any external necessity. The ground for our praise of God's perfections is that He has them from Himself. The angels, he continues, are worthy of praise in their sinlessness for that same reason, that they have it from themselves. St. Anselm's task, then, is to show how the angels resemble God in this respect, and, by defeating Boso's logic at this point, to prepare the way for asserting the freedom and praiseworthiness of Christ's righteousness. The righteousness of the angels is to be praised, not because they had the opportunity to sin and refrained from doing so, but because they have now achieved a sinless or righteous condition. This condition they may be said to have conferred upon themselves, on the general principle that he who does not prevent something from occurring is responsible for its occurrence; they did not stand in the way, by availing themselves of the opportunity to sin, and prevent themselves from becoming sinless, and are accordingly to be regarded as the authors of their own sinlessness. St. Anselm here equates "having conferred sinlessness on oneself" with "having sinlessness from oneself" (the phrase *a se* having already been applied to God), and he has to add that this is the only way in which a creature can have something from himself. For this righteousness the angels deserve our praise. In a quick stroke St. Anselm adds that since there is no constraint or prohibition [63] their righteousness does not follow from necessity but from free will. St. Anselm has laid the basis for the final assertion towards which he has been moving, that since the God-man will have *a se* every good quality that He possesses, the human nature deriving the attributes of the Divine through union with it in one Person, then His sinlessness will follow from free will and not from necessity.

The conflict of opinion between Boso and St. Anselm, brought out so clearly in Bk. II.10, p. 107, l. 10—end, is fairly closely paralleled in the history of Kantian and post-Kantian ethics, and particularly in the controversy over "the right and the good".[64] Boso's position is, in principle, the Kantian position, namely, that moral worth and praiseworthiness cannot be established unless the action is done in the face of morally unworthy alternatives; Boso would summarise these under the *posse peccare* and Kant would speak of "inclinations". It is significant that Kant, beginning from premises similar to those used by Boso, encounters precisely Boso's difficulty about God's goodness. Kant meets the situation [65] by saying that the perfectly good will is not obliged to obey moral laws, obligation existing only for beings with "subjective imperfection of the will", i.e. beings who experience inclinations, and that "ought" is here out of place because the holy will of God is "of itself necessarily in union with the law".[66] This was exactly the conclusion which Boso realised to be incompatible with his premises,[67] and it is generally agreed that Kant would have to modify his previous analysis of the good will to allow for a more consistent account than he gives of the goodness of God's will. If Christian piety supports Kant, logic favours Boso. St. Anselm, on the other hand, observes the goodness of a person whose actions are good, not because they are always done in resistance to temptation, but because they flow from an upright character. As Professor A. E. Taylor once said: "We have no high regard for the character of the person, who has to go through an intense moral struggle with temptation every time he passes a public-house, or sees loose change lying on a friend's desk." For a truly great moral character, many of the temptations which afflict weaker beings do not exist as live possibilities. In short, the goodness of the character effects rightness and praiseworthiness of actions even when no conflicting inclinations are present to provide opportunity to sin. St. Anselm, then, regards the goodness of God as normative of all goodness—whether it be of the angels, of man before the Fall, or of the *Deus-homo*—and in giving priority to the good over the right he has been followed, albeit unwittingly, by the theistic moral philosophers, such as A. E. Taylor, L. Arnaud Reid, M. C. D'Arcy and W. G. de Burgh. If Boso was aware that by taking as his starting-point an analysis which covered the righteousness of creatures he was involved in grave difficulties in trying to describe the goodness of God, then St. Anselm realised that his was the converse problem of describing the goodness of creatures in terms of the kind of goodness and praiseworthiness that he ascribed to God. He has, therefore, to explain why God's goodness is not to be called necessary but is spontaneously free and therefore laudable, and in what way the goodness of angels is describable in analogical terms.

The nature of the freedom of the will—whether in God, angels, man or the God-man—is therefore the chief issue between Boso and St. Anselm. In their dialogue it is possible to detect three views of freedom. According to the first, freedom consists in the power to choose between sinning and not sinning. Such is Boso's conception. Secondly, freedom is the power to act without constraint or prohibition of any kind from without. Thirdly, freedom is self-determination, the ability to act in accordance with one's own nature, and with the properties of that nature, properties which one has *a se* and not from any other person. Both these latter views appear in St. Anselm's speech (II.10, pp. 107, l. 27, to 108, l. 12), and while the former view suggests that St. Anselm is committed to complete indeterminism, which is a true account neither of Divine nor of human action, the latter represents his more fundamental position. It is, in addition, the position which is the proper counter to Boso's previous speech, for there Boso had maintained in reply to St. Anselm that the sinlessness of the God-man must be unpraiseworthy because it was the necessary outcome of the sinless Divine nature in Him. St. Anselm's counter is, in effect, that the self is truly free only when it is self-determined, when its actions are the expression of its true nature. What Boso had called action *ex necessitate* St. Anselm would call action of the truly free will, because it is action *a se*. In God, Whose nature is goodness, truth, mercy and so on, His actions are praiseworthy because the nature from which they proceed is praiseworthy. In the case of the angels, who are sinless, their actions may follow in a sense necessarily from their being, but they have their sinlessness *a se* and are therefore, St. Anselm holds, completely free in their volitions. It would be unwarrantable to develop St. Anselm's position further, because he states it all too briefly and without illustration, but we shall consider it immediately in the light of the evidence of the *De Libertate Arbitrii*. It would not require much elaboration to develop from St. Anselm's description of freedom the view which Hastings Rashdall [68] adopts in his reaction against determinism on the one hand and indeterminism on the other. Once more it is to be noted that the notion of *aseitas*, which St. Anselm had used in describing God's freedom in electing to save mankind, is employed in his crowning argument, this time for the sinlessness of Jesus Christ and for the freedom on which it is based. Yet it would be foolish to shut our eyes to the defects in St. Anselm's presentation of his case. For example, he does not provide a really convincing argument for the similarity of the *aseitas* of God and that of the angels. In fact, he ought to have realised that *aseitas* belongs properly only to God and not to any of His creatures, however righteous. But, as so often in St. Anselm, he says a true thing in a wrong way, and we must give him the credit for the true thing.

(6.3.2.3) St. Anselm's views on the freedom of the will stated in the *Cur Deus Homo*, Bk. II.10, may be amplified by reference to what he says in the *De Libertate Arbitrii*. In this treatise St. Anselm is discussing the precise issue of whether and in what way freedom of the will can be attributed to the apostate angels and the first man who fell; nevertheless, throughout he makes many assertions on true freedom of the will which render a comparison with the *Cur Deus Homo* valuable. In the *De Libertate Arbitrii* he expounds at length two views with which we are already familiar. The first is the negative view that sin does not consist in the power to sin or not to sin,[69] for then freedom of the will must be denied to God. Consequently, the definition to be given of freedom of the will must be such as to include both human and Divine freedom, which is exactly the point which St. Anselm makes in suggesting to Boso that his theory of moral praiseworthiness would prevent us from praising God, Who is not equally free to sin or not to sin.[70] In other words, ability to sin must not be included in any definition of freedom of the will.[71] The second view expounded is that freedom consists in the absence of coercive or preventative power [72]—an echo of the indeterminist view of the *Cur Deus Homo*. There appears, however, a third view in the earlier treatise, namely, that the power of preserving righteousness of will solely "for righteousness' sake" is a perfect definition of freedom of will.[73] He has prepared for this conclusion by a lengthy discussion in c. 3 of the non-utilitarian character of willing righteousness—a fact to be emphasised centuries later by Kant in his theory of the autonomy of the good will. The free will is the will which wills righteousness for its own sake and not for any extraneous reasons. It might appear that this account of freedom is somewhat different from the self-determination theory of the *Cur Deus Homo*, Bk. II.10, but this is not exactly so. In the latter passage St. Anselm regards Divine freedom, righteousness and praiseworthiness as the type, and these attributes in the angels as ectypal. In the *De Libertate Arbitrii* the type which he is discussing is the freedom of creaturely wills—those of man and angels, whose freedom consists in being determined by righteousness. Had he applied this type of freedom to God, then, since righteousness is one of the perfections of God's nature, God's freedom would be seen in determination by that righteousness which belongs to the essence of His being, i.e. in self-determination. Nevertheless, had St. Anselm in his analysis of the righteousness of angels in the *Cur Deus Homo* passage [74] used the *De Libertate Arbitrii* conception of freedom as determination by righteousness, then he would have arrived at an explanation of why we praise the angels for their righteousness less artificial than that they confer sinlessness upon themselves, and therefore have it *a se*. For he establishes the analogy between the freedom of God and the freedom of the angels at the wrong point. Both God and the angels are free in their actions in that they are determined by righteousness and integrity, but whereas, since these perfections are essentially one with God's Being and Nature, He has them *a se*, the angels have them *a Deo*, and only in a creaturely and derivative sense *a se*. We praise the angels for their sinlessness, which consists in complete determination by the righteousness of God, and God for that righteousness which He Himself is.

(6.4) After the elaborate arguments of II.10, designed to establish the sinlessness of the God-man, it is a surprise to find St. Anselm at II.16 advancing a position of "reverent agnosticism" in regard to the manner in which God assumes humanity sinlessly from the sinful mass of the human race. If II.10 was addressed to the *that* of Christ's sinlessness, II.16 deals with the *how* of Christ's sinlessness. Once again Boso's importunity provides the occasion for the declaration of the Anselmic view. If it be true that all men have come under the curse of the sin of Adam and are born sinners,[75] and if, too, satisfaction is to be made only by one who is born of that lineage,[76] how is it possible for someone so born to be sinless, and so to achieve the necessary satisfaction? St. Anselm's reply,[77] repeated in this same chapter,[78] is that if we cannot understand how, for the purpose of reconciliation between God and man, God takes a human nature that is sinless, then we must accept the fact, reverently admitting that

in the hidden secrets of so lofty a subject there are matters which
lie beyond our knowledge. This we do know: that the salvation
of man could not be achieved unless God in His wisdom and power
took the sinless human nature which would alone be adequate
for His great purpose. This "inscrutable work" of God surpasses human thought and penetration.

While the spirit in which this chapter is written cannot but
compel our admiration, coming in the midst of so many "arguments about it and about", nevertheless it represents what some
critics would regard as a defection on St. Anselm's part, in two
directions, from the main principles of the *Cur Deus Homo*. On
the one hand, it might be pointed out, while it is simple for the
purposes of exposition to maintain that II.10 examines the *that*
of Christ's sinlessness and II.16 the *how* of His sinlessness, it is
yet wrong to believe that the two issues are isolable. No matter
how convincing his arguments for the sinlessness of Jesus Christ
may be, if he cannot demonstrate how this sinlessness is possible,
then his purposes are defeated. II.10 requires for its completion
the demonstration of the subject of II.16; otherwise, the possibility and the reality of the God-man remain open questions.
On the other hand, St. Anselm's appeal to reverent agnosticism
could be construed as a virtual admission that his attempt at
intellectus fidei has failed at a crucial point, and that the question
of whether man's salvation can be accomplished is not to be
settled purely by a theoretical examination of the possible qualities
of the *Deus-homo*.

While a fair case can be made for the criticism that St. Anselm
has failed in these two directions, it is not so serious as might at
first appear, for the following reasons:

(6.4.1) The case for the sinlessness of Jesus Christ is more
accurately related to the Atonement than to the Incarnation.
What, in fact, St. Anselm goes on to do—and here, in his judgment, lies the justification for the sinlessness of Jesus Christ—is
to show that the Atonement is not possible except on the basis of
Christ's sinlessness. In fact, a strong position would be to argue
that the assertion of the sinlessness of Jesus Christ is an inference
backwards from the Atonement, and not a direct implication of
the Incarnation. For most theologians who affirm the sinlessness

of Jesus Christ do so on the ground that otherwise He could not be the Saviour of sinners.

(6.4.2) It might be added that if St. Anselm achieves proof only of the *that* but not of the *how* of the sinlessness of Jesus Christ, then he has achieved all that he requires for the purpose of his soteriological theory. The *that* and the *how* may be inextricably linked up, but if St. Anselm has satisfactorily demonstrated the *that*, however complete his failure in regard to the *how*, his subsequent argument is not thereby invalidated. In fact, some of the worst errors in the field of dogmatic science have arisen when theologians have either professed an excessive and unwarranted knowledge of the *how* of God's Being and actions, or, on the other hand, having discovered the difficulties of establishing the *how*, have prematurely denied the *that*.

(6.4.3) Should it be granted that St. Anselm has failed to demonstrate the *how* of Christ's sinlessness, it is doubtful whether this admission is a really serious criticism of his theological ability, for few theologians, if any, who have agreed with St. Anselm's premises concerning sin and the solidarity of Christ with sinners have ever achieved success in this regard. Some have even regarded their failure as a good reason for the contention that Christ assumed a sinful human nature. St. Anselm evidently prefers his reverent agnosticism to that alternative, which would have too many disadvantageous implications for the rest of his theology.

CHAPTER FOUR

ILLA REDEMPTIO : SOTERIOLOGY

St. ANSELM'S presentation of the doctrine of the Atonement consists of four themes: (1) the voluntary nature of the Death of Our Lord; (2) the value of His Death; (3) the application of the merits of His Death; and (4) His Death as an example to men. The interest in their presentation lies not solely in the development of each particular theme, but perhaps more so in the relation which each of these themes bears to the others, and all of them to the previous treatment of the Person of Jesus Christ.

1

St. Anselm passes from his treatment of the Person of Jesus Christ to that of His Work by means of a discussion [1] of the question whether Our Lord died of necessity or not. That discussion at II.10,11, is somewhat brief and out of proportion to its importance for his view of the value of Christ's Death. What is there stated can, however, be amplified by reference to two other accounts of the same matter—I.8-10 and II.16,17—which occur in the examination of other problems. Since it is our contention that St. Anselm is best understood in the light of all that he has to say on any particular subject, and since it was also St. Anselm's practice to take as read arguments that he had used elsewhere, we shall bring together for single treatment his several discussions of the voluntary nature of the Death of Our Lord.

(1.1) In Bk. I, before St. Anselm has properly begun his argument concerning the reason for the existence of a God-man, and while he is still apparently bandying words with Boso, he devotes much energy to the discussion of the question whether Christ's Death was voluntary or not. In I.8, Boso states the problem which St. Anselm must face, and with him, all theologians who have ever maintained the orthodox position in whatever century. Granted that the Will of God is never unreasonable,[2] how is it possible for Him to submit that man, who was His Beloved Son,

154

to the ignominy of Crucifixion, or even to permit such a thing to happen to Him? Boso further refines the problem to a dilemma.

If God could not save sinners except by this unjust (which, for Boso, is also unreasonable) treatment of an innocent man, what of His omnipotence? Yet, if He could and refused to do so, what of His wisdom and righteousness? In his immediate attempt to deal with Boso's problem St. Anselm endeavours to save God's wisdom, righteousness and omnipotence by the doubtful method of proving that God neither willed nor permitted Christ to die against His Will, and that Christ's Death is to be properly understood in terms not of His obedience to the compelling Will of the Father, but of His own free will. This method is doubtful, because not only does it involve St. Anselm in some strained exegesis of certain Scriptural passages which Boso promptly cites (e.g. Phil. ii. 8 ff.; St. Matt. xxvi. 39), but in addition it conflicts with St. Anselm's main thesis that the salvation of man was initiated by God and executed in the Person of the Eternal Son made flesh. As to Boso's dilemma, the whole work is an attempt to resolve it, and to show how, through the suffering of the innocent for the guilty, no compromise is suffered by God's wisdom, righteousness and omnipotence; or, more strongly, how it is only so that God's attributes can be properly indicated. St. Anselm's present answer to Boso's question is not irrelevant, for it provides us with his tentative first attack on a major theme of his soteriology.

(1.2) In I.9,10, St. Anselm gives a fuller account of the relation of Christ's Death to the Will of the Father, and to His own free will, but since this account is almost certainly the most obscure passage in the whole work, it is difficult to determine what St. Anselm wants to prove, and what he does actually prove, and not to convict him of downright self-contradiction. In the course of the argument he adopts the following positions:

(1.2.1) To begin with,[3] he maintains that Christ's Death was not due to His obedience to the specific volition of the Father that He should die but followed as a direct consequence of His allegiance, demanded by God, to truth and of His righteousness. That is, God enjoins that in every situation the rational creature shall not diverge from truth or righteousness, but He cannot be said to require the actual individual acts of obedience in the precise

situations in which rational creatures find themselves in endeavouring to fulfil His injunctions. He does not require Christ to die
—but He does require of Him, as of all rational creatures, that
He should invariably keep His laws of truth and righteousness.

Two comments may be made on this short discussion and they
serve to show how confusing St. Anselm's argument really is.
First, he violates the simple logical principle of *de omne et de ullo*:
whatever is true of all members of a class is true of any one of
them singly. He wants to say, on the one hand, that God requires
of Jesus Christ obedience to His laws in every situation, and, on
the other hand, that God does not require just that particular
act of obedience which issues in the situation of His crucifixion.
Secondly, he is speaking of Jesus Christ as if He were only a
rational creature (a position which he reaffirms in I.9, and later
at a most important point of His argument II.11), a statement
permissible perhaps in the case of extreme Kenoticists, but not
in one who holds so firmly the compresence of the two natures
in Our Lord's Person.

(1.2.2) Next,[4] and continuing with his establishment of the view
that God did not require the Death of Christ, he submits the
ground of the sinlessness of Christ. It would be lamentable for
God to compel a just man to perish; therefore, Christ must have
died of His own free will. St. Anselm chooses this point [5] to
return to the theme which he has just left, throwing Boso and his
readers into confusion by allowing that God may legitimately be
said to have demanded of Christ His death. God commanded
Christ to drink the cup that led to His Death, which is a perfectly
Scriptural view, but one which is a refutation of that which he
had been upholding at the beginning of I.9. He takes the matter
further still when at I.9, p. 62, ll. 23 ff., he says that the Son, with
the Father and the Holy Spirit, had decreed that He should show
forth the wonder of God's mercy "not otherwise than by His
Death". St. Anselm, then, has tacitly admitted part of Boso's
position, namely, that Christ suffers death in obedience to God's
will—a position which he had hoped at first to avoid. His task
now becomes that of showing that even on this admission Christ's
will to die is His own free will.

(1.2.3) Towards the end of I.9,[6] in discussion of. Our Lord's statement, "Father, if it be possible, let this cup pass from me; nevertheless, not what I will but what Thou willest", St. Anselm explains that the "my will" referred to by Jesus Christ is the natural human will to self-preservation. Earlier in this same chapter [7] he has referred to the "upright" human will of Jesus Christ, as deriving not from humanity but from Divinity, so that the will to self-preservation is not itself an evil thing, the presence of which in Christ makes Him sinful, nor is it allowed to become an evil thing by opposing the Divine Will in Christ. Such is the unity of Christ's nature that the human will in Him is always subordinated to the Divine. "The Will of the Father", the nature of which he now ingeniously explains,[8] is not that the Son should die, but that the human race should not be restored except man do something equal in value to the Death of the Son. In effect St. Anselm is saying that the Father's Will is that either man offers something equal in value to the Death of Christ, or man shall not be saved. It is the Son Who effectively wills the first of these alternatives, and He does so recognising that the second alternative is not a real alternative for a good and omnipotent God, Who cannot remain what He is and see His creation of man stultified by human sin. The Father then may be said to will the Death of the Son, because He virtually leaves the Son no alternative but death, if man is to be saved. The Son, by reason of the uprightness of His Will, makes that Will of the Father His own, or, perhaps more accurately, the Father wills what the Son wills, once the Son wills what is acceptable to the Father.

This argument is so tortuous that it deserves further examination.

(1.2.3.1) In the middle of the argument St. Anselm reaffirms the position which he had previously been maintaining, that the Father does not will the Death of Jesus Christ. He seems to feel obliged to do so in answer to Boso's statement, at the end of I.8, that Christ died more through a compelling will to obedience than of His spontaneous volition. Yet his whole scheme of soteriology breaks down that position and he ends by allowing, with qualifications which concede the whole point, that the Father did will the Death of the Son.

(1.2.3.2) Throughout the latter half of I.9 St. Anselm seems most of the time to be saying that the Will of Jesus Christ is merely a human will, and that its uprightness is a gift of grace, given by the Father to the man, Jesus. In fact, much of St. Anselm's difficulty in meeting Boso's statement at the end of I.8 arises from this very view. How can a human will be other than under the compulsion of obedience to the Divine Will? Yet, with the two-nature theory of the Person of Our Lord which St. Anselm accepts, it should have been possible—in fact, it would appear necessary—for him to say that Jesus Christ has uprightness of will *a se*, and not, as if it were another thing, *a Deo*.[9] His Will and God's Will are one, so that the obedience under which Jesus Christ is placed does not originate from outside Himself but is an inner compulsion, and free because self-originating. This position St. Anselm does state in I.10, but it comes almost as an afterthought and is not properly related to the difficulties he has been encountering in I.9, and of which it is his only proper solution.

(1.2.3.3) The turning-point in St. Anselm's argument, namely, his interpretation of the Will of God as being that He will not allow the human race to be saved unless man does something equal in value to that Death [10] which the *Deus-homo* suffers, is a statement which is quite meaningless at that stage of the book. It is a reference to the theory which he develops at I.21 and II.6 that the satisfaction for his sin to be offered by man to God must be something greater than all that is not God, and that the *Deus-homo* is the only Person Who can make such an offering. In effect, God enacts that, unless man can offer as satisfaction to Him for sins committed something which has the infinite value of the Death of Christ, an offering which man as sinner cannot make, then he will be denied salvation. The reference is at the same time of interest, for in Bk. II St. Anselm never *explicitly* says that the Death of Christ is greater in value than all that is not God, though the argument of Bk. I would have led us to expect this proposition. The introduction of so important a theme in such a casual and obscure manner is further evidence of the confusion of this whole chapter.

(1.2.3.4) Despite the complexities and even the self-contradictoriness of these views of St. Anselm's, they supply sufficient evidence to dispose of T. H. Hughes' criticism,[11] that satisfaction to God "must have come not from the sufferings and death of

Jesus, but from His willing surrender to the Divine Will and purpose, from His obedience to the consciousness of vocation from God and all this involved". Apart from the fact that in the paragraph from which this quotation is taken Hughes seems almost to equate satisfaction with contentment, and not to have any technical meaning in mind at all, to the confusion of his whole criticism, by failing to follow the tortuous route which St. Anselm's argument takes he has grossly oversimplified the Anselmic theory.

(1.3) When we continue in I.10, which purports to throw further light on this same theme of the relation of Christ's Will to that of the Father, we find that St. Anselm, while reaffirming previous accounts of the matter and advancing additional ones, does not yet solve Boso's problem. In fact, St. Anselm now states the several ways in which the Father may be said to have willed the Death of the Son:

(1.3.1) The Father, we are now told,[12] gives the Son the will to die, for, according to His humanity, He has not the will to act rightly—a step further than even Boso wanted to go. Once again St. Anselm seems to overlook completely the presence in Christ of a Divine nature; so far, in I.9 and I.10, he is mono-thelite in his interpretation of Christ's decision to die. This fact is explicitly stated later,[13] when "Christ's making Himself obedient unto Death" is presented as a perfect example of the free obedience of "the rational creature" who willingly follows God's Will for him. The part which the Divine nature plays in His choice of death is completely ignored at this stage, and the oversight is all the more serious in view of the importance which St. Anselm attaches to the presence of the Divine nature as giving *value* to the Death of Christ.

(1.3.2) Again,[14] the Father commanded the Son to die of His own free will, which almost makes an absurdity of the paradox of the Divine imperative and human freedom. Besides, his statement becomes unnecessary once the previous view—of the Father giving the upright Will to the Son—is accepted. That Will would by its nature be free, and it is therefore superfluous for God to require it to be free.

(1.3.3) God, adds St. Anselm, may be understood as willing the Death of Christ, on the one hand because He approves of the end which Christ seeks to accomplish thereby, namely the salvation of man, and on the other hand because He does not actually prohibit Him from dying. These two interpretations of the manner in which God wills the Death of Christ come as an anticlimax after the others, and they follow from the distinction between the legislative and the permissive Will of God—a distinction later rejected so vigorously by Jean Calvin. Nor do they really solve Boso's problem, which was: does God will the Death of Christ, and, if so, is Christ's obedience free? St. Anselm is now saying that God wills Christ's Death *after* it takes place—a view which, if taken on its own as a full account of the matter, is a contradiction of what he has just said.

(1.3.4) It comes rather as a surprise that St. Anselm should suddenly at this point [15] introduce the omnipotence of Jesus Christ as a ground for His free acceptance of His Death in obedience to God's Will. Commenting upon St. John x. 19 f., where Our Lord says that He lays down His Life of Himself, because He has the power both to do so and to take it up again, St. Anselm sees the Death of Christ as issuing from the power and Will of Christ, and rightly affirms that it is freely willed by Christ, without any external compulsion. This view, while it is an essential part of St. Anselm's answer to Boso's problem, comes too late in the present discussion to be of any real value. For not only does St. Anselm not relate the Will of the Omnipotent Son to that of the "rational creature" in whom He is incarnate—he seems to be quite content with two totally separate wills which in no way interact—but, also, he does not integrate this explanation of Christ's freedom with the others already given. As the late Professor A. E. Taylor said in another connection, it savours somewhat of knocking his opponent down with the butt, having failed to discharge him with the bullets. It is rather significant that after St. Anselm's display of arguments Boso should repeat what he had said at I.8—that it is improper for God to permit the Son to die this kind of death, adding that the willingness of the Son does not reduce the impropriety. The motivating problem of the whole book then comes into focus: why should the Death of Christ be the only means by which man can be saved?

(1.4) At II.10 and II.11, after he has described the Person of Jesus Christ, and before he goes on to state the nature of His Death, St. Anselm returns to the question discussed at I.8-10, i.e. the voluntary nature of that Death. This discussion is the basis upon which the later analysis of the value of Christ's Death rests, for St. Anselm will show that Christ must offer to God something which He does not owe to God as a debt. That offering will be His own Death; therefore, it must be established that Christ died freely, and without any externally imposed compulsion to do so. His arguments this time, by comparison with those of I.8,10, are brief, and being a repetition of two already given, need only be stated. In II.10 he maintains that the voluntary nature of Christ's Death rests upon His sinlessness. It is only sinners who are obliged to die. If He dies, He dies freely and of His own choice. In II.11 the argument used late in II.11 is reaffirmed: since Christ was according to His Divine nature omnipotent, then He had power to lay down His Life and take it up again.

(1.5) But the theme of the voluntary nature of Christ's Death has a relentless hold on St. Anselm and he returns to it once more in II.16. This time the problem arises in relation to the sinlessness of Mary, the mother of Jesus. He has been maintaining [16] that Mary participated in the cleansing from sins accomplished by the Death of Christ, and that in that purity of hers He was born. It was necessary, so it would seem, that He should die to ensure the purity of His own birth of a virgin. St. Anselm takes the matter up at considerable length.

Repeating briefly the results of the discussion held in II.10 as to whether Christ could lie or not, namely that Christ could lie if He willed to lie, but because of His nature He does not will, and that the virtue involved in not lying springs from Himself (*a se*) and is not imposed on Him by any power beyond Himself, St. Anselm, arguing analogically, suggests that beyond doubt Christ could refrain from dying if He willed to, but He did not will to, and this "willing not to die" is *a se*. Accordingly, it was freely and not by any compulsion that He died. Boso [17] fails to understand how Christ has the will to die *a se*, and consequently St. Anselm has to expand his argument. The immutable Will of God is constrained by no necessity external to itself, and even, as was demonstrated in II.5, when He appears to act necessarily because of some promise which He has made, He acts freely in the first instance in making the promise. The *Deus-homo* is one with God as regards His Divinity. Christ's Will has the same characteristic as God's Will. It acts of its own power, and without constraint from anybody. Therefore, His Will to die is self-originating and free. In other words, He has the volition to die *a se*. Boso still steadfastly refuses [18] to see how Christ did not die of necessity, and endeavours to turn the dialectic against St. Anselm by arguing that, if Christ were free to die, He was free not to die, and free therefore to make a true statement (namely, that He had willed immutably to die) false. St. Anselm, after charging Boso with boggling over nothing, sets out afresh at II.17 to show how the categories of necessity and impossibility are inapplicable to God.[19] What is true of God from eternity to eternity is true also both of the nature and of the Will of the *Deus-homo*. When it is affirmed that Christ could not but die, no inference is to be drawn that He was impotent to continue in life, but rather that, He having willed to die, nothing could constrain that immutable Will to change. Even the Virgin herself, accepting the prophecy of Isa. liii. 9, believed that He died solely because He willed to die.

St. Anselm now, as a result of his reference to prophecy, endeavours to show that the existence of a prophetic statement concerning Christ's Death does not compel Him necessarily to die. He employs Aristotle's distinction [20] between prior (*praecedens*) and posterior (*sequens*) necessity, the former efficient and causative, the latter not effecting anything, but merely occurring as in itself an effect. The former is illustrated in such a statement as: "The sky revolves because it is necessary that it should do so," [21] and the latter in such a statement as: "You talk of necessity because you talk." The distinction could be stated more formally, in this way: an example of the first kind of necessity is, "A occurs because it is necessary that it should occur," and of the second, "It is necessary that B should occur because it occurs." In the former case the occurrence is a deduction from the necessity, and in the latter the necessity is a deduction from the occurrence. Natural events in the physical order obey the former necessity; the latter applies to acts of human volition, which issue spontaneously from the will and are not determined by anything outside of themselves, and, St. Anselm adds, include the singular and future propositions mentioned by Aristotle.[22] In the *De Concordia* [23] St. Anselm, discussing the question of whether God's foreknowledge of human action affects the freedom of the persons acting, employs this same distinction in order to affirm that what God foreknows is the posterior necessity, and that His foreknowledge does not imply prior necessity. While he uses the same distinction, he illustrates it in a somewhat different way, which clarifies further the description given in the *Cur Deus Homo*. "A stick is not always necessarily white, for at some time before it was white it could not have been white." [24] But a white stick is at the moment of its being white necessarily white, because neither before nor after it was white could it be at the same time both white and not white.[25] What, in fact, St. Anselm here affirms as a form of necessity is the Law of Contradiction. A cannot be both B and not-B at the same time, and necessity attaches to this impossibility. He goes on to apply this interpretation to past, present and future, saying, in effect, that pastness is necessarily a characteristic of past events, and so on for present and future. When this *De Concordia* illustration is used in the interpretation of the example of posterior necessity in the *Cur Deus Homo*, then that example is to be understood thus: "You talk of necessity because you talk; for it is impossible that you should be both talking and not talking at the same time." Of course, it is doubtful whether this posterior necessity is properly called necessity at all—though the problem becomes nominal once we discover what St. Anselm is endeavouring to say. The *De Concordia* illustration is inadequate, on the other hand, in so far as it employs an inanimate object rather than a human will to show how posterior necessity operates.

To return, then, to the relation of prophecy to the Death of Christ. In the *Cur Deus Homo* St. Anselm concludes that the relation is not one of prior necessity, as Boso is trying to say, but of posterior necessity, because the Death of Christ originates from His Will and is freely chosen by Him. If the significance of the analogy of the *De Concordia* may be drawn out: just as there is in the nature of whiteness itself—apart from what the stick may or may not have been in the past—that which necessarily prevents a stick from being both white and not white at the same time, and since it is white, it is necessarily so and necessarily not other than white, so the necessity for Christ's Death is to be discovered not in any circumstances beyond Himself, particularly in past prophecies which compel Him to die by prior necessity, but in the nature of His Will itself. "No necessity preceded His Will." [26] To complete the argument: "Christ died; therefore prophecies concerning His Death were necessarily true" is the true statement. The false one is: "The prophecies were true; therefore they made Christ's Death necessary."

Much of this discussion of the voluntary nature of the Death of Christ covers ground that is now familiar, but certain features of it require closer examination:

(1.5.1) In contrast to the arguments he used in I.8-10, St. Anselm is now basing the voluntariness of Christ's Death almost exclusively on His Divine nature, and on the fact that His Will has the same characteristics as that of God Himself. It was only late in I.10 that he took account of the Divine nature of the *Deus-homo*, and then it was the idea of omnipotence (mentioned also at II.11) and not that of *aseitas* that provided the solution. It is clear that much of Boso's difficulty at II.16 and 17 arises from the facts that previously St. Anselm has been talking of the will of the rational creature, of the *humanitas* of Christ's Person, and that he does not now attempt in the slightest way to show how the will of the rational creature is integrated with or overcome by the Will of the *Divinitas*. It undoubtedly does credit to St. Anselm's honesty as a thinker that he should repeat so frequently Boso's objections, and his doing so is an indication that he is well aware of all the difficulties involved in saying that the Will of the Eternal Son Incarnate is identical with the Will of God Eternal. Once again he anticipates later developments in Christological thought, for Boso's objections, if followed to logical conclusions, would lead to the depotentiated Logos of Kenoticism. But St. Anselm is clearly aware that the difficulties attendant upon such a view—for example, concerning the nature of the "freedom" of

Christ in choosing death—are greater than those encountered by his own position, that the Will of the *Deus-homo* is the Will of God.

(1.5.2) The arguments provided in II.16,17, are further evidence of the supreme importance in the theology of St. Anselm of the concept of the *aseitas* of God. It is not quite accurate to describe this concept as an attribute of God, for it is essential to all of His attributes, and even seems to determine the form which they take. For example, his interpretation of God's omnipotence is based entirely on this idea. It is, therefore, a description of God's entire nature, and just as it is often said that God is identical with His attributes—for example, that God is Love, rather than loving —so it is perhaps truer still to say that God's nature *is aseitas*. It is not easy to find any single word to translate this, for it represents a number of English ideas: self-sufficiency (for example, at II.18, p. 129, Jesus Christ is said to be *perfecte sibi sufficiens* in His Divine nature), independence, self-origination in volition, freedom and, above all, grace and graciousness. The concept is, as we should expect, to be found influencing most of St. Anselm's accounts of God and of His actions: it enters into his description of God's grace, of God's initiative in purposing man's salvation, of His volitional acts, of Christ's sinlessness and that of the angels, and of Christ's decision to die, while it affects, too, his analysis of human behaviour. Significantly enough, it is the argument based upon the *aseitas* of God which finally silences the indomitable Boso, and would appear, therefore, to be the argument which St. Anselm considered the strongest of all. Allowing, as was previously mentioned, that he does not seriously consider how the Divine Will is related to the human will in Jesus Christ, we may say that it is the argument which is most convincing to the modern theologian who seeks in God Himself the grounds for His actions and finds in Him the criterion of revelation.

(1.5.3) By introducing the distinction between prior and posterior necessity St. Anselm really contributes nothing to his immediate argument which is not already implicit in the notion of *aseitas*. Besides, he makes the task of his interpreter more difficult by equating the distinction between these two types of necessity with that between causal necessity and spontaneous

human volition, and virtually with that between universal propositions on the one hand, and singular and future propositions
on the other.   In the end he has to return anyway to the notion
of *aseitas* to account for the fact that it is posterior and not prior
necessity that attaches to Christ's Will: He died because He
willed to die, and no prior necessity compelled him.

Unsatisfactory as this philosophical excursus is, it does throw
light obliquely on St. Anselm's conception of his whole task in
writing concerning *Cur Deus Homo*.   In establishing the reasons
why there should be a God-man he is not thinking of logical
premises which, as it were, causally compelled God to become
man, of a prior necessity which determined God to act in this
way and in no other, so that, given the premises or knowledge of
this necessity, we could have forecast the Incarnation.   It is
posterior necessity which attaches to the Incarnation, because,
God having willed it, His Will is free.   The Incarnation took
place, therefore it was necessary that it should take place; and not
—it took place because it was necessary that it should take place.
When, therefore, we seek the reasons for the Incarnation, we do
so remembering that these did not compel God to act as He did,
for His volition was *a se* and spontaneous.   But we are wise after
the event, and being so we look for the posterior necessity.   It is
by setting St. Anselm's distinction in this wider context that we
understand what it really means.   In natural occurrences, if we
know antecedents *a b c d . . . n*, we can deduce that event *x* will
occur in accordance with certain previously known established
causal laws.   In situations where human volitions are involved,
even if we know *a b c d . . . n*, we do *not* know that *x* will necessarily occur, for we do not know whether the agent will will to
act in just that way; the friends whom we know best not infrequently act out of character.   It is the will of the agent, which
up to the moment of his acting is not fully knowable, which
determines the event.   Now St. Anselm does not deny that even
in situations in which human agents act, antecedents *a b c d . . . n*
are present, and to that extent he is not a complete voluntarist in
ethical psychology.   He does deny that the event is explicable
purely in terms of *a b c d . . . n* as its complete cause; its "real
necessity" (his phrase) lies in the will of the agent.   So, when he
examines why God became man, he can hold, on the one hand,

that this decision issues spontaneously from God's Will, and, on the other hand, that the antecedents *a b c d . . . n* (God's purpose in creating man, man's disobedience and sin, the replacement of the fallen angels by man, the need for satisfaction to be made by a God-man, and so on) may be investigated and set down at length.   Had St. Anselm held that the Will of God was alone relevant to the Incarnation, and that the Incarnation was unrelated to any antecedents, then he would not have written this work. By regarding the antecedents as related to the Incarnation by a posterior necessity, he establishes at one and the same time the facts that this Event issued from the Will of God, and that, nevertheless, it took its form from the circumstances in relation to which it occurred.

(1.5.4) It is noteworthy that Harnack,[27] largely again following Ritschl, has ignored the significance of the arguments of II.16 to prove the voluntary nature of Christ's Death, and the place of the notion of *aseitas* in that argument.   Instead he sees, on the one hand, St. Anselm's attempts at proving the freedom of the man in the God-man, and, on the other, the contradictions in which he is involved in this proof; for example, that this Man, like all rational creatures, must in all His actions, including His Death, seek the honour of God in full obedience, and therefore cannot die freely.   But, as we have seen, St. Anselm, by his continued return to the question of the voluntary nature of Christ's Death, reveals his own dissatisfaction with the earlier arguments, and he makes it plain that when advancing the case in which he really believes he bases Christ's freedom upon His *Divinitas* and, more particularly, upon His *aseitas*.   It is doubtful, then, whether these earlier accounts are properly described as contradictions: they are rather first approximations at an answer, tentative solutions of a problem, and their inadequacy is to be seen—by us, as it was by St. Anselm himself—in the light of his maturest judgment.   Harnack's ignoring of the notion of *aseitas* in St. Anselm, and of the emphasis laid by him upon the Divine nature in describing the true character of Christ's freedom in dying, is to be explained, but not justified, by his desire to interpret St. Anselm as holding "that it was the *man* Jesus who died and that he is our Mediator".[28]

2

When we come to examine the theme of "the value of Christ's Death", we are approaching the climax of St. Anselm's argument in the *Cur Deus Homo*, and it is characteristic of this book, though not of his other works, that he should condense his arguments into a chapter and a half—II.11 and II.14. Once again the brevity creates difficulties which could easily have been resolved had he seen fit to give to this subject the extended study which he allows to others less important. In establishing the value of the Death of Christ St. Anselm endeavours to answer two questions: the first,[29] why the Death of the *Deus-homo* should be especially valuable and acceptable in God's sight; the second,[30] why the offering made in this Death should outweigh the sins committed by man for which the *Deus-homo* is required to make satisfaction.

(2.1) The answer to the first question follows very swiftly from those premises to which St. Anselm has argued in other parts of the book. The first is that an offering must be made which will satisfy the honour of God. The need for satisfaction was the case made in I.11,12,19, etc., as the only alternative to punishment, which meant annihilation for the sinner. The second premise is that this satisfaction can only take the form of an offering which is greater than everything that is not God, or is less than God, or is under God.[31] This offering the *Deus-homo* must make from Himself, for nothing outside of Himself will be of sufficiently great value. To give Himself, in obedient living, to God is not adequate either, for such is the debt which every rational creature owes to God. It is only by giving Himself to death for the sake of God's honour that He makes sufficient satisfaction to God. This offering He can make because He is without sin, and not under the necessity of death. There, then, is the third premise of the argument: this offering which Christ makes, He makes completely freely.[32] It is only by dying of His own free will that the *Deus-homo* can make to God sufficiently great satisfaction for the dishonour done to God by man in sinning. Such is the central core of the argument, but St. Anselm complicates it both near the beginning and towards the end. Early

in the argument, after stating the first premise mentioned above
and saying that the *Deus-homo* must offer Himself or something
from Himself, he writes,[33] "He will not be able to give Himself
or anything from Himself to God, as if to someone who did not
have it, so that it might become His own, since every creature
belongs to God." This sentence is difficult in many ways. It
contradicts the immediately previous speech of "Anselm". It
suggests that the *Deus-homo* is a creature whose relation to God
is the same as that of other creatures—a suggestion which is
reaffirmed two speeches later [34] and one which misrepresents St.
Anselm's conception of the Person of Jesus Christ. Moreover,
it would, if taken literally, stultify the remainder of his argument,
for it implies that the creature cannot give to God anything which
is not already God's, and that this man cannot, therefore, offer
to God even His Death. In fact, this sentence, taken with that
of two speeches later, together lay St. Anselm open to the charge
that he regards Christ as a *man* in His Life, and as *God-man* in
His Death. The only possible interpretation of the sentence
under debate which will integrate it with the previous speech
could be stated thus: The offering of Himself, or of something
from Himself, which the *Deus-homo* makes to God is of a kind
different from that made by "every creature", who because of
his creatureliness can only give to God what is already God's by
right. But, even so, this interpretation cannot be reconciled with
the words stated two speeches later, where the *Deus-homo* is said,
by obeying God in upright living, to be giving God what "every
rational creature" owes to God. The conclusion seems inevitable
that the sentence cannot, as it stands, be rationalised. The solid
presence of the clause, *quoniam omnis creatura Dei est*, makes any
simple textual adjustment well-nigh impossible, and there the
matter must rest.

The other complication of the argument offered by St. Anselm
to account for Christ's Death comes when he discusses [35] the
"rational fittingness" of the *death* of the person making satisfaction to God. The argument he offers is analogical and it consists of several consecutive questions which make the same point.
If man sinned out of self-indulgence, is it not fitting that he should
make satisfaction to God in suffering? If, allowing the Devil
to conquer him, he dishonoured God, is it not right that he should

satisfy God's honour by conquering the Devil? Is it not seemly that he who removed himself as far as possible from God by his sin should make the maximum self-surrender to God, by way of satisfaction? Man can achieve this most difficult and most painful kind of satisfaction only if he gives himself to death for the sake of God's honour. The character of the argument implied by these questions must be carefully noted: it is not calculated to establish the logical necessity of Christ's Death. St. Anselm has already done so in the previous speeches of II.11. He is now saying that, given the necessity of Christ's Death, it may also be seen to be fitting and proper that He should die to make adequate satisfaction to God, but this fittingness and propriety are seen only by the believer, or by the person who has accepted the previous arguments. That is, a certain aesthetic quality attaches to the Death of Christ in St. Anselm's opinion, but the demonstration of that quality is not, in itself, sufficient to prove why Christ died.

Before proceeding to the examination of II.14, which is really the completion of the argument of II.11, and keeping in mind what have been called "the complications" of the argument, it is necessary at this point to make certain observations upon the position so far established.

(2.1.1) However sympathetic we try to be in the interpretation of the earlier "complication" of St. Anselm's argument, we cannot escape the conclusion that he has virtually thought of the *homo* in the *Deus-homo* as offering to God the satisfaction which He requires for man's sin. The repetition of the term *creatura* puts this criticism beyond all question. Why he should do so, when he has so carefully argued the case that the *Deus-homo* alone can offer satisfaction, is quite inexplicable. A perfect man could have done all that St. Anselm requires of the person making satisfaction, according to II.11. It would therefore appear difficult to see why St. Anselm [36] should have reminded us that the offering made to God in satisfaction should be greater than anything apart from God, for the logical sequel to that reminder is to say that the *Deus-homo* alone can make such an offering. Certainly no creature can make it, yet it is with the offering of the "rational creature" that St. Anselm deals as his argument develops.

no Incarnation

(2.1.2) Having said that "reason taught" us that the satisfaction to be made to God for man's sin must exceed all that is not God, St. Anselm makes no attempt within this present chapter to show how the offering made by Christ in His Death is of just that value. Now he does return to this question in II.14, but some indication of the connection between the two facts is necessary at II.11, for otherwise that argument consists of a premise from which no conclusion is shown to follow.

(2.1.3) Further, St. Anselm rests his argument upon what is a very dangerous distinction between the kind of obedience which Christ showed in His Life and the relation in which He stood to God in His Death. The Holy Scriptures provide no ground for any such distinction; in fact, the evidence there provided is quite to the contrary, namely, that Christ's obedience to God, both in Life and in Death, formed one single pattern. St. Anselm seems here almost to hold that Christ's Death was not suffered in obedience to God's Will, and his soteriology would be the poorer for such an implication.

(2.1.4) It is, again, regrettable that the connection between sin and death is so fortuitous in St. Anselm's present presentation of his theory. The *Deus-homo* cannot offer up anything of His life to God as an adequate satisfaction; the alternative is that He offers His Death, which is a possible satisfaction, since being sinless He is not required to die. If any other offering would have been adequate, He could equally well have made it. There is no inner necessity which requires the Death of Christ *rather than* anything else as the proper satisfaction. The aesthetic arguments of the "second complication" really carry no weight in this matter, for they rest, for such logical strength as they have, upon the demonstration of the value of Christ's Death.

(2.1.5) Perhaps the most interesting feature of this argument of II.11 is the fact that, in order to establish the value of the *Death* of Christ (as against the life which He lived as a *creatura rationalis*, steadfastly obedient to the Will of God), he has to employ the notion of *supererogation*. The idea upon which the whole argument turns is that Christ in dying does something extra which God's Will does not enjoin, and which His own nature does not necessitate.   In other words, the notion of merit is intimately conjoined with that of satisfaction; in fact, the latter cannot be understood except in terms of the former.   It is especially important to take notice of this connection, for Ritschl's suggestion [37] that, at II.19, St. Anselm "substitutes for the idea of satisfaction the different one of merit" is quite inaccurate. Already at II.11 St. Anselm has used the two ideas together: it is because the *Deus-homo* is able to give God something which God does not require of Him (and so to establish "merit") that He can make the necessary satisfaction to God.

(2.1.6) As to the actual characterisation of the position which St. Anselm reaches in II.11, while St. Anselm does not draw his argument to any conclusive statement, we may fairly say that the position is one of vicarious or representative satisfaction.   The *Deus-homo*, as *homo* and representative of the human race, makes that offering to God for human sin which the race cannot make for itself.   If the word "substitution" were not so frequently used in the phrase "penal substitution"—and St. Anselm's theory cannot without considerable explanation be called "penal"—then the phrase "substitutionary satisfaction" would not be inappropriate.   Man ought to make the satisfaction, but the *Deus-homo* substitutes Himself for man and achieves that end to the honour of God.

(2.2) Having demonstrated that the Death of Christ is particularly valuable (or meritorious) in the sight of God, St. Anselm has now to face the question of how its value is sufficiently great to exceed the sins of all mankind and to render it the satisfaction which God requires.   In II.14 he endeavours to deal with this problem.   After the discussion, in II.12 and 13, of the topic of whether the *Deus-homo* shares in the infirmities and in the ignorance of ordinary mankind, Boso presses for an answer to the question: if, as was shown in I.21, a single glance contrary to the Will of God shall not be taken, even though an infinite number of worlds is to be saved thereby, how can the Death of the *Deus-homo* exceed the numerous and enormous sins of all mankind?

(2.2.1) The several steps of the argument demonstrate the logic St. Anselm adopts to reach his conclusion:

(2.2.1.1) He begins by compelling Boso's agreement to certain statements; for example, that he would not slay the *Deus-homo*, even if by so doing he could save from destruction everything that is not God, nor would he do Him the slightest hurt for that end.

(2.2.1.2) This "judgment of the heart" is justified on the ground that a sin done upon His Person immeasurably exceeds one conceived apart from Him.

(2.2.1.3) The problem then becomes: why is it that no sins (apart from sins done to the Person of God) can exceed the harm done to the bodily Life of this man? Or, how great a good is that (Life), the destruction of which is so evil?

(2.2.1.4) Goods are proportionate in their goodness to the evil of their destruction. If the evil of destroying that Life exceeds the mass of human sin as an evil, then that Life is an incomparably greater good than these sins are evil.

(2.2.1.5) Sins are despicable in proportion to their evil character and that Life of the *Deus-homo* is lovable in proportion to its goodness, and more lovable than the sins are despicable.

(2.2.1.6) Therefore, Christ's giving of this so good and so lovable Life (which is the equivalent of His receiving death) is sufficient to pay the debt owed for the sins of the whole world. This giving is said also to conquer all sins and to exceed them all in value—with the exception of sins that touch the Person of God.

(2.2.2) While it is necessary, for the purposes of the fuller commentary which is to follow, to have the complete argument before us, it is possible to state it in a much condensed form, as follows: It is a moral and psychological impossibility to contemplate the committing of any hurt to Christ, even to save the whole world from its sins. One sin done in hurt to Christ exceeds all other sins. Therefore, His Life is so incomparably great a good that it surpasses all human sins; and when offered to God in Christ's acceptance of death it pays off the debt resulting from human sin. Let us, then, examine the argument more closely:

(2.2.2.1) St. Anselm takes as his premise a psychological judgment—*cor tuum indicat* [38]—as to the evil of doing bodily harm to Christ, and draws a conclusion about how great a good His Life is as an offering to God. Here he has committed the fallacy of *hysteron-proteron*. We judge it repugnant to do bodily harm to Christ, because we know how good and lovable He is, and it is incorrect to argue that His Life is an incomparably great good because we are unable to think of doing Him hurt. So, too, it is a prior truth that the evil involved in the destruction of goods is proportionate to their goodness, and not the reverse. Having mentioned the impossibility of our doing Christ bodily harm, St. Anselm would have been expected to add that this impossibility springs from our knowledge of Who He is, the *Deus-homo* —an expectation created by his elaborate analysis [39] of the moral qualities of the *Deus-homo*. The purely psychological premise from which he commences is grossly inadequate to support the important conclusion which he endeavours to draw from it.

(2.2.2.2) It is difficult to reconcile what St. Anselm says in this chapter about the "great goodness" of the Life of Christ with his remarks in II.11, that in abiding steadfastly in righteousness, He gives to God only that which God requires of Him as a due debt. His Life as such has no special merit, for we must interpret it in terms of deeds done and words spoken, and in these terms it cannot be an offering (*datio*) adequate to satisfy the honour of God. There must be something more involved in the *acceptio mortis* than there is in the *datio vitae*, and St. Anselm, by identifying the two, has obscured the real point at issue, which is: why is a peculiar, additional value to be attached to the Death of Christ which is not found simply in His Life? Two answers to this question are possible. The customarily accepted view is that answer can only be given once we establish an internal relation between human sin and Christ's Death, and that St. Anselm's failure to establish that relation amounts to a virtual breakdown of his argument at this, perhaps its most important, turning-point. On the other hand, and this is the view for which we shall later argue,[40] St. Anselm may revise his contention that Christ owes God His Life but is free to die, and say that because of His *aseitas*, that important attribute of the Divine nature of which St. Anselm makes so much in this work, all that Christ does, in Life or Death,

is done freely. The *datio vitae* then becomes the offering of something that has abundant merit in the sight of God.

(2.2.2.3) On two occasions during the argument [41] St. Anselm
refers to sins done against the Person of God—on the first, saying
that no sins except one done to the Person of God exceed violation
of Christ's physical body, and, on the second, that Christ's accepting of death outweighs all the sins of men which do not affect the
Person of God. The first reference is in line with the general
trend of the discussion, but the second raises queries. The sins
for which satisfaction must be made by the *Deus-homo are* sins
done to the Person of God; why, therefore, should St. Anselm
suggest that these are to be excluded from the number which the
Death of Christ exceeds in value? And how, if they are excluded,
can the Death of Christ be regarded as adequate satisfaction?
The answer to the latter question is that the Death of Christ
would not be adequate satisfaction under such circumstances,
and that, therefore, St. Anselm has not yet solved his problem of
how the Death of Christ exceeds the many sins of mankind, for
the chief sins for which satisfaction ought to be made are, as he
has so extensively shown in Bk. I, those which dishonour God
and do injustice to His Person. The answer to the former
question is to be found in the fact that St. Anselm has been
deceived by his own argumentation. Thus, from the premise:
a sin done in hurt to Christ is greater than all the sins done apart
from His Person, with the exception of sins done to the Person of
God (a true statement, for hurt done to Christ is a sin against the
Person of God), he concludes that the Death of Christ (the offering
of the "great good" of His Life) exceeds, and therefore makes
satisfaction for, all the sins committed by men, with the exception
of sins done to the Person of God (a statement which contradicts
what he has said several times previously,[42] that the offering of
Christ's Life is sufficient to remove the debt owed as a result of
the sins of the whole world—*totius mundi*—and one which does
not follow self-evidently from the premise). St. Anselm's argument on this point is most unsatisfactory.

(2.2.2.4) In interpreting the relation between II.11 and II.14
we have maintained that the former depends on the latter for its
completion. II.11 is designed to prove that the Death of Christ

exceeds the sins of men, and II.14 to show how it exceeds them. The upshot is that II.14 fails in its purpose, and, in fact, yields the opposite result, that the Death of Christ is not sufficient to remove those sins for which satisfaction is most urgently required, namely, injustices against the Person of God.

(2.3) Before proceeding to the third theme it is necessary to deal briefly with a subject which is related to both the second and the third themes, namely, how the Death of Christ is effectual for the salvation of those who were not alive at the time of His Death. The subject is dealt with in II.16.[43] The problem is solved by means of an illustration. A king is so offended by all his subjects that he requires of them the penalty of death. One person, however, who is innocent and beloved of the king, promises to reconcile all the guilty people, who will accept his counsel, by some outstanding service on a date fixed by the king. Whoever is unable to be present on that date is, nevertheless, not cut off from pardon, for he may plead the deed at any time before or after its occurrence as a basis for forgiveness for all past sins. Should it happen that any, after receiving forgiveness, should again fall into error, then, provided they make worthy satisfaction and mend their ways, they will again receive pardon through the efficacy of the same covenant. In the same way, the efficacy of the Death of Christ extends beyond His contemporaries. This brief analogical argument has certain noteworthy features:

(2.3.1) To begin with, St. Anselm has rightly drawn attention to the universal efficacy in time and space of the Death of Christ, and of the Atonement achieved by Him. He sees the Death of Christ as the basis of all the forgiveness which God has offered to men in history—not only after Christ but also before Him, and he insists on the latter because he is anxious to ensure the purity of the Virgin of whom Jesus was born.

(2.3.2) It must not be held against St. Anselm that he speaks of the man who sins after receiving forgiveness as required to make worthy satisfaction. No doubt the satisfaction which St. Anselm has in mind is that of the penitential system: penitence, fastings, bodily labours (cf. I.20). But he cannot be thought, as a result, to be accepting these as adequate for man's redemption, and to be renouncing the views of I.20. On the contrary, he is plainly speaking of the man who has already received forgiveness through the efficacy of the covenant. Such a person, he says quite rightly, must produce evidence of his contrition and new resolve to be a better man; the word *satisfacere* [44] carries no further implication. In addition, this satisfaction is offered only through "the efficacy of the covenant", and the forgiveness which ensues comes not simply as a result of the satisfaction but through the continuing efficacy of that covenant. Aulén completely misses the point when he writes [45] that, as regards penance for sins committed after Baptism, "Anselm, like other Latin theologians, allows that men can earn merit in God's sight". That is just where St. Anselm is completely and characteristically different from "other Latin theologians". St. Anselm's views are here both theologically sound and practically realistic: on the one hand, he recognises that the penitential practices do not of themselves remove the debt owed to God for human sin—only the *Deus-homo* can do that; on the other hand, he is well aware that even the redeemed man lapses into sin, that he requires the disciplines of fasting and bodily labours as the vehicles of contrition, and that in submitting to these disciplines he is not establishing any rights to forgiveness, for forgiveness is made effectual only through the efficacy of the covenant established between the king and his beloved subject.

(2.3.3) It is clear, then, that St. Anselm corrects the dangerously false theology at the basis of the penitential system, but he is also most explicit where Tertullian, at the best, only leaves us guessing. In the *De Poenitentia* Tertullian fails to relate penitence after baptism, the subject concerning which the work is written, to the Atonement wrought by God in Christ, whereby, consequent upon penitence, forgiveness of sins is possible for sinners. He even suggests in c. 5 that the original penitence after which the sinner receives his first forgiveness is itself satisfaction offered to God. Admittedly, St. Anselm uses the word *satisfacere*, as we have already observed, in relation to penitence after the first forgiveness of sins, but nowhere does he suggest, as does Tertullian, that the original forgiveness was offered as a result of penitence which in itself satisfied God. It is easy to see how a

suggestion such as Tertullian's, which regards penitence as itself
the satisfaction required by God in order that He should forgive
sins, could develop into the excesses of the penitential system,
and to a neglect of emphasis upon the Work of Christ as the condition, not only of forgiveness, but also of repentance itself. St.
Anselm, with his simple illustration of the king, his rebellious
subjects and the beloved subject, integrates sanctification with
justification, and is never in danger of confusing the former with
the latter, or *vice versa.*

3

In passing to the third theme of St. Anselm's presentation of
his soteriological scheme, namely, the application of the merits
of the Death of Christ, we must first state his case as he conceives
it,[46] returning in our commentary to discuss the question of the
relation of his treatment of this theme to that of the previous one.
His main intention is to demonstrate in what way the merits
achieved by Christ in dying, freely and without obligation to God
to do so, are made available for men, who owe to God an infinite
debt for their sins against Him. Affirming [47] that St. Anselm has
already sufficiently clearly proved the immeasurable value of the
Life of Christ as payment for the debt created by human sin,
Boso asks his teacher to show *in what way* it is adequate payment
for human sin. The *that* has been established; the *how* is yet to
be proved.

(3.1) After a preliminary objection by Boso concerning the value
of Christ's Death as an example of adherence to righteousness
in the face of persecution, on the ground that many others have
set such an example apart from Christ, and St. Anselm's reply
that none apart from Christ has done so *freely*, the argument
settles down to a discussion of whether Christ did not really owe
His Death to God, once He knew that that was what was most
pleasing in God's sight. The general principle cited by Boso
is that every creature owes to God all that he is and knows and
is capable of achieving.[48] In developing the discussion, St.
Anselm in effect takes two lines: the first being of great importance for the view which he will finally present of the value of
Christ's Death for sinners; the second being a parallel argument

to those he presented concerning the application of the notions of "impossibility" and "necessity" to God's actions.[49] We shall deal with the two lines in St. Anselm's order.

(3.1.1) In the Christian life there arise from time to time moral situations in which the Christian is faced with two alternative courses of action, either of which is morally permissible, and neither of which is definitely commanded by the moral law, though one is better and more acceptable in God's sight; for example, virginity and marriage. From this distinction St. Anselm draws two inferences. On the one hand, the person who chooses virginity, say, may legitimately expect some reward from God for doing what is in excess of duty, and it is to be remembered that St. Anselm is here referring to creatures, and not to the *Deus-homo* specifically.[50] This inference is taken up again in relation to Christ's Death in II.19. On the other hand, once the person has made his preference, say in favour of virginity as before, then it may fairly be held that he *ought* to pursue that course—a view which leads on to the examination of the notion of "oughtness" as applied to God's actions. When, therefore, it is said that a man owes as a debt to God (or "ought" to take) a certain course of action, which represents his maximum and optimum of achievement, the statement is true only with the qualification that only when God actually *wills* such a course is it owed to God. If God does not will it, then the term "ought" is applied in the secondary sense already mentioned: a man ought to abide by his decision once he has made it, though he ought not necessarily to make that decision rather than the other, equally permissible under God's Will.

(3.1.2) The treatment of "oughtness" in reference to God's actions takes a form which is now familiar. It belongs to God to make or not to make creatures, but once He has decided to create, then He ought to abide by that decision. It is an "oughtness" which springs *a se* and is not imposed on Him from without. In the same way, it belonged to Christ to die or not to die, but once He had made His decision, then He was bound to achieve what He willed. In respect of His Divine nature, Christ is self-sufficient and under debt to no one, so that He requires to render nothing to any person. His decision to die arises from Himself [51] and He is free in His choice of death; but once He has made His choice, He is bound by it.

(3.2) The way is now prepared for what is, in effect, the final argument of the *Cur Deus Homo*.[52]   Other statements are made in the remaining chapters but no major addition is made to the position now reached.   As St. Anselm himself says: "Let us now observe by how convincing an argument human salvation can be deduced from these premises."[53]   The Son, by reason of His free Death which He offered to God as a gift, must needs be recompensed by God for this great deed.   But since all that is the Father's is His also, and since, too, He has committed no sins which God might forgive in return for this gift and thus cancel the debt to God created by them, the question arises of how God can make recompense for the Death of Christ.   The answer given by St. Anselm is that God makes over the reward to those for whose salvation the Son became man, and to whom He held up the example of persisting in righteousness even unto death.   When this transaction is completed, the sinful men are forgiven the debts they owe, for they are given that which by reason of their sins they lacked.   Concerning the achievement of participation in such grace and the manner in which he is to live by it, Holy Scriptures everywhere provide instruction.

(3.3) Most of the important aspects of this third theme of St. Anselm's emerge from a comparison of it with the previous theme, as follows:

(3.3.1) Against Ritschl's suggestion[54] that it represents an alternative account of the nature of Christ's Death—a subtle change from the notion of satisfaction to that of merit—we must insist that his third theme is a development of the second.   At II.14, where the second theme is completed, we are assured that the "great good" of the Death of Christ is adequate to remove the debt of human sin.   At II.18,19, we are shown how in fact it comes about that the offering made by Christ can redound to the good of sinful men.   We have already seen how "vicarious satisfaction" seems to be a fair description of the view given in II.14.   In II.18,19,[55] St. Anselm uses the term *satisfactio* but once—which fact may lend a *prima facie* plausibility to Ritschl's

case—and, on this occasion, in a recapitulatory speech which is
not closely related to the rest of the argument of the chapter.
But he does use the notions of debt, payment and cancellation
(or forgiveness), which clearly indicate that he is still within the
realm of discourse of satisfaction. The comparison of II.11 with
II.14 has already yielded the conclusion that the notion of satisfaction requires that of merit for its completion; the final speeches
of II.19 show that the merits won by Christ would be vain if not
diverted to the purpose of paying man's debt to God incurred by
his sinning. That is, satisfaction without merit would be impossible; merit without satisfaction would be purposeless. In any
case, while satisfaction is not mentioned in II.18, it clearly under-
lies the whole of the introductory speeches.

At a first glance, also, the notion of "vicariousness" seems to
be absent from this third theme. In II.19 particularly, the
situation is not that Christ offers His Death to God on behalf of,
or in the stead of, man for his sin, but rather that Christ offers
His Death to God as a gift which He is not required to give,
whereupon God makes over to Christ's brethren the reward due
to Christ. The final stage of the transaction, in which men pay
back the gift to God, for they have not anything else with which
to pay, is left unstated but definitely implied. It is not just to
say that St. Anselm has abandoned vicariousness for some totally
different conception of Christ's offering of His Death to God;
it is much nearer the truth to hold that St. Anselm, by the more
extensive description, is endeavouring to show how "vicariousness" works, how it is effectual unto the cancelling of the debt
of human sin. Conceived of in this way, II.18,19 present a
development of the themes of "vicarious satisfaction" and
"merit", and provide fuller evidence of how the two are insepar-
ably related in St. Anselm's soteriology.

(3.3.2) Harnack [56] follows Ritschl in making the same mistake
of failing to see the connection between merit and satisfaction
in the Anselmic scheme. "If God's suffering establishes *merit*,
it does not contain strict reparation; but if it contains satisfaction
it establishes no merit." His general contention is that merit
is foreign to the satisfaction theory. In this view Harnack shows
himself curiously unaware of the long association of merit and

satisfaction in, for example, Tertullian, but still more conspicuously in the penance system, and of the consequence that merit had become in fact part of the satisfaction theory.   But more strictly in St. Anselm Christ's suffering establishes merit, the reward for which is received not by Christ but by the sinners, who need that very thing to make adequate satisfaction (reparation) to God; and it contains vicarious satisfaction just because it establishes merit.   Harnack's contention is admittedly true superficially, and if held without any close examination of how St. Anselm has worked out his theory: it is that if Christ by His Death is engaged in making satisfaction, then He is paying what is owed to God, and is not establishing merit.   St. Anselm's problem, as we have seen, is the slightly different one: how *is* Christ able to make satisfaction and how does vicariousness work ? His answer is: by Christ's establishing merit which is transferred to sinners.   It is quite wrong for Harnack to say [57] that St. Anselm passes beyond his theory of satisfaction when he deals with the merit of Christ, for the third theme of his soteriological argument is an essential development of the second, both merit and satisfaction being involved in the two arguments, as the text both indicates and implies.

(3.3.3) Franks [58] uses this same line of thought to make a different criticism of St. Anselm.   "If Christ's satisfaction only exactly purchases the remission of sins, it is clear that there can be no superfluous merit to win eternal life." [59]   Franks gives us no indication either as to the textual source in St. Anselm of his premise, or as to the relevance of the conclusion to St. Anselm's theory of Atonement.   Nowhere does St. Anselm speak of Christ's Death *exactly* purchasing remission of sins: exact quantities are alien to his description of the value of Christ's Death.   On the other hand, it is doubtful whether Franks' conclusion would trouble St. Anselm at all.   His position has been that sin has prevented man from fulfilling that destiny which God intended for him when He first created him.   Once proper satisfaction is made for that sin, the way is open for God to fulfil in man His purpose for him, a purpose which would include eternal life, in addition to other things which St. Anselm specifically mentions, such as everlasting happiness and enjoyment of Himself.   Satisfaction, by removing the debt of sin, secures for him the other ends which God intended for him. St. Anselm is not like the Greek Fathers, exclusively interested in the Death of Christ as the basis or source of eternal life, and Franks' statement amounts almost to a criticism of St. Anselm for being a Latin and not a Greek theologian!

(3.3.4) The treatment of this third theme corrects what we discovered to be a major defect in the second. There we saw [60] that St. Anselm, by speaking on two occasions, in II.11, of the *creatura*, who makes to God in death an offering not required of him by God as a debt, gives the impression that it is the *homo* in the *Deus-homo* who makes the satisfaction to God; and that, in II.14, he did not draw upon his view of the moral character of the *Deus-homo* to prove why His Life and Death should have sufficient value to conquer the sins of mankind. Continuing for a time in this same strain in II.18, and still using the word *creatura*,[61] St. Anselm eventually makes it clear that it is the *Deus-homo* Who offers to God the gift of excess merit, and that He is able to do so because He has all things *a se*. In respect of His Divine nature He owes no one anything at any time; He is self-sufficient. The excess merit through which adequate satisfaction can be made to God for human sin originates in the Person of the *Deus-homo*. It is both interesting and important that St. Anselm should produce this account of the nature and value of Christ's Death as his final argument, for the following reasons:

(3.3.4.1) It justifies the lengthy discussion which St. Anselm had previously conducted on the Person of the *Deus-homo*. As already mentioned,[62] in II.11 and II.14, St. Anselm seemed almost to affirm that the excess merit required to cancel the debt due to God as a result of human sin could be achieved by a perfectly good man, who was under no necessity to die, and who could therefore offer to God the gift of His Death. At that stage the analysis of the Person of Jesus Christ appeared to have been unnecessary. Now it is clearly stated that the value of the Death of Christ derives from the value of His Person. *Only* the *Deus-homo* could achieve this excess of merit.

(3.3.4.2) St. Anselm's transition to emphasis upon the importance of the Divine nature of Jesus Christ within his scheme, and his use at that point once again of the notion of *aseitas*, are parallel to his method of treatment of the *freedom* of Christ in electing to die for mankind. There the argument based on *aseitas* finally settled the doubts of Boso; here, when St. Anselm has used the concept *a se* in yet another reference, namely, to show how it is through the merits of Christ that men are saved, Boso exclaims: "Nothing more reasonable, acceptable or desirable, could the world hear." [63] In both cases it would be wrong to suggest that the production of the concept so late in the argument was accidental. The evidence to the contrary is too compelling. St. Anselm, having offered certain arguments which may be well received by some, but which he himself rejects, keeps his best wine until the end, and bases both the freedom of Christ in choosing to die and the merit which attaches to that Death upon the *aseitas* of the Divine nature. In both cases the final argument removes the difficulties which Boso and his readers feel to be inherent in the preliminary accounts of necessity and the merits of Christ's Death. For example, the difficulties raised by St. Anselm's statement[64] that the death of this man exceeds the sins of all mankind, except those that touch the Person of God, are removed when it is made clear that sins against the *Deus-homo* are sins against God, and that these are the very sins for which satisfaction is to be made and can be made. Also, in the treatment of the second theme of the soteriology, particularly at the end of II.14, the argument broke down because St. Anselm had not been able to show how *acceptio mortis* was particularly meritorious in the sight of God if it was identified with *datio vitae*, and that *vita* was one of obligatory righteousness. When the notion of *aseitas* is introduced, then whatever the *Deus-homo* does, in Life or Death, is full of merit, for He owes no one anything. If, therefore, we are anxious to find any difference between the second and third themes of St. Anselm's account of the Atonement, we must not, with Ritschl, Harnack and Franks, define it as a transition from satisfaction to merit; the real difference lies in the fact that in the former the notion of *aseitas* is absent, and in the latter it is present.

(3.3.4.3) We can now enforce more strongly that conclusion which was stated in our earlier discussion of the relation of *aseitas* to freedom in Christ,[65] the conclusion concerning the supreme importance of this concept in the Anselmic theology. We have already seen how it recurs in his treatment of many subjects; it appears now as the means by which St. Anselm solves the chief problems of his book—why Christ should die and how His Death accomplishes the salvation of sinners. It must therefore be maintained that this is the dominant idea of the whole book, and as such is to be regarded as regulative of St. Anselm's conception of God's nature—as justice, righteousness, mercy and love—and of God's actions in Creation and Redemption. As has already been upheld in Chapter Two, any analysis of the argumentation of the *Cur Deus Homo* which interprets it as simply an analogical inference from Teutonic law or early medieval penance-systems has missed the deeper significance of the work, for while analogies from these spheres are present, they are nevertheless set in subordination to the dominant notion of the *aseitas* of God, and in that setting are radically transformed. For that reason the *Cur Deus Homo* provides excellent proof of the close relation of St. Anselm's soteriology to his general theology, not only in methodology, but also in essential subject-matter.

4

On several occasions, in his discussions of his second and third themes, St. Anselm introduces the idea of the Death of Christ as an example of steadfast perseverance in the way of righteousness, no matter the misery or the suffering which it entails. The popular distinction is drawn between subjective and objective theories of Atonement, and it is therefore of interest that St. Anselm, who is normally presented as an exponent of the latter, should find a place within his scheme for the former kind of theory. The references are of two kinds:

(4.1) In II.11,[66] II.18,[67] the general contention is that the Death of Christ does not have only a God-ward reference, nor is its significance exhausted in the fact that Christ offers it up as a gift to God by way of private transaction. His Death is a public event, with, as it were, a horizontal reference. It provides an example of the price that is to be paid by those who earnestly seek to obey God's Will.

(4.2) In II.19 [68] a different emphasis appears: "In vain will men be imitators of His example (of dying for righteousness' sake) if they do not share in His merit." The difference is of importance, for in this sentence St. Anselm has criticised effectively all theories of the Atonement which find the full significance of the Death of Christ solely in its exemplary character. It is only redeemed man, man who has shared in the fruits of Christ's Work, who can begin to follow Christ's example, and who can make an offering acceptable to God. Unredeemed man is still so overwhelmed by the burden of debt that he knows nothing of the righteousness in which to persevere. In terms of the popular distinction, a subjective theory by itself is a mockery of man's condition, but it is not so totally false that it cannot find a place within a more complete account of the Atonement. That St. Anselm should observe this fact, and that he should anticipate later criticisms of subjective theories, does him great credit.

5

It must by this time be obvious that St. Anselm's *Cur Deus Homo* is one of the most severely criticised of all the important writings on the Atonement, and that the criticism comes from thinkers of every shade of thought. The major criticisms are reserved for that section of his work which we have just examined —his specific treatment of the Death of Christ. A source-criticism of the criticisms of the *Cur Deus Homo* is an interesting study, for arguments appear and reappear in the commentators, each mixing "the tradition" with his own private variations.[69] While, therefore, each produces a formidable list of fallacies, errors or demerits in the soteriology of St. Anselm, they are, because of repetition, reducible to a number much smaller than the aggregate.

(5.1) The most searching criticisms of St. Anselm are submitted by A. Harnack,[70] those of the other commentators being variations of, or deductions from, what Harnack had said.

(5.1.1) One of the earliest charges brought up by Harnack [71] is that St. Anselm is content with "the doctrine of salvation, as demonstrating the possibility of the redemption of the individual from sin". It carries no assurance, no *certitudo salutis*, to the distressed conscience of sinful men that they personally are redeemed. At the most, according to Harnack, St. Anselm says to *some* that if they live piously they will be saved, thus: "If thou fulfillest the commandments of Scripture, then the great provision of the God-man has an effect for thee."

On behalf of St. Anselm certain definite replies must be made to Harnack's charges:

(5.1.1.1) To begin with, it is wrong to say that St. Anselm demonstrates only "the possibility of the individual's redemption from sin". The possibility of the redemption of the individual, if it enters into the argument at all, is a deduction from what St. Anselm actually demonstrates, namely, the objective ground of human salvation. In his own terminology, he was concerned with the "rational necessity" of man's salvation by the God-man, but even when we transcribe this notion into the more modern one of "objective ground" we are still dealing with something different from possibility. For the believer he was endeavouring to answer the question: upon what basis does the forgiveness of sins, which I know to be a reality, rest? And for the unbeliever the questions he was answering were: is it necessary for my sins to be forgiven, and if so, how is this end to be accomplished? The question of the possibility does not arise for the believer; if it does for the unbeliever, it is a question secondary to those with which St. Anselm deals. Thus granted that it is necessary, the unbeliever might say, for my sins to be forgiven, and that the ground for such forgiveness has been established in Jesus Christ and His Death, then it is legitimate for me to deduce that it is *possible* for my sins to be forgiven. Such a deduction is permissible from St. Anselm's argument, but it is *not* the subject with which he is primarily concerned. It is, accordingly, inaccurate to accuse St. Anselm of demonstrating only the possibility of redemption.

When it is maintained that St. Anselm, in the first instance, addresses himself to the question of the objective ground of salvation, we are saying no more and no less than we would say of any theologian who expounds a theory of the Atonement. The purpose of such a theory is to set forth the objective ground or condition of salvation, and this statement is as true of the so-

called "subjective" theories as of the "objective", for both agree
that salvation comes from a source beyond the sinner himself,
whether it be the moral influence of an example of utter self-
sacrifice, or the payment of a debt, or the endurance of vicarious
punishment. The inadequacy of this criticism of Harnack's is
due to the fact that he has ignored what we might call "the
paradox of redemption". In one sense, mankind is redeemed
by the Death of Our Lord; in another and equally true sense, we
are not yet redeemed, for we are still *in via*. We have been saved;
yet we are being saved (σωζόμενοι). For the most part, St.
Anselm, like many other theologians in treating of the Atonement,
deals more with the former statement than with the latter.

(5.1.1.2) Harnack has a very strange view of the way in which
certitudo salutis arises: he seems to think that it can come as a
deduction from a theory of the Atonement. On these terms—
to take the extreme case—an agnostic logician could deduce his
own salvation from the statements in a "universalist" account
of the Atonement; yet his conclusion would be far removed from
what we know as *certitudo salutis*. In fact, such *certitudo* comes in
an entirely different way—through the moving of the Holy Spirit
in the heart of the sinner, so that in penitence and in response
to the offer of God's grace in Christ Crucified and Risen he receives
forgiveness of sins. And, further, there may be—and there often
is—forgiveness of sins and redemption without *certitudo salutis*.
Many people would miss forgiveness if they waited until they had
certitudo, and many people would have *certitudo* who missed
forgiveness, if *certitudo* were deducible logically from a theory, as
Harnack suggests it should be. One is grateful that it cannot be
derived from St. Anselm's theory: the theory is all the better for
such a defect.

(5.1.1.3) It is a great pity that Harnack should reduce St.
Anselm's concern for the individual—which is not absent from
his work, though he deals primarily, as we have seen, with the
question of the objective ground of salvation—to the gross caricature that if the sinner obeys the commands of Scripture, then the
work of the God-man is effectual for him, or, as he says later, that
it is those who live piously who shall be redeemed, and redeemed
because they live piously. Harnack seems to be bent upon making

St. Anselm's theory one of justification by works—what he calls
"an old-world, medieval, *Catholic* Christian theory". Nothing
could be further from the truth. What St. Anselm actually says
is as follows [72]: God will not reject anyone who approaches Him
in the name of Jesus Christ. In order to enter into and participate
in the Divine Grace and live in it, we must follow the proper
method of approach to God set down in the Scriptures. What he
means is this: that though God's Grace has been so abundantly
at work in the Death of Christ, nevertheless these events do not
magically achieve the redemption of individuals. Each sinner
must do what the Scriptures prescribe; hear the Gospel, repent
of his sins, turn to Christ for forgiveness and salvation, and give
evidence of his having been forgiven by his new way of life. The
"pious living" so disdainfully referred to by Harnack is for St.
Anselm part of the consequence of receiving the redemption
offered in Christ, and not a condition of receiving it. Salvation
is *sola gratia* in the *Cur Deus Homo,* as can be seen so unmistakably
in II.20, where St. Anselm explicitly says that the sinner has
nothing wherewith to redeem himself. God, we are told, says
to the sinner: "Take my Only-Begotten Son and offer Him for
thyself," and the Son says: "Take Me, and redeem thyself."
Curiously enough, Harnack quotes this very passage himself,[73]
but fails to see how completely it refutes his previous criticism.
Incidentally, it creates difficulties for the doctrine of particular
salvation which St. Anselm had advocated at II.16-18—a point
which Harnack again misses.

(5.1.2) Another of Harnack's major criticisms [74] (echoed by
Denney [75]) is that, whereas St. Anselm claims that he establishes
all the details of the doctrine of the Atonement by strictly logical
steps, at one of the most important turning-points of his arguments he substitutes the *convenientius* for the *necessarium.*[76] Jesus
Christ, having offered the gift of His Life to God in death, must
receive from Him the reward due for so great a deed. Upon
whom then, St. Anselm asks, should He *more fittingly* bestow the
reward than on men? We have previously seen [77] how St. Anselm
uses two forms of argument, the one normally for acceptance
by believers, the other for unbelievers as well as for believers, so
that Harnack's criticism is superficially convincing, though not

unanswerable. The answer is, in fact, to be found in the same speech in St. Anselm's writing. For he goes on to say that those to whom God assigns the benefit are those for whom—as the logic of his discussion has demonstrated—the Son was made man: His own kindred and brethren. The *convenientius*, then, is not absolute; it is relative to a *necessarium* already established. In fact, it would be superfluous for St. Anselm to reintroduce the *necessarium* at this point, for he has already shown why the God-man should necessarily die, namely, for the salvation of His fellow-men.[78] The argument of II.19 must therefore be taken along with its premise as stated in II.7 and 8, and in that context the *convenientius* loses its force and, we might add, its apparent arbitrariness. Denney's statement [79] that "(Christ) has no definite use for His Death"—which is in the same tone as Harnack's criticism—also loses its point when it is realised that the use to which Christ shall put His Death has been determined by St. Anselm in the earlier chapters of the book.

(5.1.3) Much is made by Harnack, as well as by others,[80] of the criticism that "the Death of Christ is entirely severed from His life-work on earth and isolated",[81] and that this God-man need not have preached, and founded a kingdom, and gathered disciples, he only required to die.[82]

Certain immediate reflections may be made upon these words of Harnack's. It is to be admitted, for example, that St. Anselm holds that the relation of Christ's Life to God's Will is different from that of His Death to God's Will,[83] and he has to face the difficulty that if the *acceptio mortis* is equivalent to the *datio vitae*, then Christ is only offering to God something which has no merit in itself. We have already urged that that interpretation of St. Anselm, while justified by his statements in one part of his work, is to be corrected in the light of his later employment [84] of the concept of *aseitas* to describe the whole of the Incarnation, both the Life and Death of Jesus Christ. On the latter interpretation, Christ offers to God in His Death the Life, so fully described in the Gospels, of mercy and loving kindness, of goodwill and steadfast obedience to God, so that by means of the notion of *aseitas* St. Anselm, so far from isolating the Life from the Death of Christ, links them together in one single pattern of Divine action and self-offering. At the same time, it is rather extreme of Harnack to suggest that the *Deus-homo* "only required to die". Granted that, while St. Anselm's work is called *Cur Deus Homo*, he treats only of the Atonement, and not of the many other aspects of the Incarnation, suggesting perhaps to some that he ignores the significance of such other aspects, nevertheless, from the start St. Anselm makes it clear that he intends to deal only with the Atonement, and that this is the limit within which he proposes *quaerere intellectum*. After all, he was not writing a complete dogmatic which could be expected to include even a complete Christology; the *Epistola de Incarnatione Verbi* in itself shows that St. Anselm had other things to say concerning the Incarnation which do not appear in the *Cur Deus Homo*. But St. Anselm would claim—and his claim would be correct—that the Atonement was the purpose of the Incarnation. We may make many other statements concerning the Incarnation—about its essentially revelatory nature, about the moral enlightenment that resulted, about its influence upon history—but the reason for its taking place was that God might redeem man from sin. It is with that issue that St. Anselm comes to grips, admittedly for the time ignoring other very important matters, but rightly convinced that that subject merited separate treatment. "For to this end was He man, that He might die" [8b] is a proposition which no Christian can finally deny. But it is fallacious to think that this proposition logically implies that His Life was valueless or unimportant, or that St. Anselm thought it so.

(5.1.4) Harnack, in a disappointingly brief statement,[86] charges St. Anselm's theory with a "quite Gnostic antagonism between justice and goodness". Of all the antinomies or contradictions alleged to exist in the theory this is perhaps the most difficult to comprehend. St. Anselm says often that God is Himself good and the source of all goodness, while the Son Whose Will is one with the Father's is in full agreement with the decision that the honour and justice of God are to be satisfied. It is quite impossible to make any case for the distinction of qualities of Father and Son, or to cite any convincing texts in support.

(5.1.5) A more important criticism comes from Harnack [87] when he says that in St. Anselm "the category of the inner moral

necessity of the good and holy even for God is consistently con-
founded with that of reason (ratio)". Denney [88] has the same
charge: "(The Atonement) is deduced by what St. Anselm calls
a rational necessity, and belongs to the world of metaphysics, not
of spiritual experience." The value of these criticisms lies in the
manner in which they serve to elicit what have now been proved
to be the fundamental concepts and characteristics of this much
misunderstood work.

(5.1.5.1) Harnack is correct when he suggests that St. Anselm
equates "the category of inner moral necessity" with *ratio*. His
error—and it affects his entire interpretation of St. Anselm—is his
description of this equation as a "confusion" in St. Anselm's
mind. For there is no confusion in the sense that St. Anselm
regards as identical two things which are different, namely, moral
necessity and *ratio*. In fact, St. Anselm is saying that these two
things are one. *Ratio* as it exists in God is the *archetype* of all
rationality. Consequently, as we have seen,[89] in his definition of
rationality in man St. Anselm includes the notion of morality.
When, therefore, at I.8 [90] St. Anselm says that "the Will of God
is never unreasonable", he does not mean that a rational necessity
external to God's nature constrains Him to abide by its laws, but
rather that the *ratio* by which His Will is directed is His own
essential Being, moral as well as reasonable. "The inner moral
necessity of the good and the holy" which Harnack so insistently
claims is absent from St. Anselm, is what St. Anselm means in
fact by *ratio*. This reply removes the second part of Denney's
criticism also; the first part is almost identical with Harnack's.
The rational necessity with which St. Anselm deals is a theological
and religious, and not simply a metaphysical, category, except
perhaps in the widest sense of the term. It belongs to "the world
of spiritual experience"—though St. Anselm would happily not
have used that kind of phrase—because *ratio* is essential to God's
nature. "Rational necessity" in St. Anselm is not to be interpreted as a characteristic of the steps of his argument, but rather
as a quality of his theory as a whole, and the *ratio* by which it is
held together is the *ratio* of God's Being. St. Anselm has here
drawn our attention to a most important aspect of theological
doctrines, namely, that we do not accept them only because they

are established by a series of arguments, each of which is logically valid and unassailable, but because, as a whole, they convince us of their rationality, and because we see in them the expression of the *ratio* of God Himself. It is this *ratio* which we discover to be absent from agnostic or atheistic theories, however valid their steps of reasoning may be.

(5.1.5.2) It is most surprising that both Harnack and Denney should make this kind of criticism in view of St. Anselm's repeated analyses of the application of necessity to God's actions, and to those of Jesus Christ. These analyses may be at times confused; if we do not follow carefully the sequence of St. Anselm's thought, we may even call them contradictory. But their sheer frequency makes any ignoring of their major content inexcusable. The conclusion of all these analyses is uniform—namely, that God is not compelled to act, or prohibited from acting, by anything outside of Himself, whether it be a natural or a rational necessity. When He wills to act righteously and justly He does so spontaneously and with a view to maintaining His self-consistency. In Him we find inner moral necessity at its highest and purest, and it takes the form of self-determination.[91] When He promises to act mercifully and graciously towards His creatures He necessarily does so, but this necessity springs from His own nature, which will not permit Him to promise falsely but constrains Him to abide by His given word.

(5.1.5.3) The previous reply to the two writers quoted—and it is applicable to all who write in a similar strain [92]—may be alternatively stated thus: that they have failed to realise the importance of the concept of *aseitas* in the *Cur Deus Homo*. For St. Anselm's final view on the application of *necessitas* to God requires this concept for its proper exposition. The necessity which constrains Him to be self-consistent and maintain His integrity springs from Himself (*a se*) and from no other person or thing. When we become fully aware of this concept, we discover that at the heart of the *Cur Deus Homo* there is not rational necessity but Divine Grace, and that even God's justice expresses itself only in accordance with the demands of His *aseitas*. From this interpretation of the work two important consequences follow. First, it is no longer possible to argue, as Mozley does,[93] that there is a sheer dualism at the heart of it between different moral qualities, justice and love or mercy, for they are synthesised within the notion of *aseitas*. Omit that consideration, as do Mozley and the others, and dualism is the inevitable result. Secondly, we are compelled to take a different view of St. Anselm's methodology from that adopted by those who see it as purely rationalistic. No atheistic or non-Christian rationalism could arrive at St. Anselm's conclusions from general first principles. His conclusions spring from an understanding of a God Whose nature is supremely *aseitas*, and his purpose in the *Cur Deus Homo* is as much to create that understanding in the unbeliever's heart as it is to convince him of the cogency of his arguments. It is, accordingly, as true to say that his conclusions are calculated to support his premises as it is to maintain the opposite. Belief in the total scheme of salvation or, more accurately still, faith in the God Who has thus acted so mightily unto salvation, is St. Anselm's end. If the clumsiness of the abstracts may be pardoned, he intends to establish the *necessitas* of *aseitas*, not the necessity involved in formal logic or natural law.

(5.1.5.4) Of course it would be quite permissible to take a "short way" with Harnack and Denney, and draw their attention to II.20, where St. Anselm asserts, in effect, that the framework of the whole argument of the *Cur Deus Homo*, so often concerned with God's justice and man's sin, is a framework of Divine Grace. Nothing could be plainer than that God willed to save the world by the *Deus-homo*, not primarily to satisfy His justice, or to meet the demands of logical necessity, nor yet to avoid frustration of purpose, but for mercy's sake. When, therefore, the Father and the Son make their appeal to the sinner, they plead the challenge of mercy, and not the irresistible character of the logic which somehow necessitated the Atonement. This chapter may be dismissed as a devotional aberration from the chilly rationalism of the rest of the book. On the contrary, if we regard *aseitas* as the supreme interpretative concept of the rest of the book, we discover that II.20 says in simple language what St. Anselm has been saying in a much more complicated theological style elsewhere.

(5.1.6) One of the greatest failures of St. Anselm's theory—in the opinion of Harnack and Denney—is that it does not regard the Death of Christ as *penal* in character. "Here no innocent one suffers *penalty* for the guilty," says Harnack,[94] and Denney, elaborating the verdict, holds that "Anselm, by defining Christ's Death merely as an *alternative* to the punishment of sin . . . has practically made it meaningless".[95] Despite the importance which they both attach to this criticism, neither is it so final as they suppose nor does it justify the extreme conclusions which they draw from it as to its badness or its meaninglessness.

The following considerations, unnoticed by either, must be borne in mind:

(5.1.6.1) Those who agree that the term "penal" ought to be applied *simpliciter* in describing the Death of Christ have ignored two important points. The first is that the notion of punishment cannot be defined in a manner acceptable to all. It has been variously described as retributive, reformative and deterrent in character, so that to say that the Death of Christ is penal is to beg a very large question, and is, in fact, to mislead a generation which has, through advances in social theory, become acutely aware of the variety of possible interpretations to be given to the notion of punishment. The second fact which has been ignored is that even if the idea of retribution is held to be the dominant element in punishment, nevertheless the term "penal" cannot be applied *simpliciter* to the Death of Christ. For in retributive punishment three factors are involved—the retrospection to the crime previously committed, the proportioning of the pain inflicted to the degree of badness of the crime, and the visitation of that pain upon the person committing the crime. It is this third factor—one which is essential to the concept, for without it crime would go scot-free and the idea of retribution would be negated—which must be absent from any account of the Death of Christ. Even the most rigid penal substitutionary theory, which bases its position upon the fact that Our Lord stands substitute for the entire fallen human race, has to face this difficulty, and to admit that the Death of Christ can, at best, if we are going to insist on literal meanings, be described as quasi-penal. Such being the case, it is possible to make either of two replies on behalf of St. Anselm to his critics.

On the one hand, it could be argued, since the *primary* sense of "penal" is not applicable anyway to the Death of Christ, St. Anselm is free to employ some other form of description which incorporates the first two factors involved in the notion of punishment but which stops short of using the term "penal" because of the absence of the third. In fact, that is very much what St. Anselm does: he takes account of the enormity of the crime which is human sin, and he proportionately relates the suffering of Christ to that crime. On the other hand, it could be simply said that the term "penalty" is only secondarily used in reference to the Death of Christ, to signify that which Christ suffers as a result of human sin, and that, in this sense, provided the qualification is clearly stated, the Death of Christ is a penalty. So heinous was man's disobedience to God that nothing short of the *datio vitae* of the Eternal Son of God could atone for it. That *datio* is surely penalty in as strong a sense as any held by penal substitutionary theories. That view surely refutes also the repeated criticism of Denney that in St. Anselm there is no *real* connection between sin and the Death of Christ: it is this *real* connection which holds the entire book together in a single piece.

(5.1.6.2) Both Denney and Harnack, however, also fail to recognise the meaning of *poena* in St. Anselm's disjunction: *aut poena aut satisfactio*. The punishment which St. Anselm envisages for sin, for which no satisfaction has been offered in the manner described in his argument, is the annihilation of the sinner (*mors aeterna*) [96] or, at least, the eternal torments of hell. With that extreme notion of punishment in his mind, it is not surprising that he does not regard satisfaction as penal. For that kind of punishment there can be no substitute punishment. What, therefore, St. Anselm presents is the alternative method by which God deals with the great fact of human sin, namely, satisfaction. It would not be inaccurate either to conjecture that recent or contemporary abuse of the penitential system affected St. Anselm in the formulation of his rigid disjunction. Tertullian had hinted [97] that the penitential performances of the sinner discharged eternal punishment, but commutation of so many of these performances into less exacting tasks had almost removed the element of punishment. Substitute punishments for the eternal punishment of God had, one might say, lost all significance in ecclesiastical thought and practice by St. Anselm's time. He affirms therefore that there is but one punishment for sins, however great or small, and that the only alternative thereto is not some easily made offering to a priest or abbot, but the Incarnation and Death of the Eternal Son of God, which has its roots in Divine mercy and grace. In such a context it becomes more obvious why St. Anselm should himself be reluctant to transfer the notion of punishment from one side of his disjunction to the other.

(5.2) In his criticism of St. Anselm Gustav Aulén (*Christus Victor*) raises matters neglected by most other critics, for they spring chiefly from his own theory concerning the "classic idea" of the Atonement. The variety is refreshing, though some of his criticisms stand or fall with his own thesis.

(5.2.1) On the basis of the "classic idea" of the Atonement, according to which God reconciles the world to Himself, as being both Reconciler and Reconciled, by carrying through in Christ a victorious struggle with the powers of evil, Aulén puts the question: "Does Anselm treat the atoning work of Christ as the work of God Himself from start to finish?" [98] Aulén recognises that in St. Anselm it is God Who initiates the whole scheme of redemption, but emphasises that this fact does not answer his question. For, in St. Anselm's theory, it is man who has sinned, and it is man who must make the satisfaction. Man ought to do it, but cannot; God ought not, but can. Therefore "God becomes man". His argument, Aulén continues, is designed "to show how the Man appears who is able to give the satisfaction which God absolutely demands"; [99] and he concludes that in St. Anselm the satisfaction offered by Christ "is not in the full sense God's work of redemption".[100]

(5.2.1.1) It is at once obvious that Aulén has derived his criticism from a mistaken conception of the *Deus-homo*, of the relation of the two natures in this one Person, and of their respective relations to the *satisfactio* offered in the Death of Christ. The mistake is one of emphasis rather than of outright misrepresentation. According to Aulén, St. Anselm says that satisfaction is offered to God by a *Man*, Who is also God. What St. Anselm does say is that satisfaction is offered to God by the God-man.

Aulén ignores St. Anselm's uses of the name *Deus-homo* as a single concept, and he misses the point of the title of the work, which is not "Why did God become man?" but "Why the God-man?". In fact, the sentence "*Deus homo factus est*" occurs most infrequently in the course of the work, St. Anselm preferring to speak of the *Deus-homo*, with the suggestion of hyphenation which Schmitt uses so regularly. Indeed, the burden of St. Anselm's work, as Aulén recognises, though he does not appreciate the implications of such recognition, is that man *cannot* make the satisfaction required by God. It is the Divine nature of the *Deus-homo* which achieves sufficient merit for that purpose. There is, as we have noticed, much evidence for a theory of *communicatio idiomatum* in St. Anselm's Christology, but it does not involve the view, which Aulén thinks St. Anselm holds, that the *homo* takes over all the attributes of the *Deus* and, as it were on his own, offers to God satisfaction adequate to atone for the sins of all mankind. That discontinuity in Divine action, in Incarnation and Atonement, which Aulén is so anxious to establish as a feature of the Latin theory of the Atonement, as against the continuity affirmed in the "classic idea", is not rightly attributed to the Anselmic theory. God's decision to redeem men, to become incarnate in the *Deus-homo*, to suffer and to die, forms for St. Anselm a continuous line, and Aulén's case is not complete.

(5.2.1.2) Once this initial reply is made to Aulén's criticism it immediately becomes evident that either St. Anselm's theory is in much the same position as the "classic idea" so greatly favoured by Aulén or the latter is theologically inadequate. On the one hand, just as God in Jesus Christ conquers the powers of evil which held man in bondage and so effects reconciliation between man and Himself, so God-in-Jesus Christ, the *Deus-homo*, makes the satisfaction to Himself which He Himself requires. In both cases God takes the initiative; He is incarnate, but it is the Divine nature in Jesus Christ which does the work which is effectual unto salvation. The Atonement is as "directly the work of God" [101] in one case as in the other. On the other hand, if Aulén holds that on the "classic idea" the atoning work of Christ is *literally* the work of God from start to finish, then he is committed to a theologically inadequate view of the Person of Jesus Christ, for he reduces to zero the part played by the human nature of Our Lord in the Incarnation and the Atonement. In fact, he would find difficulty in avoiding either the charge of Docetism or the criticism that he regards the human nature of Christ as an instrument used by the Divine nature to achieve its victory over the Devil and the powers of evil. At this point the Anselmic theory is closer to the truth than the "classic idea" as Aulén presents it; indeed, Aulén's criticism of St. Anselm has brought to light a very important defect either in the "classic idea" or in Aulén's presentation of it.

(5.2.2) The other criticisms which Aulén makes of the Anselmic soteriology are much less important than the first, but they are significant and must be considered. After making much of the juridical conceptions implied by the notion of satisfaction, and identifying St. Anselm with "the legalism of the medieval outlook",[102] he expresses amazement that the post-Reformation theologians should accept the Anselmic theory as the basis of their soteriology, even though this was so completely at one with the tradition which the Reformers rejected with their theme of *sola gratia*. It is now unnecessary for us to repeat our views on St. Anselm's use and mastery of his legal analogies, but it must be maintained that Aulén has misconstrued both St. Anselm's relation to "the medieval outlook" and the central theme of the *Cur Deus Homo*. There is much that St. Anselm does not share with "the medieval outlook"—for example, his theological methodology, his conception of the relation of faith to reason, his views on penance—the reaction of the Thomists and the Neo-Thomists to St. Anselm being confirmatory evidence of this contention. Further, it is *sola gratia* that is St. Anselm's theme, and only the most unsympathetic and superficial reflection upon his argument could yield any other conclusion. In fact, in some ways, St. Anselm by lightly touching upon the "penal" character of the Death of Christ could legitimately be said to be closer to the principle of *sola gratia* than some, at least, of the post-Reformation theologians, who reduced the scheme of salvation to a tidy system of punishment. That continuity in the order of justice which Aulén alleges to be so marked a feature of the Latin type of theory of the Atonement is not so conspicuously present in St. Anselm as Aulén thinks it is. Aulén's all too facile classification of St.

Anselm with the post-Reformation theologians, as if he were their complete prototype, has led to a certain falsification on his part of St. Anselm's view. To this unsatisfactory state of affairs must be added Aulén's too ready willingness to reject whatever does not agree with the "classic idea"—for example, St. Anselm's repudiation of the idea of a ransom paid to the Devil—a willingness which is due to his failure to recognise that the "classic idea" of the Atonement is not properly called a "theory" of the Atonement, and that the seed thoughts of other "ideas" or "theories" are as scriptural as those for the *Christus Victor* view.

(5.3) A very serious criticism of the Anselmic theory is briefly made by J. K. Mozley [103] when he says that St. Anselm, by working out a satisfaction which more than pays the debt owed to God by man as a result of his sin, robs the idea of forgiveness of all relevance. It does so because, once the adequate satisfaction has been made and the grievous dishonour done to God atoned for, then there is nothing left for God to forgive.

A consideration of this criticism will reveal some of its essential fallacies:

(5.3.1) First, the criticism rests upon, or at least strongly suggests, an entirely wrong conception of forgiveness, namely, that of God's indulgent condonation of the sins committed against Him. Mozley feels dissatisfied about the fact that St. Anselm has so effectively estimated the extent of the satisfaction offered by Christ that no possibility is left of God waiving consideration of any sins that man may have committed. Mozley is correct in saying that, in St. Anselm's judgment, there are no sins which God can treat in this way: his discussion of "the single glance forbidden by God" is sufficient evidence on that score. But St. Anselm would go further and insist that such connivance on God's part as Mozley suggests is not forgiveness (cf. I.12).

(5.3.2) What Mozley fails to recognise is that the whole process of satisfaction, initiated within the Godhead and continued in the Incarnation of the Eternal Son and in the Death of Jesus Christ, is regarded by St. Anselm as that which forms the ground of God's forgiveness and through which it takes place. This is what Atonement means, and this is how forgiveness works. There is, then, actually nothing left over which God could be thought to deal with in some other and quite arbitrary way. In his statement of the inner nature of the Atonement St. Anselm has shown that there are three attributes of God which must in no way be compromised—God's freedom, His justice and His love. His freedom is compromised if God is solely determined in His Will to save the world by some inner necessity of His own Being, or by the sinful condition of man; His justice is compromised if He allows sin to go scot-free; and His love if He has no regard for the final blessedness of those whom He once created. A theory of the Atonement has to be evolved within these limits, and forgiveness must be conceived of as falling within them. St. Anselm's is a theory about forgiveness or it is nothing at all. Mozley's criticism that it is not a theory of forgiveness misses the whole point of St. Anselm's discussion.

(5.3.3) Finally, it might simply be said of Mozley's criticism that it could be brought against any theory of the Atonement with the exception of one which regards forgiveness as God's mere condonation of sin and remission of it without cost to Himself or to man. Any proper theory of the Atonement endeavours to set forth the grounds upon which, or the conditions under which, forgiveness is made possible for God without compromise to His essential nature in one attribute or another. Penal substitutionary theories show how One has undergone God's punishment in the place of the many guilty; the "classic idea" bases the possibility of God's forgiveness upon the reconciliation achieved by His own victory over the Devil and the powers of evil; the theory of "vicarious penitence" regards Christ as alone achieving, on behalf of sinners, that depth of penitence which the gravity of their sin merits and which makes forgiveness a possibility for them—to mention but a few examples. In each case the idea of forgiveness is made irrelevant—in Mozley's sense of the term—for there is nothing left for God to forgive, if by "forgive" we mean "to remit unconditionally". On the other hand, each of these theories, including St. Anselm's, recognises, and indeed rests upon, the assumption that forgiveness can take place only when certain conditions are fulfilled, even though God Himself through the God-man is the only Person Who can possibly fulfil them.

6

It is now possible, after this detailed examination of the many criticisms of St. Anselm's theory of the Atonement, to summarise the chief errors from which these criticisms have arisen, and to indicate the dominant themes of the *Cur Deus Homo*.

(6.1) Perhaps the most obvious error committed by the critics is their failure to appreciate the Anselmic dialectic. The dialogue in which the study of the Death of Christ is cast is more than a useful but somewhat unnecessary form, as it sometimes becomes in later dialogues of Plato. It is a live discussion and moves as such a discussion would, when a persistent interlocutor refuses immediately to be put off with unsatisfactory answers, or when he returns later, after the discussion has moved on, to criticise answers which, upon reflection, reveal certain fallacies. Boso has a real personality and is no mere foil for a clever master. That fact requires us, in assessing St. Anselm's views on any topic, to survey his complete judgment, and not to criticise him on any penultimate statements. Almost invariably he keeps his good wine to the end. Many of the so-called contradictions in St. Anselm are therefore to be discovered by comparing the tentative answers which he has given to Boso's questions—for example, his various accounts of the freedom of God or of Jesus Christ. But they are regarded as contradictions, or set down as defects of his theory, only so long as we fail to recognise that he himself regards them as but partial solutions to problems for which he has reserved final solutions to be given later in the book.

(6.2) St. Anselm's use of analogy, and indeed the use of analogy in general, has been consistently misunderstood by his critics. Any writer is free to employ whatever appropriate analogy he chooses, but he is not fettered to every element in the source of his analogy. The history of the part played by such terms as οὐσία and ὑπόστασις in the development of the Doctrine of the Trinity would otherwise need to be rewritten. The energy expounded upon the sources of St. Anselm's analogies reveals great historical and critical acumen but little sound theological judgment. In his hands concepts that may be shown to have kinship with Roman or Teutonic law or with the penance-system undergo transformation in the new contexts in which he sets them. Their theological reference alters them in some cases beyond recognition. Concentration upon the origins of the analogies was no doubt inevitable in a period when "the argument from origins" was so widely accepted, not only in secular but also in theological fields of study. Once the fallacies of that argument are pointed out it is possible to do greater justice to St. Anselm's use of analogies.

(6.3) Too little trouble has been taken, even by critics as sympathetic as James Denney, to understand what St. Anselm means by rational necessity, or, in general, what his methodological procedure is. To put the case briefly: St. Anselm's purpose is to show how the Atonement follows from the nature and Will of God Himself, and not, as the critics hold, from some rational necessity external to God which constrains Him to act as He does, initiating a process which results in the satisfaction offered by the God-man instead of the punishment of sinners by the torments of eternal fire. Nor, even in terms of that stricter purpose, is St. Anselm maintaining that the Atonement follows by a rational necessity from God's essential Being, as if God could not be God without redeeming mankind. His prolonged examination of the propriety of applying the term "necessity" to God's actions and to Christ's in deciding to die for the sins of His brethren, together with his emphasis upon God's mercy as the source of salvation, leaves us in no doubt that for St. Anselm the Atonement was an outflowing of Divine Grace, unmerited by man and granted as God's greatest gift to him in Jesus Christ. Rational necessity enters only at the next stage of the discussion, when, granted that God of His Grace wills to save sinners, St. Anselm endeavours to show the form which such salvation will take. But it is a rational necessity of a limited kind, for it is operative only within a limited sphere of reference, and it is not likely to be accepted by those who reject these limits, or who equate it with the rational necessity of a formal logical system. In other words, St. Anselm is maintaining that in order to interpret aright the Death of Christ we must understand the reasons why He died. In setting forth these reasons he does what the exponent of any soteriological theory does, and is therefore no more open than any other to criticism directed at his notion of rational necessity, for it is the rational necessity, in the limited sense denoted above, which all theories seek to expound. St. Anselm's exposition has the merit, above many others, of bringing out clearly the relation of necessity to Grace within the scheme of salvation from its origin to its completion.

(6.4) The gravest error committed by those who have paraphrased the *Cur Deus Homo* and criticised it in such detail has been their failure to detect the part played in the argument by the notion of *aseitas* or, more simply, by the phrase *a se*. This error is serious on two accounts. On the one hand, this idea, recurring as it so frequently does at the climax of St. Anselm's discussion of the major topics of the book, acts as a thread holding the whole argument together. If we neglect it, the argument becomes a disjointed series of discussions with no sustained interest, the point of the argument of the book, simply as an argument, passes unobserved, and the dramatic unity of the work is misunderstood. On the other hand, St. Anselm's conception of God and of His purpose to redeem mankind is utterly falsified. It is only by drawing out the full implications of this notion of *aseitas* that we can refute the charges that the book is an exercise in Scholastic logic at its worst, that God's justice is overemphasised at the expense of God's mercy, that for St. Anselm God is simply a feudal baron writ large, and that forgiveness is commercialised, if not rendered impossible, by the interpretation he gives of it. When, however, the importance of this concept is fully appreciated, the *Cur Deus Homo* emerges as the greatest theological work of St. Anselm—greatest not simply because, in relation to the theory of the Atonement, he achieves his most original work, but even more because in it he gives, though in less systematic form than in the other works, his most mature account of the Nature of God.

NOTES

CHAPTER ONE

1. *Sancti Anselmi Opera Omnia* (edidit F. S. Schmitt, O.S.B.), vol. I, *Proslogion*, 1, p. 100, l. 18.
2. Published by Thos. Nelson and Sons. All references are to this edition of St. Anselm's works.
3. *Mocanensis Latinus* 21248.
4. *Neapolitanus Sangallensis* 287, 801; *Turicensis Rhinangiensis* 124; *Vindobensis* 691; *Mellicensis* 154.
5. *Cantab. Emman. Coll.* 135.
6. *Londiniensis Lambethianus* 59; *Cantab. Corpus Christi Coll.* 135.
7. *Duacensis* 352; *Paris* 13414.
8. *Opera*, vol. II, p. 40, ll. 1 ff.
9. Cf. Vg. Isa. vii. 9: "*Si non credideritis, non permanebitis.*"
10. *Opera*, vol. II, p. 40, ll. 10-12.
11. I.1, p. 48, ll. 16-18.
12. *Intelligere*; St. Anselm uses *comprehendere* two lines lower with no difference of intention.
13. *Opera*, vol. II, *Praef.*, p. 42, ll. 11-13.
14. E.g. at I.10, p. 67, ll. 12 ff.; II.10, p. 107, ll. 10, 11.
15. P. 95, ll. 1-6.
16. *Vide supra*, pp. 3-4.
17. *Proslogion*, 1, p. 100, ll. 15-19.
18. Id., 2, p. 101, ll. 3-5.
19. Id., 1, p. 98, ll. 12-15.
20. Id., 26, pp. 120, l. 25, to 121, l. 1.
21. Id., 2, p. 101, l. 3: "*Et quidem credimus te esse aliquid quo nihil maius cogitari possit.*"
22. *Opera*, vol. II, pp. 1 ff.
23. Vol. III, pp. 270-271.
24. Id., pp. 279-281.
25. *Epistola de Incarnatione Verbi*, I, p. 9, ll. 5, 6.
26. Ibid.
27. C. 1, p. 7, ll. 5-9.
28. C. 80, p. 86, ll. 17-18.
29. *Prologus*, p. 7, ll. 7-8.
30. P. 13, l. 11.
31. *Monologion*, 1, p. 13, ll. 5-6.
32. Cf. *De Processione Spiritus Sancti.*
33. Op. cit., p. 160.
34. Id., pp. 178, 179.
35. Id., p. 179.
36. *Our Knowledge of God*, p. 135.
37. Op. cit., p. 159.

38. *La Philosophie au Moyen Âge*, p. 242.
39. *L'Esprit de la Philosophie Médiévale*, p. 29.
40. *The Faith of a Moralist*, vol. II, pp. 200-201.
41. *Our Knowledge of God*, pp. 134-143.
42. Op cit.
43. Italics mine.
44. Op. cit.
45. Id., p. 141.
46. Id., p. 143.
47. *Fides Quaerens Intellectum* and *Kirchliche Dogmatik*.
48. *Fides Quaerens Intellectum*, p. 13.
49. *The Christian in Philosophy*.
50. *Fides Quaerens Intellectum*, p. 17.
51. Ibid.
52. Id., p. 8.
53. Id., p. 7.
54. Id., p. 20.
55. Ibid.
56. If so, why *CUR Deus Homo*?
57. *Fides Quaerens Intellectum*, p. 37.
58. Id., p. 39.
59. Ibid.
60. Id., p. 40.
61. *The Doctrine of the Word of God*, English translation, pp. 16-17.
62. *Kirchliche Dogmatik*, I/2, p. 9.
63. Id., II/1, p. 101.
64. *Fides Quaerens Intellectum*, p. 54.
65. Id., p. 55.
66. Given in the *Kirchliche Dogmatik*, I/2, p. 9.
67. *Fides Quaerens Intellectum*, pp. 56-57.
68. *The Doctrine of the Word of God*, English translation, p. 264.
69. *Fides Quaerens Intellectum*, pp. 59-60.
70. At (2.4.4) *supra*.
71. *Fides Quaerens Intellectum*, p. 54.
72. II.22, p. 133, ll. 6, 7.
73. *Fides Quaerens Intellectum*, p. 59
74. Ibid.
75. B. B. Warfield, *The Inspiration and the Authority of the Bible*, 1948, p. 210.
76. *Fides Quaerens Intellectum, passim*.

CHAPTER TWO

1. I.3, p. 51, l. 5.
2. Id., l. 3.
3. Schmitt, in his footnotes on p. 51, gives representative references to the sources of these views: Leo Magnus, *Sermo XXV*, c. V

(PL 54, 211 s); cf. also Romans v.19, and xii—for the first;
Tertullian, *De Carne Christi*, c. XVII (PL 2, 827 s); Ambrose,
Expositio in Lucam, I.11, n. 28; Augustine, *Sermo* CCXXXII,
c. 11, n. 2—for the second. Gustav Aulén, *Christus Victor*,
amply illustrates the third.

4. In I.4 and I.6.
5. I.4, p. 51, l. 16.
6. Id., l. 21.
7. E.g. in *The Glass of Vision*.
8. I.6.
9. I.8.
10. Cf. *infra*, Chapter II, Part B (2.3).
11. Cf. *infra*, Chapter III (5) and (6).
12. Cf. *infra*, Chapter IV (1).
13. I.4.
14. *Vide* I.4; I.9; II.4, etc.
15. Cf. *De Concordia*, I [6], p. 257, ll. 5 ff. (vol. II, *Opera*).
16. *Vide* (1.1.1).
17. I.11.
18. *Christ in Modern Theology*, p. 124.
19. I.11.
20. I.3.
21. I.5.
22. E.g. II.11.
23. E.g., A. M. Fairbairn, *Christ in Modern Theology*, p. 122, n. 1; H. N.
    Oxenham, *The Catholic Doctrine of the Atonement*, pp. 181 ff.
24. *Sponte*, I.24, p. 92.
25. *Vide infra* (3), *passim*.
26. II.8.
27. Cf. *De Conceptu et de Originali Peccato*.
28. Chapter III (6).
29. *The Atonement*, p. 34.
30. *Atonement and Personality*, pp. 370-371.
31. I.11, p. 68, l. 10.
32. Op. cit., p. 370.
33. James Denney, *The Christian Doctrine of Reconciliation*, p. 67.
34. Cf. Part B (1.4.3) of this present chapter, *supra*.
35. Cf. Part B (3.1.2.3) of this present chapter, *infra*.
36. *The Christian Doctrine of Reconciliation*, p. 73.
37. *The Christian Doctrine of Salvation*, pp. 241 f.
38. Id., p. 241.
39. Id., p. 242.
40. Ibid.
41. *Vide* Part B (3.1.1.1) of this present chapter, *infra*.
42. *The Atonement*, pp. 33-35.
43. Op. cit., p. 34.
44. I.11, p. 69, ll. 1-2.

45. I.21, p. 89, l. 18.
46. Id., ll. 22-23.
47. Cf. I.21, l. 27; II.1.
48. At p. 89, ll. 27, 28.
49. Cf. Part B (3.2.3) of this present chapter, *infra.*
50. I.22, ll. 20-23.
51. Cf. II.14.
52. *Vide* I.19.
53. I.19, ll. 22-24.
54. The most important discussions of this topic are to be found in the following writings:
    A. Harnack, *History of Dogma*, English translation, vol. VI, pp. 56-58.
    R. S. Franks, *A History of the Doctrine of the Work of Christ*, vol. I, pp. 101-153, 164 ff.
    J. Denney, *The Christian Doctrine of Reconciliation*, pp. 46 ff.
    Cremer, *Stud. u. Krit.*, 1880, pp. 7 ff.; 1893, pp. 316-345.
    Schultz, id., 1894, pp. 1-50, 245-314, 554-614.
    Loofs, *Dogmengeschichte*, I.4, p. 493, n. 3.
55. Op. cit.
56. Sim. 5.3.3, quoted by Franks, op. cit., pp. 104 f.
57. *De Poenitentia*, c. 2.
58. It is a defect in Franks' exposition (op. cit.), pp. 105 f., that instead of stating Tertullian's account of satisfaction to begin with, he proceeds, immediately after describing the idea of merit, to discuss whether *satisfactio* is *poena* or *venia.*
59. *De Poenitentia*, c. 7.
60. Id., c. 6.
61. Id., c. 9.
62. *Vide* Harnack, op. cit., p. 57, footnote; cf. Denney, op. cit., p. 48.
63. Tertullian, *De Poenitentia*, c. 9; cf. St. Augustine, *Sermo* XXIX, *ad fin.*
64. *De Pudicitia*, c. 2.
65. Op. cit., p. 57, footnote.
66. Franks, op. cit., p. 106.
67. The Pseudo-Augustinian *De Vera et Falsa Religione* (19.35), quoted by Franks, op. cit., p. 153, and by Denney, op. cit., p. 57.
68. Op. cit.
69. *A Critical History of the Christian Doctrine of Reconciliation and Justification*, English translation, pp. 29-31.
70. J. K. Mozley, *The Doctrine of the Atonement*, p. 130, follows all too closely this criticism of Ritschl's.
71. *Cur Deus Homo*, I.11, p. 68, ll. 23 ff.
72. Cf. Part B (3.1.1.3) of this present chapter, *supra.*
73. Op. cit., pp. 181 f. The criticism occurs, though in a less developed form, in Harnack, op. cit., pp. 72 f.
74. Op. cit., p. 21.
75. I.11, p. 68, ll. 26-27.

76. I.20, p. 86, l. 19; I.21, p. 89, l. 24
77. Op. cit., p. 81.
78. Op. cit., p. 76.
79. Cf. *supra*, Part A (3.1) of this present chapter.
80. *Vide supra*, Part B (3.3) at the beginning; also I.12, l. 11.
81. St. Matt. vi. 12.
82. Cf. I.12, p. 69, ll. 29-30.
83. I.12, p. 70, ll. 1-4.
84. St. Matt. xviii. 23-25.
85. I.12, ll. 11 ff; I.13.
86. I.13.
87. P. 70 n.
88. Cf. *supra*, Part B (1.1.4) of this present chapter.
89. I.12, p. 69, ll. 29-30.
90. I.24, p. 94, l. 8.
91. I.13, l. 17.
92. Quoted *supra*, Part B (3.3.2) of this present chapter.
93. I.12, p. 69, ll. 29-30.
94. I.19, p. 86, ll. 1-5.
95. Id., ll. 3-4.
96. Id., ll. 2-3.
97. Id., ll. 6 ff.
98. Cf. II.19, p. 131, ll. 7-10.
99. P. 86, ll. 6 ff.
100. *History of Dogma*, English translation, vol. VI, p. 77.
101. I.19, p. 93, ll. 25-28.
102. Cf. I.13, ll. 16-17.
103. I.12.
104. Cf. Part B (3.3.1) of this present chapter, *supra*.
105. I.24, p. 94, ll. 8-9.
106. Particularly in I.12,13,19,24.
107. Cf. *infra*, Chapter IV (5.3).
108. I.14, p. 72, l. 25.
109. I.15.
110. Id., p. 72, l. 29.
111. Cf. St. Augustine, *De Ordine*, Bks. I and II; Calvin, *Institutio*, I.18.
112. I.15, p. 73, l. 17.
113. Id., ll. 14-16.
114. The two English translations commence I.25 at I.25, p. 95, l. 9, of Schmitt's edition. As throughout, we follow Schmitt's division of the chapters.
115. I.25, p. 95, l. 24 to end.
116. Id., ll. 18-19.
117. I.e. I.25, p. 95, ll. 9-23.

CHAPTER THREE

1. Ancient and Modern Library of Theological Literature.
2. The Religious Tract Society.
3. II.5, p. 99, ll. 23 f.
4. Id., p. 100, ll. 20-21.
5. P. 123, l. 23.
6. Cf. *infra* (6.3.2.2) of this chapter; also Chapter IV (1.5.2).
7. Cf. *De Concordia*, I (2), p. 247, ll. 6 ff.
8. II.6, p. 101, ll. 3, 4.
9. *Vide supra*, Chapter II, Part B (3.1.1.3).
10. St. Anselm at II.6, p. 101, l. 7, uses *sub Deo*; cf. at id., l. 4, *praeter Deum*; and, previously, at I.21, p. 89, l. 2, *quidquid Deus non est*. These phrases all seem to be equivalent to each other.
11. II.8, p. 69, ll. 5-8.
12. In II.10.
13. II.8, p. 103, l. 4.
14. Id., ll. 7-9.
15. P. 102.
16. Cf. *supra*, Chapter II, Part B (3.3).
17. Cf. Chapter II, Part B (1.2.2).
18. It is to be noted that St. Anselm once again uses *oportet* at II.8, p. 104, l. 20, which is varied with *decet* on the same page.
19. II.8, p. 104, l. 25.
20. Id., ll. 16, 21, 23.
21. VI.v.2, pp. 56-57.
22. *History of Dogma*, English translation, vol. VI, c. 1, p. 74.
23. Cf. *infra*, Chapter IV (5.1.5.1).
24. Cf. *supra*, Chapter I (1.2).
25. *Ep. de Inc. Verbi*, p. 4, ll. 6-9; p. 10, l. 22 to p. 11, l. 1. Cf. *Ep. Ioh. ad Ans.*, No. 128, ll. 8-11.
26. Cf. M. H. Carré, *Realists and Nominalists*.
27. I.e. p. 9, l. 20, to p. 10, l. 13.
28. Carré, op. cit., p. 41.
29. Quoted at the beginning of the present sub-section (5.3).
30. *Opera*, vol. III, No. 136, p. 279, ll. 3, 4, 6, 7.
31. C. 3, p. 15, ll. 18-19.
32. C. 4 ff.
33. C. 9.
34. C. 10.
35. C. 7.
36. C. 8.
37. C. 13.
38. C. 9, p. 23, ll. 13-16; cf. c. 2, p. 14, l. 6.
39. Id., p. 24, l. 30.
40. Id., p. 23, ll. 16 ff.

41. C. 2, p. 14, l. 3.
42. Id., l. 6.
43. C. 9, p. 24, ll. 9-10.
44. Id., l. 15, to p. 25, l. 4.
45. Cf. c. 10, pp. 27, l. 18, to 28, l. 9.
46. Cf. c. 6, p. 21, ll. 23-25.
47. *Reformed Dogmatics*, English translation, pp. 114, 115.
48. II.7, p. 102, ll. 17-18: "*Servata integritate utriusque naturae.*"
49. *Vide supra* (4) of this chapter.
50. II.10, p. 106, l. 16; id., p. 108, ll. 11-12; II.13, p. 113, ll. 14-15.
51. II.11.
52. II.16, pp. 116, l. 16, to 118, l. 5.
53. *The Person of Jesus Christ*, p. 240.
54. II.11, p. 109, l. 22.
55. II.13, p. 113, l. 15.
56. C. II.11, p. 29, ll. 3, 4.
57. Id., l. 21.
58. Id., p. 30, ll. 3, 4.
59. Id., p. 29, ll. 11-12.
60. Id., ll. 14, 15, 17.
61. II.10, p. 107, ll. 1-6.
62. II.5, p. 100, l. 21.
63. Cf. II.5, p. 100, l. 21.
64. Cf. the book by W. D. Ross on this very subject.
65. "Fundamental Principles of the Metaphysic of Morals", p. 31, in
    T. K. Abbott, *Kant's Theory of Ethics*.
66. Ibid.
67. II.10, p. 107, ll. 25, 26.
68. *The Theory of Good and Evil*, vol. II, bk. II, c. 3.
69. *Opera*, vol. I, c. 1, p. 207, ll. 11, 12. Cf. Augustine, *Contra Jul.*,
    I. vi, n. x (1518), quoted by Schmitt, pp. 207-208 n.
70. *Cur Deus Homo*, II.10, p. 107, ll. 21-23.
71 *De Libertate Arbitrii*, c. 1, p. 208, ll. 21-23.
72. Id., c. 2, p. 210, ll. 3-5, 10; c. 5, p. 216, ll. 13, 14.
73. Id., c. 13, p. 225, ll. 2-3; cf. id., c. 3, p. 212, ll. 19-20, 22-25.
74. II.10.
75. II.8, p. 103, ll. 3-4.
76. Id., ll. 4-5.
77. II.16, p. 117, ll. 1 ff.
78. Id., pp. 117, l. 22, to 118, l. 3.

CHAPTER FOUR

1. II.10,11.
2. I.8, p. 59, l. 11.
3. I.9, p. 61, ll. 8-24.
4. Id., l. 25, to p. 62, l. 8.

5. I.9, p. 62, ll. 9 ff.
6. At p. 63, ll. 25 ff.
7. Id., ll. 21 ff.
8. At p. 63, ll. 29 ff.
9. Cf. *supra*, Chapter III (6.3.1).
10. P. 63, ll. 29 ff.
11. *The Atonement*, p. 35.
12. I.10, p. 64, ll. 18 ff.
13. Id., ll. 23-27.
14. Id., p. 65, ll. 7 ff.
15. Id., p. 66, ll. 8 ff.
16. II.16, p. 119, ll. 28 ff.
17. Id., p. 121, ll. 7-8.
18. Id., p. 122, ll. 1 ff.
19. Cf. *supra*, Chapter III (1).
20. *De Interpretatione*, 9.
21. II.17, p. 125, l. 10. It is rather absurd that the Ancient and Modern Library of Theological Literature should translate this pre-Copernican sentence thus: "The earth revolves around the sun"!
22. Op. cit.
23. I [2], pp. 248, l. 5, to 252, l. 5; cf. footnote, l. 4, p. 248.
24. *De Concordia*, I [2], p. 249, ll. 15, 16.
25. Id., ll. 17-19.
26. II.17, p. 125, ll. 29-30.
27. Op. cit., p. 73.
28. Id., p. 74.
29. II.11, p. 110, ll. 9 to end of chapter.
30. II. 14.
31. Cf. I.21, II.6; also *supra*, Chapter II, Part B (3.1.1.3).
32. Cf. II.10,11.
33. II.11, p. 110, ll. 18-20.
34. Id., ll. 27-28.
35. Id., p. 111, ll. 6 ff.
36. Id., p. 110, ll. 9-10.
37. Op. cit., p. 33.
38. II.14, p. 114, l. 8.
39. E.g. at II.10.
40. *Infra* (3.3.4.2).
41. II.14, p. 114, l. 18, and p. 115, l. 4.
42. Id., ll. 29-30.
43. P. 118, ll. 5 ff.
44. Id., l. 18.
45. *Christus Victor*, English translation, p. 108.
46. II.18,19.
47. II.18, p. 127, ll. 6-9.
48. Id., p. 128, ll. 11-12.
49. Cf. II.5 and II.17.

50. II.18, p. 128, l. 13.
51. Cf. *supra*, this chapter (1.5.1).
52. II.19.
53. Id., p. 129, ll. 29, 30.
54. *A Critical History of the Doctrine of Justification and Reconciliation*, English translation, p. 33.
55. P. 131, l. 21.
56. *History of Dogma*, English translation, vol. VI, c. I, pp. 71 ff.
57. Id., p. 71.
58. Op. cit., pp. 182 f.
59. Cf. J. K. Mozley, *The Doctrine of the Atonement*, p. 130.
60. At (2.1.1) *supra* of this chapter.
61. II.18, p. 128, ll. 13 ff.
62. At (2.1) *supra* of this chapter.
63. II.19, p. 131, ll. 2-4.
64. II.14.
65. (1.5.2) *supra* of this chapter.
66. P. 111, l. 29, to p. 112, l. 1.
67. P. 127, ll. 17 ff.
68. II.19, p. 130, ll. 30-33.
69. Cf. *supra* (3.3.1) to (3.3.3) of this chapter.
70. *History of Dogma*, English translation, vol. VI, c. I, pp. 68-78.
71. Id., p. 69.
72. *Vide* II.19, p. 131, ll. 5-10.
73. Op. cit., p. 69.
74. Id., p. 71.
75. Op. cit., p. 77.
76. II.19, p. 130, ll. 28-31.
77. *Supra*, Chapter III (4).
78. II.7,8.
79. Op. cit., p. 75.
80. E.g. Denney, op. cit., p. 75.
81. Harnack, op. cit., p. 76.
82. Ibid.
83. Cf. (2.2.1.6) and (2.2.2.1) of this chapter.
84. Cf. (3.3.4.2) of this chapter.
85. II.7, p. 120, l. 30.
86. Op. cit., p. 76.
87. Ibid.
88. Op. cit., p. 75.
89. *Vide supra*, Chapter I (1).
90. P. 59, l. 11.
91. Cf. *supra*, Chapter III (1.1).
92. E.g. Mozley, op. cit., p. 131.
93. Op. cit., p. 130.
94. Op. cit., p. 77.
95. Op. cit., p. 77.

96. I.5, p. 52, ll. 19-20.
97. Cf. *supra*, Chapter II Part B (3.1.1).
98. Op. cit., p. 102.
99. Id., p. 103.
100. Id., p. 104.
101. Id., p. 105.
102. Id., p. 108.
103. *The Doctrine of the Atonement*, p. 130.